MANUSCRIPTS & PRECIOUS BOOKS IN THE MAURITS SABBE LIBRARY · KU LEUVEN

[illegible]

Ego sum [illegible]

[illegible] per Nicolaum Mathei

Quatuor sunt [illegible]:
- Mollificativum
- Mundificativum
- [illegible]
- Diureticum

Quatuor sunt cause [illegible]

Adolescentia [illegible]

Iuventus [illegible]

Senectus [illegible]

Senium [illegible]

Semina frigida:
- Maiora: cucurbite, citrulli, melonum, cucumeris
- Minora: endivie, scariole, portulace, lactuce

Hec est [illegible]

Hec sunt [illegible]

Quatuor ex vento veniunt in corpore retento
sc. ydrops colica vertigo quatuor ista

[illegible]

Ego sum [illegible]

Diffinitio mulieris

Mulier est animal imperfectum varium fallax multis morbis passionibus subiectum
sine fide sine timore sine constantia sine pietate

Alia diffinitio

Mulier est viri [illegible] compilatrix amoris rapina [illegible]
[illegible] honoris [illegible]

[illegible]

Quare sompnus [illegible]

Sompnus est ligamentum virtutum [illegible]
[illegible] corporis superfluitates [illegible]
[illegible] sedans dolores [illegible] — Sompnus
[illegible]

Manuscripts & Precious Books

in the Maurits Sabbe Library · KU Leuven

FACULTY OF THEOLOGY AND RELIGIOUS STUDIES · KU LEUVEN
PEETERS · LEUVEN
2019

Manuscripts & Precious Books in the Maurits Sabbe Library · KU Leuven

Publisher Peeters
Bondgenotenlaan 153 · BE-3000 Leuven · Belgium
www.peeters-leuven.be

ISBN 978-90-429-4154-0
eISBN 978-90-429-4155-7
Legal deposit D/2019/0602/120

Printed in Belgium

Frontispiece Rhazes, *Nonus liber Almansoris: cum expositione eiusdem clarissimi doctoris Sillani de Nigris de Papia*, see p. 30
Cover brocate paper, see p. 116

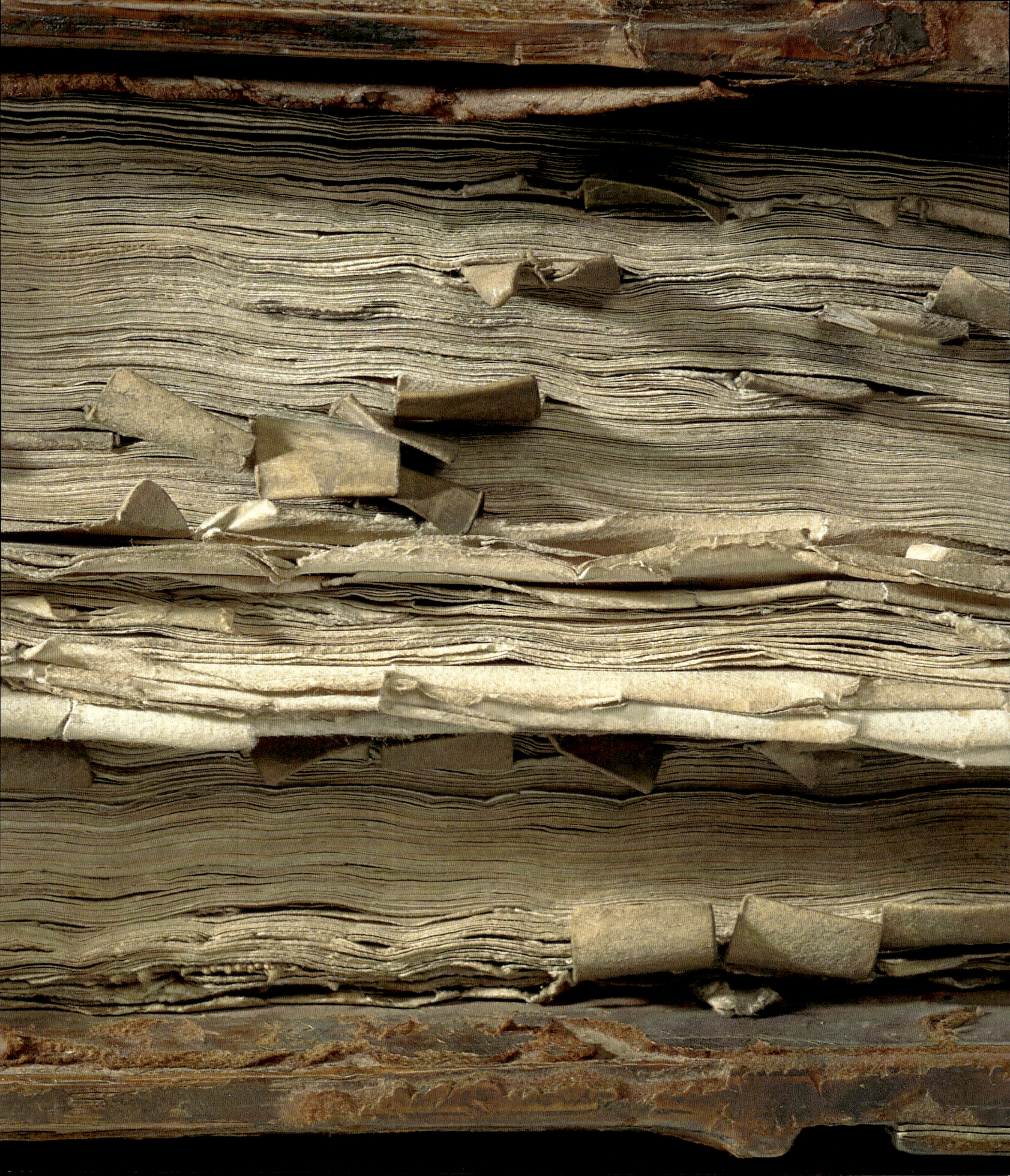

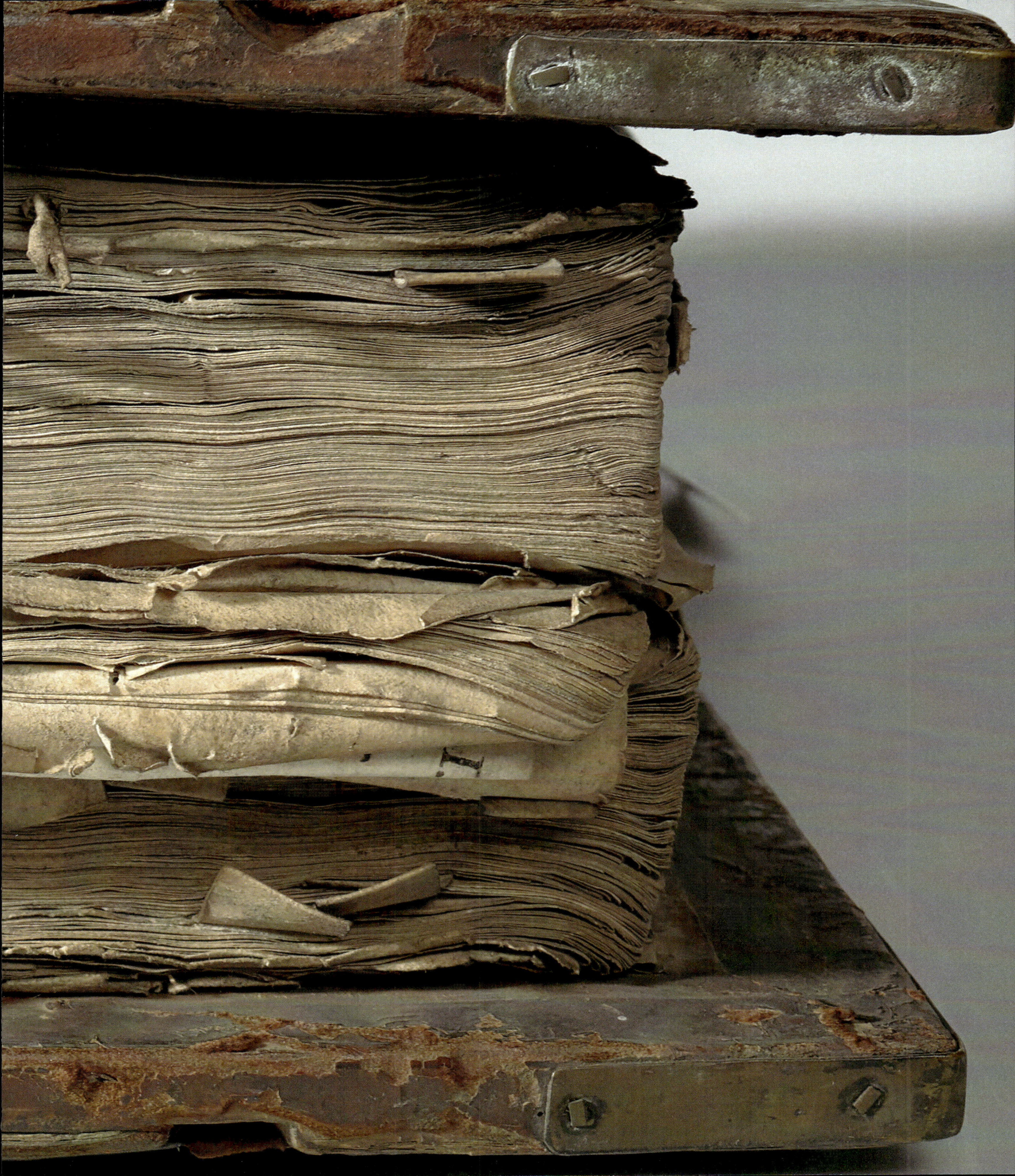

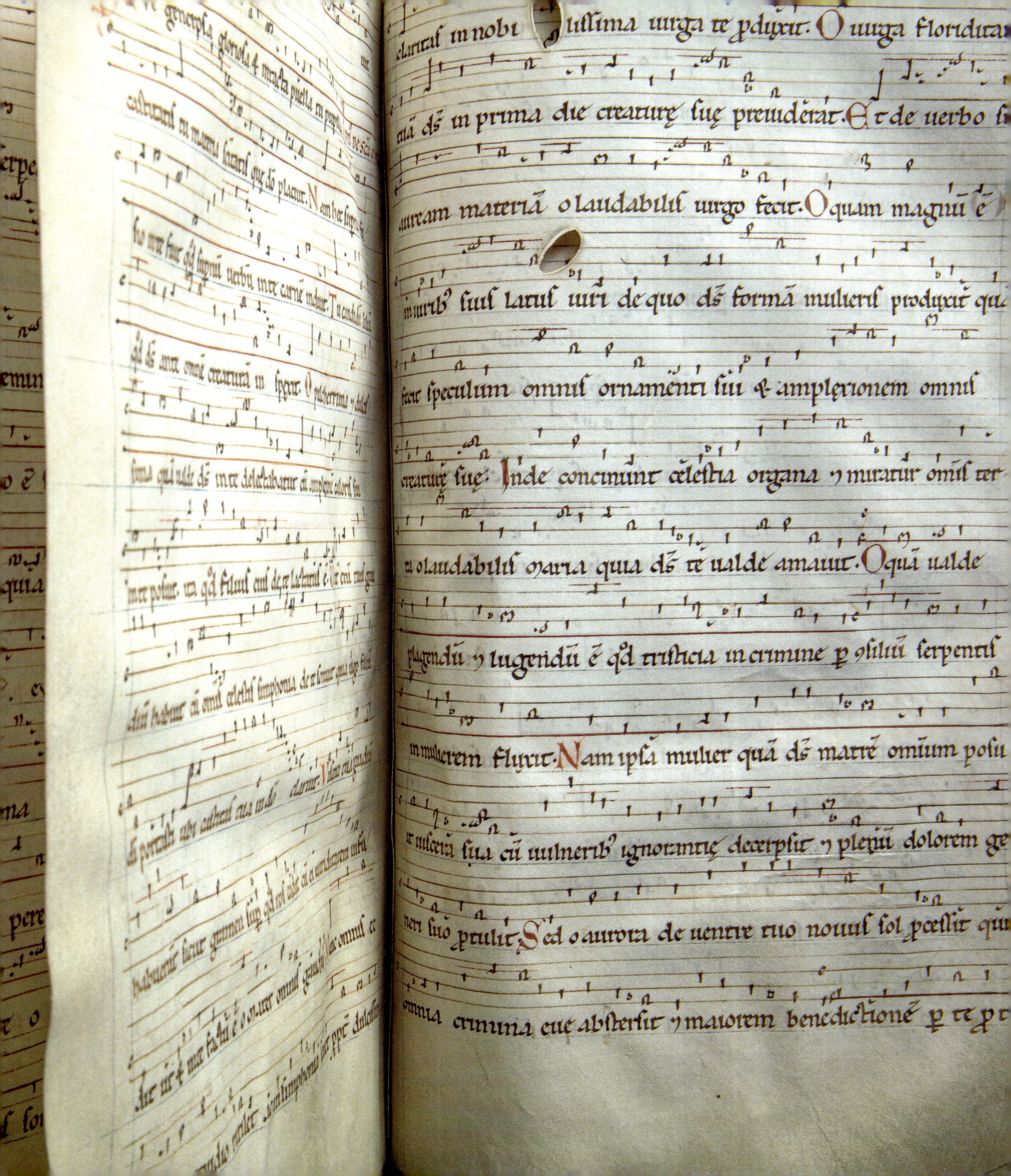
claritas in nobis ussima uirga te pduxit. O uirga floridita
quā ds in prima die creature sue preuiderat. Et de uerbo su
auream materiā o laudabilis uirgo fecit. O quam magnū ē
in uirib' suis latus uiri de quo ds formā mulieris produxit qua
fecit speculum omnis ornamenti sui & amplexionem omnis
creature sue. Inde concinunt celestia organa 7 miratur omis ter
ra o laudabilis maria quia ds te ualde amauit. O quā ualde
plangendū 7 lugendū ē quod tristicia in crimine p consiliū serpentis
in mulierem fluxit. Nam ipsa mulier quā ds matrē omnium posu
it uiscera sua cū uulnerib' ignorantie decerpsit 7 plenū dolorem ge
neri suo ptulit. Sed o aurora de uentre tuo nouus sol pcessit qui
omnia crimina eue abstersit 7 maiorem benedictionē p te p

An exceptional treasury of rare books is located in the heart of the city of Leuven, between the Saint Donatus Park and the Saint Michael's Church. The *preciosa,* the secure room for the valuable books of the Maurits Sabbe Library of the Faculty of Theology and Religious Studies of the University of Leuven (Louvain), holds an impressive collection of manuscripts and early printed books dating from the 10th to the 19th century.

The Library was created as one of the faculty libraries of the new Dutch-speaking Katholieke Universiteit Leuven (KU Leuven), established in 1969 after the separation of the Dutch and French speaking parts of the centuries-old University of Louvain. On 16 October 1974, the Library was opened in a brand new building, designed by architect Paul Van Aerschot. Under the spirited guidance of the first academic librarian, biblical scholar Maurits Sabbe, its holdings were assembled by bringing together the theology collection of the new University and two other important libraries: the theological and historical collection of the Flemish Jesuits and the library of the Major Seminary of the Archdiocese of Mechelen. Together, these collections ensured that, from the very beginning, the Faculty had available an exceptionally well equipped scholarly library, including a rich collection of more than 170,000 manuscripts and early printed books dating from the 10th to the 19th century. During the following decades, the collection was increased by further libraries, from Faculty professors and from numerous religious orders and congregations, some as donations and some as long-term deposits. The Faculty also has a dynamic purchasing policy. The number of books is presently estimated to have reached over 1,300,000 volumes, making it one of the largest and richest libraries for theology and religious studies in Europe (and even in the world). In 2004, at the thirtieth anniversary celebrations, it was named the Maurits Sabbe Library, to honor its founder and first academic librarian.

The collections holds a large number of present-day books, journals and other research facilities, and the holdings of manuscripts and early prints continue to increase, now numbering c. 1,000 manuscripts and c. 170,000 early printed books: 500 incunabula, 1,750 post-incunabula (3,000 vols.), 5,500 titles (10,000 vols.) from the late 16th century, 55,000 from the 17th century, and 105,000 from the 18th and early 19th century.

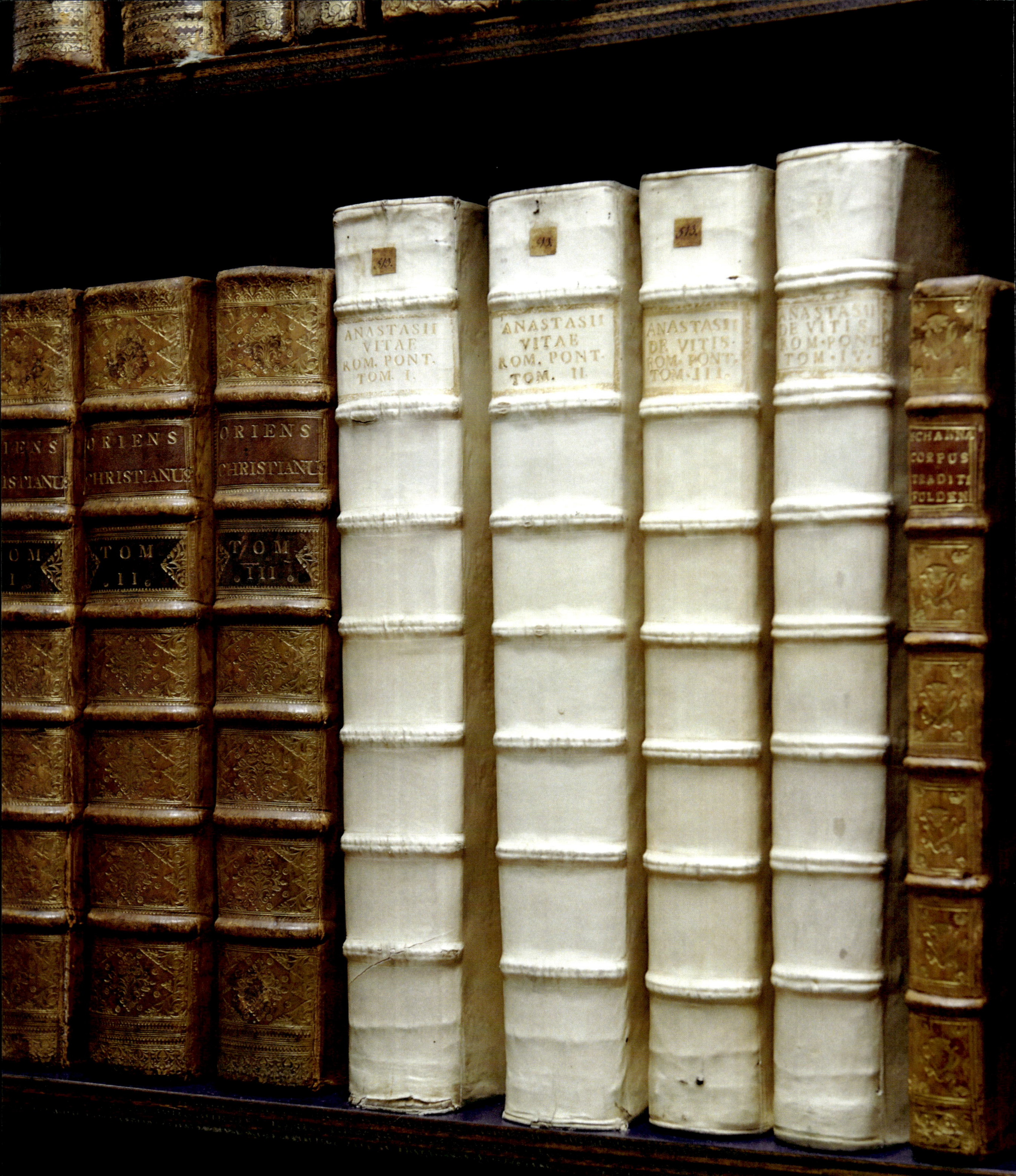
ORIENS CHRISTIANUS
TOM. II.
ORIENS CHRISTIANUS
TOM. III.
ANASTASII VITAE ROM. PONT. TOM. I.
ANASTASII VITAE ROM. PONT. TOM. II
ANASTASII DE VITIS ROM. PONT. TOM. III.
ANASTASII DE VITIS ROM. PONT. TOM. IV.

Furthermore, the Library hosts various archives, among them, the Centre for the Study of the Second Vatican Council, with a rich set of documents concerning the important Belgian representation at the Council, the Archives of the Leuven Faculty of Theology and some of its most eminent professors.

Two book series are published by the Library, *Documenta Libraria* (41 vols. published) and *Instrumenta Theologica* (41 vols. published). These series include catalogues, inventories, exhibition guides, editions of texts and documentary materials, and the proceedings of conferences related to the documents and publications preserved in the Library and its archives.

The extensive collections of the Maurits Sabbe Library are used as valuable resources for teaching, research and lecturing, and its holdings are being made widely accessible through well planned digitalisation programs. As part of KU Leuven Libraries it is a Heritage Library of the Flemish Community and holds several recognised masterpieces such as the Bible of Anjou and the large and precious library of the 18th-century Cardinal d'Alsace, Archbishop of Mechelen. Since 2016 an expert Centre for the Study and Conservation of Manuscripts and Books (the Book Heritage Lab – KU Leuven) has been housed in the Library, advancing the in-depth study of the content, codicology and condition of the collections through book-historical tools in combination with innovative technologies.

This volume includes forty-five descriptions of remarkable books representing the immense variety and richness of the Maurits Sabbe Library. The portrayed Bibles, missals, atlases, religious, devotional, historical, botanical and medical works are all reflecting the wealth of one of the most distinctive rare book collections in the Low Countries.

Wim François
Lieve Watteeuw
Leo Kenis

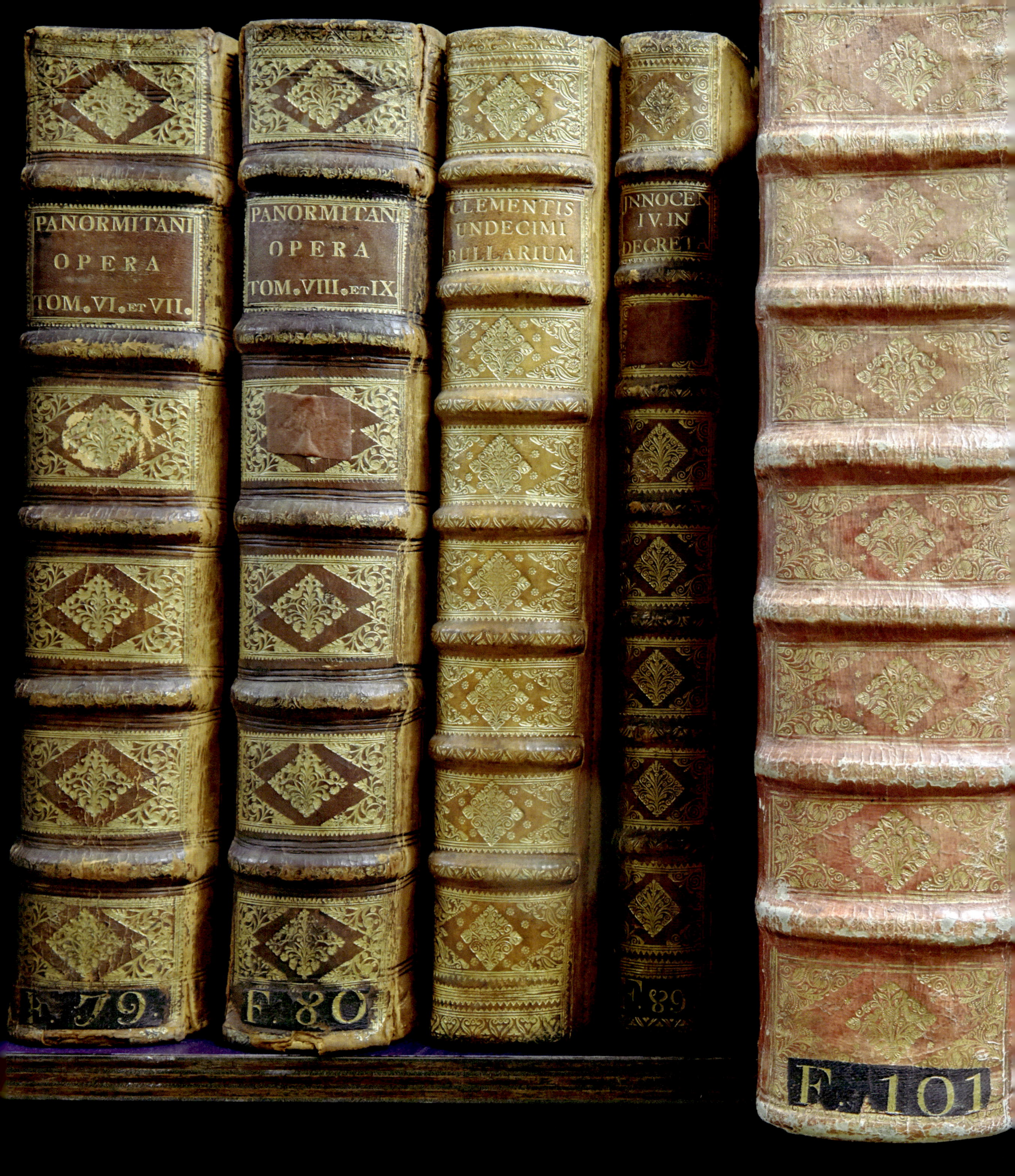
PANORMITANI
OPERA
TOM.VI.ET VII.
F.79.
PANORMITANI
OPERA
TOM.VIII.ET IX
F.80
CLEMENTIS
UNDECIMI
BULLARIUM
INNOCEN
IV.IN
DECRETA
F.89
F.101

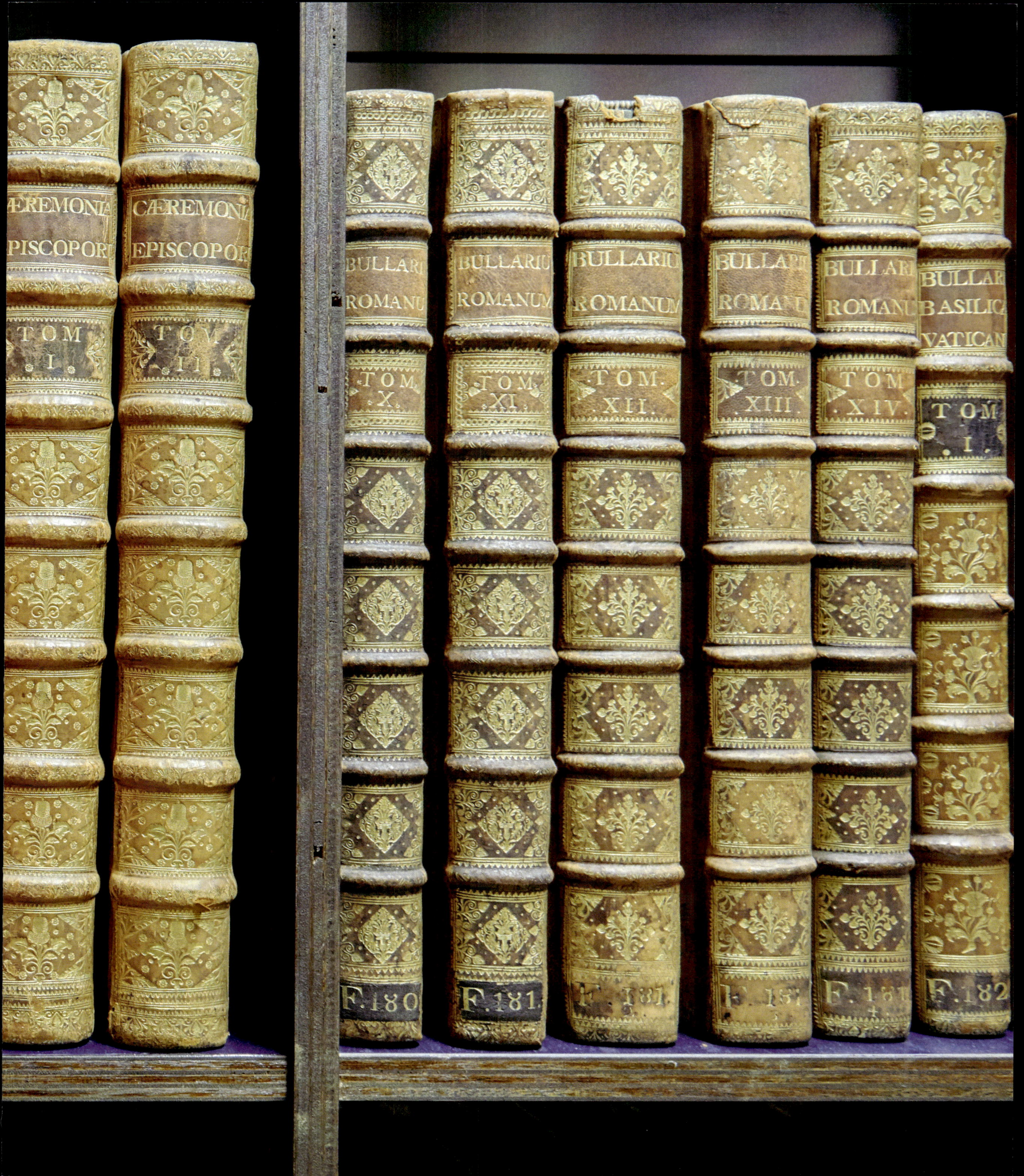
CÆREMONIA EPISCOPORU
TOM I
CÆREMONIA EPISCOPORU
TOM III
BULLARIU ROMANUM
TOM. X.
F. 180
BULLARIU ROMANUM
TOM. XI.
F. 181
BULLARIU ROMANUM
TOM. XII.
BULLARI ROMANU
TOM XIII
BULLARI ROMANU
TOM XIV.
BULLAR BASILICA VATICAN
TOM I.
F. 182

INCIPIUNT GESTA ABBATUM SANCTI TRUDONIS

Rodulfus gratia dei. sanctorum que Trudonis
et Eucherii. abbas eorum cenobii. omnibus
posteris meis. tam abbatibus quam monachis.
qui in hoc eodem cenobio deo sunt milita
turi. id fore quod profitemini. et pecca
tricis anime mee. interdum reminisci.
Sepe necnon et sepissime fratres karissimi.
totam armarii nostri reuoluens suppellectilem.
dum adhuc in carne qua nunc agoni
zatis positus essem. ardebam
uehementer me posse reperi
re. qui. et quot. et cuius professionis. utrum omnes monachi
an canonici aliqui fuissent predecessores mei. et cuius quisque
uocabuli. et quot annis prefuerit. Quod ad desiderium
meum fateor me nunquam potuisse reperire. Sed neque quisquam
erat antiquis de fratribus. qui se usquam hoc legendo repperisse
uel unquam audiendo didicisse diceret. ut ego scire querebam.
Hoc utrumne contigerit familiari semper nostris negligentia
notariorum. an inter frequentissimas loci desolationes.
amissione forsitan librorum. certum similiter habere nullo
modo potui. Dominum autem nostrum et piissime memorie.
sanctum Trudonem. clericum fuisse et sacerdotem. et cenobii
nostri primum edificatorem. vita ipsius docet. necnon et beati
Remacli tungrorum episcopi. Ubi et aliqui leguntur de principi
bus regnorum. et rectoribus ecclesiarum. quorum temporibus hoc
nostrum sanctissime puritatis lilium effloruit. Sed hoc mani
feste neque ibi. neque alias usquam datur intelligi. utrum
per eum ipsum regeret. primo edificatum cenobium nostrum.
siue per alium. clerici quoque siue monachi. fuerint. quos
in eo constituerit. et quando monachi in eo esse inceperint.
Talia que quidem dignissima essent sincera annotatione.
dum lectione aut uera relatione. sepe et ut dixi sepissime
uehementer arderem cognoscere. inueni libellum quendam
ubi uita sancti Siluestri habebatur. atque translatio sancti bene
dicti. necnon et sermo de assumptione sancte Marie semper
uirginis. In eo quantum repperi erum. hic annotare curaui.
Unde excusatum rogo habere me lectores huius mei opusculi
si minus quam uelletis certos uos reddidero. ex his de quibus
ipse certior esse non potui. Hec mea in hoc opusculo
est intentio. ut quod aliorum negligentia ferme obliteratum

¢ The first chronicle of the Abbey of Sint-Truiden ~ 1138

Rodulfus Trudonensis &
Folcardus Trudonensis
Gesta abbatum Trudonensium
Sint-Truiden, second half of
the 12th century, after 1138
92 f. · 221 × 120 mm
PM0029/V (Mechelen, Grootseminarie, codex 4)

The Abbey of Sint-Truiden was founded by Saint Trudo in Zerkingen c. 650. Although the abbey technically stood within the Diocese of Liège, the Bishops of Metz controlled the monastery, especially its material aspects. Rudolfus Trudenensis was the first writer of the Chronicle of the Abbots of Sint-Truiden (*Gesta abbatum Trudonensium*) covering the period from 628 to 1138; with 1138 marking the year of his own death, on 6 March. His work was continued by Folcardus, who was a cellerarius and cantor in 1108, and who became provost in 1112 before succeeding Rudolfus as Abbot of Sint-Truiden in 1138; he died on 11th May 1145. His contribution to the chronicle (volumes 8 and 10–13) dealt with the abbacy of Rodulfus himself (1107–1138).

The intention of Abbots Rodulfus and Folcardus was to record a series of notable facts from the history of the abbey, which were in danger of being forgotten, despite their vital role in substantiating the abbey's legal rights, both secular and ecclesiastical. A second aim was to encourage their successors to continue documenting the abbey's history. Descriptions of miracles performed by Saint Trudo and other saints of his time were included in the Chronicle, which also contains depictions of numerous political events from the time of the Franks and the German kings, in addition to many details of the Viking invasions, during which the abbey buildings were destroyed.

The text of the *Gesta abbatum Trudonensium* survives in three manuscripts. The oldest is the manuscript kept at the Maurits Sabbe Library, which contains only the work of the first authors, Rodulfus and Folcardus. The two later copies are preserved at the Royal Library of Belgium.

The text is delicately decorated with initials in blue, red, green and yellow at the beginning of each chapter; we find small initials in red, blue and green and small initials in red in the text. In the margins, multiple *maniculæ* have been added to draw attention to certain lines. Originally, all the large initials were protected with a textile veil on each page where they appear; the only one to remain is the white linen sheet on folio 98, covering the large initial F that opens chapter 9. In the 12th century, the decoration of the manuscripts of Sint-Truiden was influenced by the scriptorium of Saint-Hubert. The manuscript binding in brown leather was most probably realised under Abbot Georges Sarens (1533–1557), who rebuilt the library of Sint-Truiden. The text for the period between 999–1138, books I–XIII, was published by Dom Luc d'Achery in the series *Veterum aliquot scriptorum qui in Galliæ bibliothecis, maxime Benedictinorum, latuerunt spicilegium* (vol. VII, Paris, 1666).

Literature:
Carlo De Clercq, *Catalogue des manuscrits du Grand Séminaire de Malines* (Gembloux: J. Duculot; Paris: Les Belles Lettres, 1937), 19, 28–29; Steven Vanderputten, 'Rudolf of St. Trond', in *The Encyclopaedia of the Medieval Chronicle*, ed. Graeme Dunphy (Boston and Leiden: Brill, 2010), 1307.

¢ Hildegard von Bingen's visions in the Dendermonde Codex ~ 1175

Hildegard von Bingen
Liber Vitæ Meritorum
Elisabeth von Schönau
Liber Viarum Dei
Hildegard von Bingen
Symphonia Harmoniæ Cælestium Revelationum
Anonymous
Dialogue between a priest and the devil
Rupertsberg, Bingen-am-Rhein, c. 1175
183 f. · 290 × 200 mm
PM0045/V (Dendermonde, Abbey of Saints Peter and Paul, codex 9)

The Dendermonde Codex is one of the few extant manuscripts of works by Hildegard von Bingen that were written during her lifetime. The manuscript comprises four works: the *Liber vitæ meritorum* by Hildegard, one of her most important treatises; the *Liber viarum Dei,* a book of visions by Elisabeth of Schönau, a contemporary and friend of Hildegard; the *Symphonia harmoniæ cælestium revelationum,* a series of musical compositions by Hildegard; and finally, the so-called *Teufelsverhör,* a short exorcistic dialogue between a priest and the devil in which Hildegard herself also makes an appearance.

The manuscript was completed in approximately 1175 at the Abbey of Rupertsberg, where Hildegard was the abbess. It was made under her supervision to be sent as a gift to the Cistercian monks of the Abbey of Villers in Brabant, which was at that time under the care of Abbot Ulric (abbot from 1158 until 1184, died in 1196). The Dendermonde Codex is therefore of enormous importance to various fields. It was completed under the supervision of Hildegard herself, and is therefore imbued with her authority; it is one of only two extant manuscripts that contain musical works by Hildegard; it is an exceptional testimony to the thought of female mystics in the 12th century, and it is an important source of information about Hildegard's network and the dissemination of her theological, mystical, and musical insights.

The Dendermonde Codex is best known for Hildegard's musical works, collectively known as the *Symphonia armonie celestium revelationum.* They are not only an important part of her creative œuvre, but also more generally significant for the history of early music. The compositions channel Hildegard's visions and theological concerns by translating them into auditory compositions, and they also unite the community in the praise of God. At the same time, these works are among the greatest musical creations produced by a single person during the Middle Ages. Hildegard's compositions are most strongly related to Gregorian chants, and they regularly use forms that are typical of the Gregorian repertory. The Dendermonde Codex contains thirty-three antiphons, thirteen responsories, three hymns, five sequences, and two *symphoniæ.* Just as is the case with Gregorian chants, all these pieces had a liturgical function, such as the veneration of saints that were particularly important to Hildegard. A number of examples include Saint Disibod, the patron saint of the first convent where Hildegard lived; Saint Rupert, on whose burial site she founded her own convent; and Saint Ursula, who according to legend was martyred along with 11,000 other virgins. Hildegard was particularly devoted to Ursula.

Literature:
Peter Van Poucke, ed., *Hildegard of Bingen: Symphonia harmoniæ caelestium revelationum – Dendermonde St.-Pieters & Paulusabdij Ms. Cod. 9* (Peer: Alamire, 1991); *Hildegard of Bingen: Symphonia: A Critical Edition of the* Symphonia Armonie Celestium Revelationum *(Symphony of the Harmony of Celestial Revelations),* ed. and trans. Barbara Newman (Ithaca, NY: Cornell University Press, 1998).

lxii. Sicut talpa terram eicit, sic obstinatio queque bona euertit.

lxiii. Quod quia deus Iob ualde amauit, multas tribulationes super ipsum posuit.

lxiiii. Item de quibusdam purgatoriis penis animarum quorundam hominum qui in cupiditate peccauerant, et cur illas hoc modo sustineant.

lxv. Quomodo homines penitendo peccatum cupiditatis in se purgent.

lxvi. Quod cupiditas canibus et auibus qui non satiantur similis existens, ad illa que aliena sunt respicit.

lxvii. Item de quibusdam aliis penis purgatoriis animarum quorundam hominum qui in zelo peccata sibi attraxerant, et quare eas ita patiantur.

lxviii. Qualiter peccata discordie homines per penitentiam in corporibus suis puniant.

lxviiii. Quod qui discordiam diligunt a maligno spiritu fatigantur, ita quod discors et inpenitens homo in magno casu cadit.

lxx. Verba euangelii.

Incipit quarta pars. De uiro ad austrum et ad occidentem aspiciente.

Vidi quoque quod prefatus uir ad austrum se conuertit, ita quod et austrum et occidentem inspiciebat. Et terra in qua idem uir a genibus usque ad suras suas erat, humorem et uiriditatem ac germen in se habuit, et quasi floriditas ac decor uirtutis eidem uiro fuit, uelut uirtus ipsi per eam decorata esset, quia in diuersis generibus fertilis est, scilicet quo omnia formata in terrenis creaturis de terra producta sunt. Ipsa quoque materia operis dei in homine est, qui materia humanitatis filii dei est. Et ecce in superdicta nebula que diuersa genera uiciorum in se habuit ut prefatum est, nunc etiam octo uicia in imaginibus suis hoc modo uidebam. Nam prima imago caput ut hinnulus ceruorum habebat, et cauda ut ursus, reliquum uero corpus eius porco assimilabatur. Et eadem imago dicebat: Super quem iusticiam meam ponam? Super nullum. Nam si illum et illum inspicerem, creatura dei non essem, sed sicut asellus essem qui tarde incedit nisi per stimulum minetur. Sapientior enim et prudentior aliis sum. Solem quoque et lunam ac stellas ac ceteras creaturas scio, et unam

... & cithar

Mentes hominū de te flagrant & tabernacula animari

res ipsarū continet. Unde uoluntas ascendit & gustū

tribuit & eius lucerna ē desiderium. Intellectus te in

sono aduocat ac edificia tibi cū racionalitate parat qu

is opib⁹ sudat. Tu autē semꝑ gladiū habes illud abscid

nexiale pomum ꝑ nigerrimū homicidiū ꝓfert. Quando

uoluntatem & desideria tegit in quibus anima uolat.

et constringui ... Quando a

malū ad te gladiū suū educit tu illud in cor illi' refringis

in primo pdito angelo fecisti ubi turrim supbie illius in int

deiecisti. Et ibi aliā turrī in publicanis ⁊ peccatorib' eleuasti

tibi peccata sua cū opib' suis confitent̄. Unde om̄s creatur

de te uiuunt te laudant quia tu preciosissimum ungentum

es ⁊ fetidis uulneribus ubi illa in preciosissimas gemmas tue

Nunc dignare nos om̄s ad te colligere ⁊ ad recta itinera dirig

aris. ... u ... imo ... ure ... la ... q;

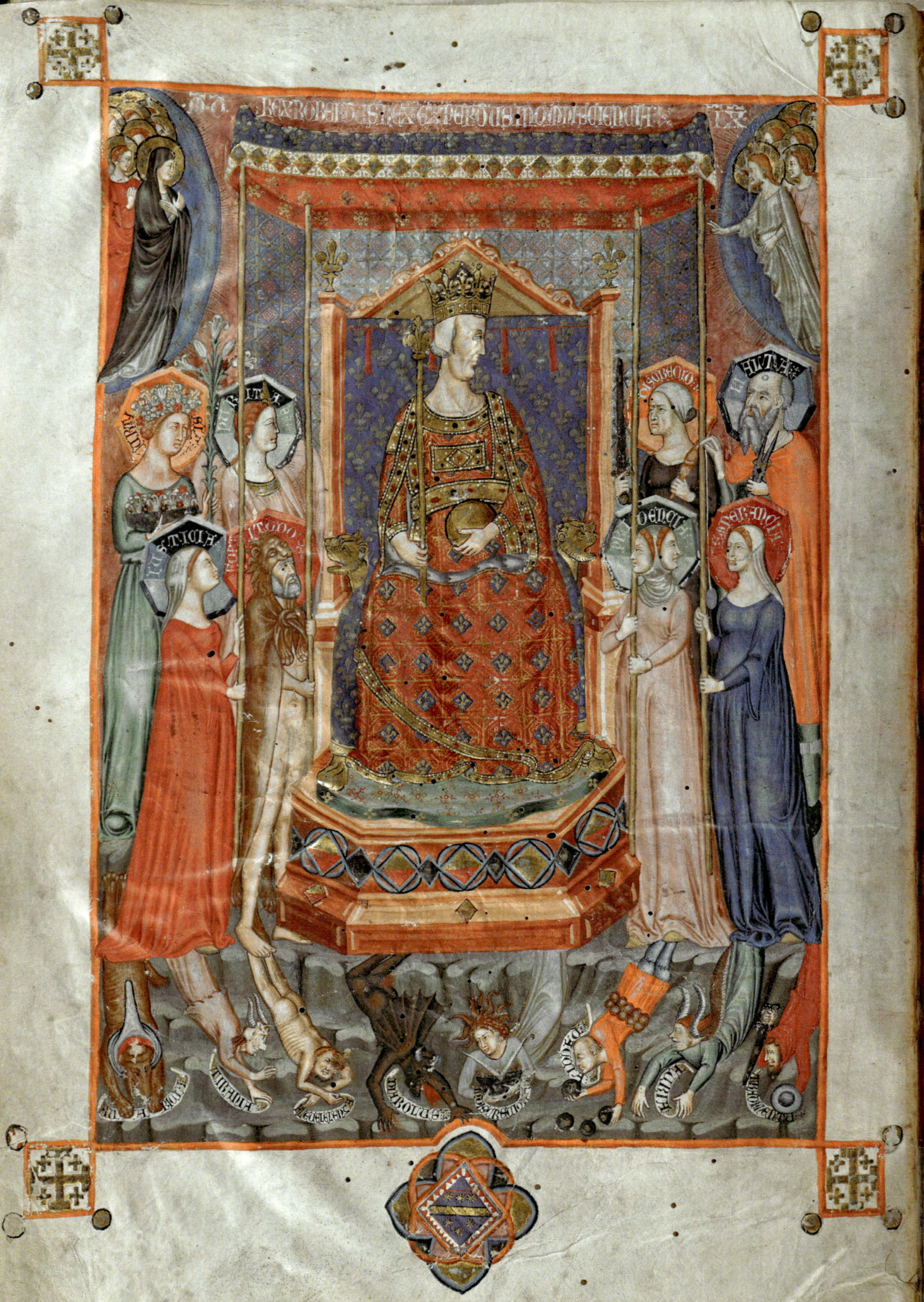

¢ A SPLENDID ILLUMINATED BIBLE FROM NAPLES ~ C. 1340

Anjou Bible
Naples, c. 1340
338 f. · 420 × 280 mm
PM0001/V (Mechelen, Grootseminarie, codex 1)

The Anjou Bible originated at the court of Robert of Anjou, King of Naples (1275–1343), who is celebrated in the opening diptych. On the left-hand page Robert is seen enthroned between virtues overcoming vices. On the right-hand page is a family tree in three registers, illustrating the history of the house of Anjou in Naples and Hungary. At the top are Charles I and his consort, Beatrice of Provence; in the centre are Charles II and his wife, Queen Mary of Hungary; with two kings, their third son Robert of Naples and the King of Hungary, either their eldest son, Charles Martel or his son Charles Robert with their heirs, the young Louis and Andrew of Hungary; below, are Robert and his wife, Queen Sancha of Majorca. Robert's only son Charles died unexpectedly in 1328, and in 1330, Charles's eldest daughter Joanna (1326–1382) was officially proclaimed successor to the Neapolitan crown; she and her sister are seen kneeling by Queen Sancha. In 1334, Joanna was betrothed to Andrew of Hungary (1327–1345), son of Charles Robert of Anjou. This is where the illustrious history of the Anjou Bible may have begun, as a gift from Robert of Anjou to Joanna and Andrew. When Robert died in 1343, intrigues at the Neapolitan court prevented Andrew from becoming king and in 1345 he was killed. It was perhaps at this moment that the Bible was acquired by Joanna's loyal chancellor, Niccolo Alunno de Alifio, as stated on folio 308: *hec est blibia* [sic] *magistri nicolai de alifio doctor*[*is*].

The manuscript contains many allusions to the royal house and its principal representatives. The book of Ecclesiastes, for instance, opens with an historiated initial of the author, the Preacher, depicted as a prince with the features of Robert of Anjou, enthroned and preaching to a crowd (fol. 79r). The reason for this is not hard to perceive: Robert was concerned not only with kingship but also with theology, often writing and delivering sermons that earned him the nickname 'the preacher king'. His credentials are put forward in the caption to his first portrait in the opening diptych: *rex expertus in omnia scientia;* translated as "king expert in all branches of knowledge." The prestigious manuscript was passed around in princely circles. In 1402, it was listed in the inventory of John, Duke of Berry (1340–1416), who was the brother of Charles V of France and a renowned lover of art and books. The identification is confirmed by Berry's inventory of 1413, which cites the opening words on the second folio. Traces of the duke's coat of arms can still be made out on the fore-edge and his partially effaced ex libris reads: "Ceste Bible est à Jehan, filz de roy de France, duc de Berry et d'Auvergne, comte de Poitou et d'Auvergne." The Bible probably reached France through the second house of Anjou which came to rule Naples: Berry's elder brother, Louis I, Duke of Anjou (1339–1384), was chosen by Joanna of Naples as her heir.

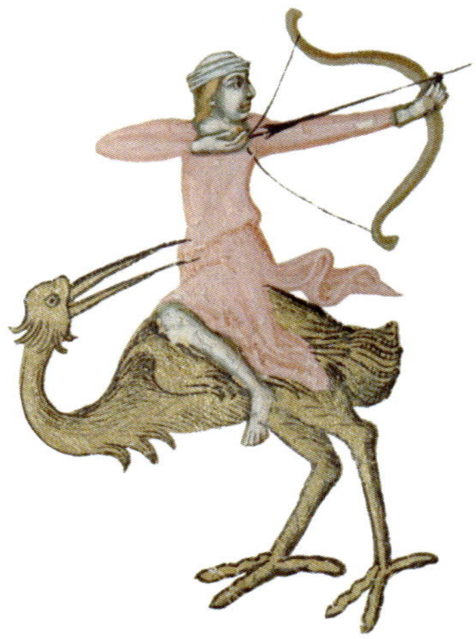

denudasti fundamenta eius usque ad collum. Maledixisti sceptris eius, capiti bellatorum eius venientibus ut turbo ad dispergendum me. Exultatio eorum sicut eius qui devorat pauperem in abscondito. Viam fecisti in mari equis tuis, in luto aquarum multarum. Audivi et conturbatus est venter meus, a voce contremuerunt labia mea. Ingrediatur putredo in ossibus meis, et subter me scateat. Ut requiescam in die tribulationis, ut ascendam ad populum accinctum nostrum. Ficus enim non florebit, et non erit germen in vineis. Mentietur opus olive, et arva non afferent cibum. Abscindetur de ovili pecus, et non erit armentum in presepibus. Ego autem in domino gaudebo, et exultabo in deo Ihesu meo. Deus dominus fortitudo mea, et ponet pedes meos quasi cervorum. Et super excelsa mea deducet me victor in psalmis canentem. Incipit prologus Sophonie prophete.

Tradunt hebrei cuiuscumque prophete pater aut avus in titulo ponitur, ipsos quoque prophetas fuisse. Verum Amos unus de duodecim prophetis qui dicit: Non sum propheta nec filius prophete, sed pastor caprarum vellicans sicomoros, patris nomen in titulo non habet. Hic vero nunc Sophonias propheta est, qui generationem in quo sunt ita dicamus prophetiam, gloriosa maiorum suorum stirpe generatus est. Sub Iosia rege Iuda prophetavit. Huius enim patrem Chusi, avum Godoliam, proavum Amasiam, atavum Ezechiam, qui ad regnum lectus velut extremus angustia complevit. Nomen Sophonie alii speculam, alii archanum domini transtulerunt. Sive igitur specula sive absconditum domini interpretetur, utrumque prophete convenit. Dicitur enim ad Ezechielem: Fili hominis speculatorem posui te domui Israel. Iste ergo propheta qui erat in specula et in sublimibus constitutus, et noverat misteria domini, filius erat Chusi, quod interpretatur humiliati. Habebat autem Godoliam, qui dicitur magnitudo domini, et proavum Amasiam, qui interpretatur in sermone domini, et atavum Ezechiam, qui sonat fortitudinem domini. De fortitudine itaque domini notus est sermo domini, et de sermone domini nata est magnitudo domini, et de magnitudine domini nata est humilitas. Ut cum venisset aliquis ad perfectum diceret: quia non sum dignus vocari apostolus, et illud in psalmis: Domine non est exaltatum cor meum, neque elati sunt oculi mei. Sophonias speculator et archanorum domini cognitor audivit clamorem a porta piscium et ululatum a secunda et contritionem a collibus. Indicat quoque ululatum habitatoribus pile, quia conticuit omnis populus chanaan, disperierunt universi qui involuti erant argento. Incipit liber Sophonie prophete.

I

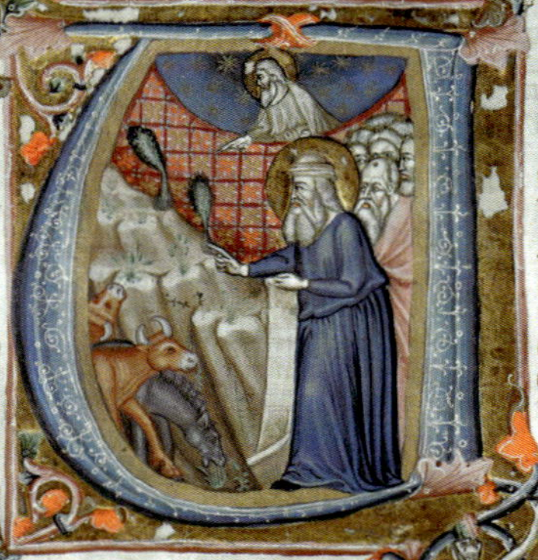

Verbum domini quod factum est ad Sophoniam filium Chusi filii Godolie filii Amasie filii Ezechie in diebus Iosie filii Amon regis Iude. Congregans congregabo omnia a facie terre, dicit dominus. Congregans hominem et pecus, congregans volatilia celi et pisces maris, et ruine impiorum erunt, et disperdam homines a facie terre, dicit dominus. Et extendam manum meam super Iudam et super omnes habitatores Ierusalem, et disperdam de loco hoc reliquias Baal et nomina edituorum cum sacerdotibus, et eos qui adorant super tecta militiam celi, et adorant et iurant in domino et iurant in Melchom, et qui avertuntur de post tergum domini, et qui non quesierunt dominum nec investigaverunt eum. Silete a facie domini dei, quia iuxta est dies domini, quia preparavit dominus hostiam, sanctificavit vocatos suos. Et erit in die hostie domini, visitabo super principes et super filios regis et super omnes qui induti sunt veste peregrina. Et visitabo super omnem qui arroganter ingreditur super limen in die illo, qui complent domum domini dei sui iniquitate et dolo. Et erit in die illa, dicit dominus, vox clamoris a porta piscium, et ululatus a secunda, et contritio magna a collibus. Ululate habitatores pile, conticuit omnis populus chanaan, disperierunt omnes involuti argento. Et erit in tempore illo, scrutabor Ierusalem in lucernis, et visitabo super viros defixos in fecibus suis, qui dicunt in cordibus suis: Non faciet bene dominus, et non faciet male. Et erit fortitudo eorum in direptionem, et domus eorum in desertum. Et edificabunt domos et non habitabunt in eis, et plantabunt vineas et non bibent vinum earum. Iuxta est dies domini magnus, iuxta et velox nimis. Vox diei domini amara, tribulabitur ibi fortis. Dies ire dies illa, dies tribulationis et angustie, dies calamitatis et miserie, dies tenebrarum et caliginis, dies nebule et turbinis, dies tube et clangoris super civitates munitas et super angulos excelsos. Et tribulabo homines et ambulabunt ut ceci, quia domino peccaverunt, et effundetur sanguis eorum sicut humus, et corpora eorum sicut stercora. Sed et argentum eorum et aurum eorum non poterit liberare eos in die ire domini. In igne zeli eius devorabitur omnis terra, quia consummationem cum festinatione faciet cunctis habitantibus terram. II

Convenite congregamini gens non amabilis, priusquam pariat iussio quasi pulverem transeuntem diem, antequam veniat super vos ira furoris domini. Querite dominum omnes mansueti terre, qui iudicium eius estis operati. Querite iustum, querite mansuetum, si quomodo abscondamini in die furoris domini. Quia Gaza destructa erit et Ascalon in desertum. Azotum in meridie eicient, et Accaron eradicabitur. Ve qui habitatis funiculum maris, gens perditorum. Verbum domini super vos, Chanaan terra Philistinorum, et disperdam te ita ut non sit inhabitator. Et erit funiculus maris requies pastorum et caule pecorum. Et erit funiculus eius qui remanserit de domo Iuda; ibi pascentur in domibus Ascalonis, ad vesperam requiescent, quia visitabit eos dominus deus eorum et avertet captivitatem eorum. Audivi obprobrium Moab et blasphemias filiorum Amon, que exprobraverunt populo meo, et magnificati sunt super terminos eorum. Propterea vivo ego, dicit dominus exercituum deus Israel, quia Moab ut Sodoma erit, et filii Amon quasi Gomorra. Siccitas spinarum et acervus salis et desertum usque in eternum. Reliquie populi mei diripient illos, et residui gentis mee possidebunt eos. Hoc enim eis eveniet pro superbia sua, quia blasphemaverunt et magnificati sunt super populum dei exerci-

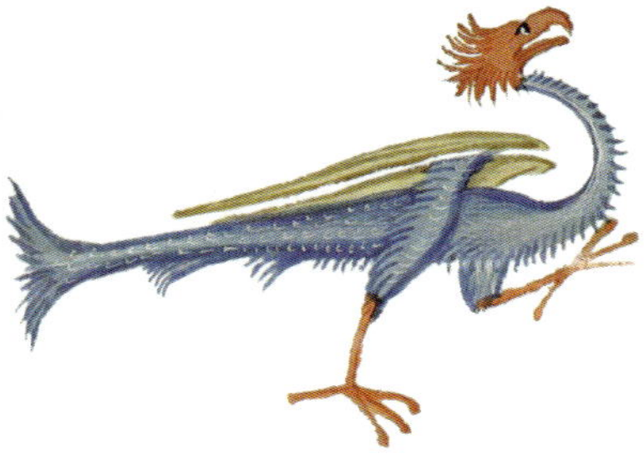

The Bible may have come to the Arras College in Louvain from its founder Nicolas de Ruistre (Ruterius), Bishop of Arras, who died in 1509. It is noted as having been at the college via a citation in the 1547 Louvain edition of the Vulgate Bible and when it was quoted in the *Notationes in Sacra Biblia* by Franciscus Lucas of Bruges, published in 1580. The manuscript catalogue of the library of the Major Seminary in Mechelen shows that it was a part of that collection between 1808 and 1821. Since 1970, it has been on permanent loan to the Maurits Sabbe Library.

In addition to the two full-page miniatures of the opening diptych, the Anjou Bible has over 160 illustrations consisting of historiated initials introducing the various books of the Bible, as well as smaller miniatures alluding to the biblical texts or historical events relating to the royal house of Naples; and on a large number of folio's there are also borders teeming with invention. The text itself is written in two columns in a characteristic Italian book hand; on the last page of the Apocalypse (fol. 311v) is the name of the scribe: *Iannutius de Matrice incepit, mediavit et finivit hoc opus*. The miniatures are the work of several Neapolitan artists, led by Cristoforo Orimina, whose name appears on folio 308: *quam illuminavit de pincello xpophorus orimina de neapoli*. He was responsible for all the 'historical' miniatures connected with the Angevin rulers of Naples that shed light on the origin of the manuscript. His style is characterized by sturdy figures, firmly rooted in reality, whose heavy faces have a Byzantine cast and are often painted in profile. The other major contributor in Orimina's workshop is an artist who concentrated on the biblical scenes and marginal decoration. The style is typical of Naples in the mid-14th century, in combining aspects of French illumination with trends that were current at the time in Florence and Siena, while still looking to the Byzantine tradition. The fantastical monsters and grotesques that can be seen among the twining stems and foliage are particularly characteristic of this style: either pursuing each other or locked in combat, they are evocative of pagan opponents to the biblical protagonists. Collectively, the miniatures and borders present an exceptionally rich spectacle, striking in its liveliness and vibrant in its storytelling.

Literature:
Lieve Watteeuw and Jan Van der Stock, eds., *The Anjou Bible: A Royal Manuscript Revealed, Naples 1340* (Leuven: Peeters, 2010).

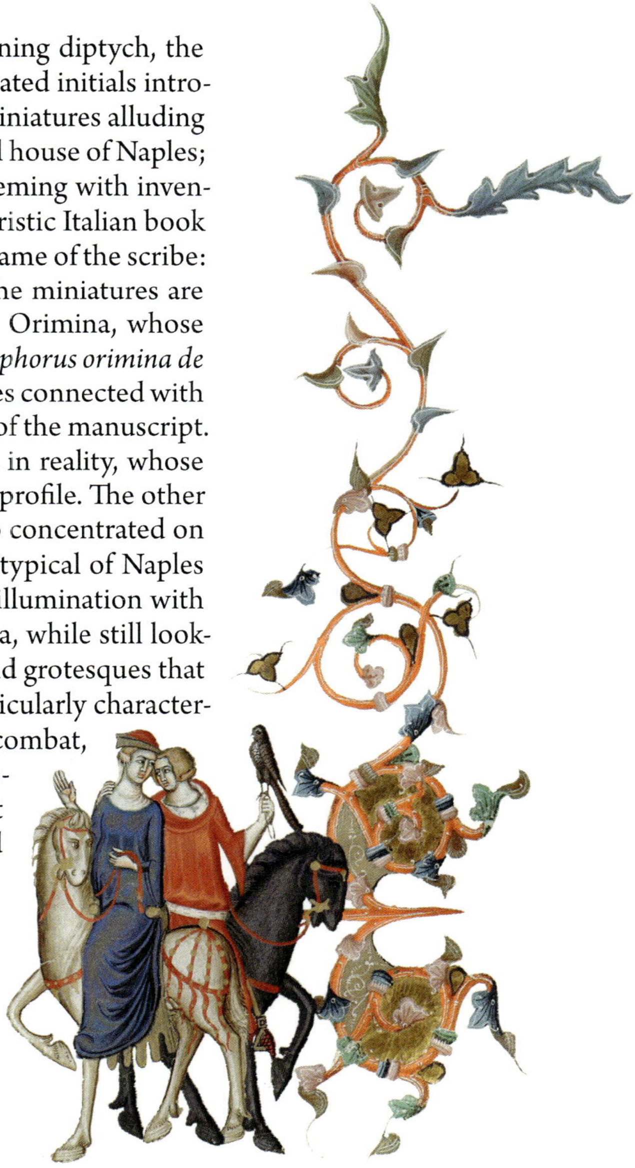

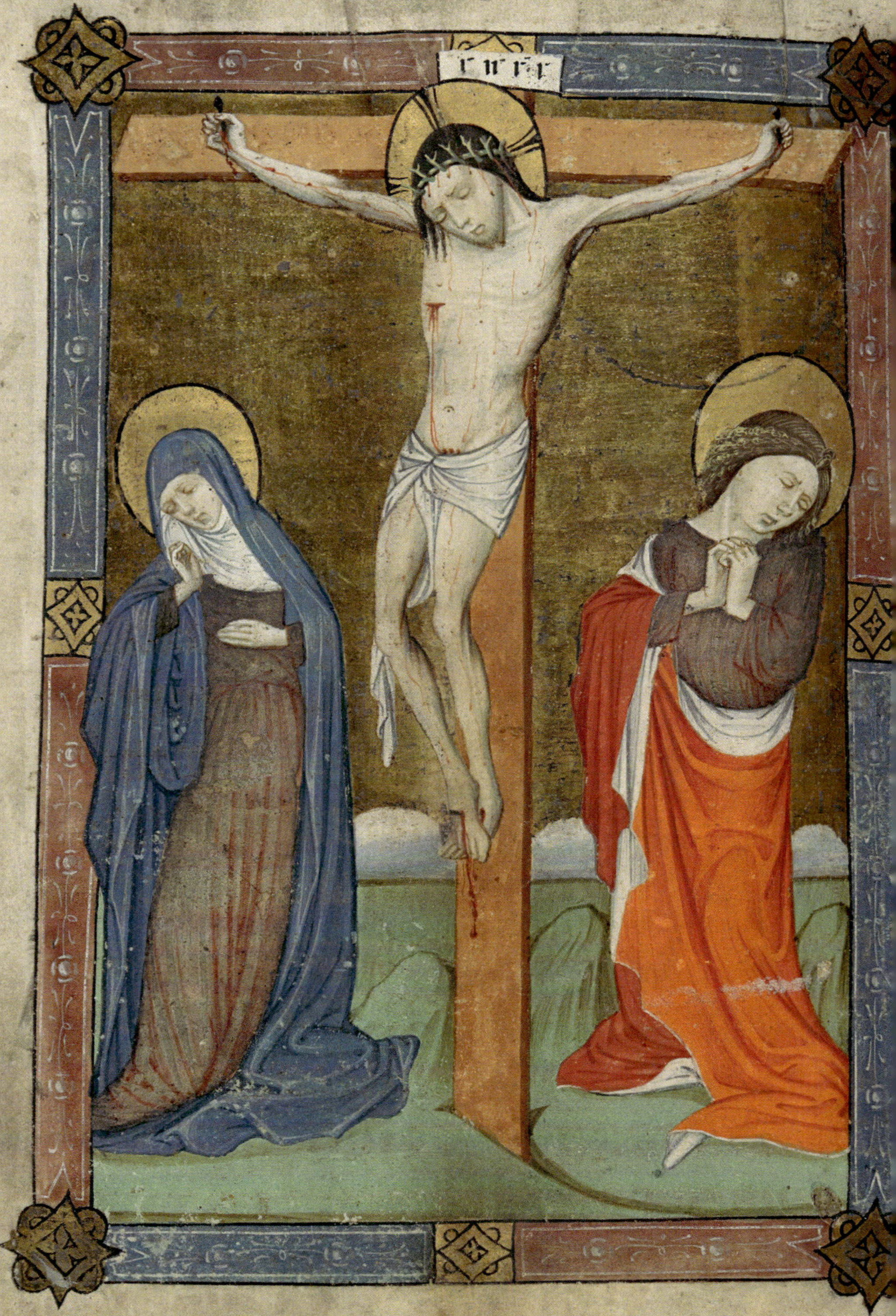

A MISSAL FOR COLOGNE MADE IN NIJMEGEN ~ C. 1450

Missale
Nijmegen (?), c. 1450
266 f. · 355 × 240 mm
PM0032/V (Nijmegen, Berchmanianum, 2 B1)

This manuscript dates from c. 1450 and its leather binding – which is of a later date – is in bad condition: both the front and the back cover have come unattached. This is a missal, i.e., a book that contains the texts and prayers used during the celebration of Mass. This missal is well-made, but by no means elaborately adorned. It does not show evidence of extensive use, except on the folios that contain the canon of the Mass. This is not surprising given that this is the part of the liturgy that is used most often. A number of folios have been left blank. We know nothing about the origin of this missal, but according to A. J. Geurts, it was intended for use in the Diocese of Cologne, and it was probably made in Nijmegen.

As is customary, the middle of the missal contains the canon, the main Eucharistic Prayer for the consecration of the bread and wine. In this missal, the canon is preceded by a full-page miniature that was probably made in Zwolle, and depicts the crucified Christ with Mary, his mother, to his left, and John the Apostle to his right. The fact that this miniature was included on precisely this page is no coincidence. Indeed, when the priest celebrates this section of the liturgy and begins the Eucharistic Prayer, he sacramentally repeats the events of the crucifixion. This miniature is therefore far more than a mere illustration; it has a performative function. It is intended to stimulate a specific spiritual attitude in the user – the priest celebrating Mass. A missal is not a book that seeks to convey knowledge or information, it is a book that functions solely in the service of a spiritual event.

The miniature in this particular missal (from the circle of the Masters of Otto of Moerdrecht) is remarkably beautiful. The eyes of the three figures are closed, emphasising the interior significance of the event. At the same time, the detailed depiction of the blood on Jesus' body renders the scene very realistic. Both Mary and John are painted to show a sense of intense but restrained emotion. Their gestures are expressive but at the same time dignified and noble. The golden tone of the background evokes the presence of the divine during the event depicted. It is surprising, however, that there are almost no decorative elements in this miniature, except for the relatively simple frame. This fully directs the viewer's gaze to the events that are transpiring.

Literature:
A. J. Geurts, *Moderne devotie: figuren en facetten: Catalogus tentoonstelling ter herdenking van het sterfjaar van Geert Grote 1384–1984* (Nijmegen: Katholieke Universiteit, Afdeling Hulpwetenschappen van de geschiedenis, 1984).

¢ The first printing of Thomas a Kempis ~ 1473

Few authors from the Low Countries have had such a profound influence on the international development of Christian culture and spirituality as has the Windesheim canon Thomas a Kempis. He is best-known for his *Imitatio Christi* (*Imitation of Christ*), but he wrote many other works. Thomas was the novice master of his monastery, Sint-Agnietenberg (Mount Saint Agnes) in Zwolle, and the majority of his works were written as spiritual treatises intended to help novices to develop their spiritual lives, as a way to develop a personal relationship with God. Thomas is one of the most-celebrated representatives of the *Devotio Moderna,* a late-medieval spiritual movement that was inspired by the desire to experience the profundity of the Christian faith and the relationship with God both externally and internally, in the most personal way possible. Thomas' œuvre is entirely devoted to this goal.

Thomas died in 1471 and his works appeared in print not long after. The printing press was a relatively new medium ('block books' had begun to appear in the West c. 1440), and Thomas' confreres commissioned the Utrecht printers Nicolaus Ketelaer and Gherardus de Leempt to print his treatises. The very first printed version of Thomas' works does not contain the four texts that constitute the *Imitation of Christ.* His *Soliloquium animæ* (*Soliloquy of the Soul*) was not included either. In other words, though this is a large volume, it does not contain Thomas' complete œuvre. Research has demonstrated that this first printing is very close to Thomas' autograph. It is striking that in printing these works, the particular punctuation mark known as the *flexa* was preserved. The *flexa* indicated the specific rhythm required when reading the text aloud. This print is thus a fine example of the way in which early printed books initially retained the typical characteristics of texts in manuscripts. While printing would eventually lead to the possibility for all readers to possess their own copy of a book, early printers did not take this possibility into account. Indeed, this edition of Thomas' works was clearly intended to be read aloud. Furthermore, the fact that the *flexa* was retained in the printed version is a clear indication that the printers were aware of the literary quality of Thomas' work, which could be fully expressed when read aloud.

Thomas a Kempis
Sermones, epistolæ et alia opuscula
[Utrecht: Nicolaus Ketelaer – Gerard de Leempt, 1473?
[246] f. · in 2°
P Inc 83B13

Literature:
Thomæ Hemerken a Kempis Opera Omnia, ed. Michael J. Pohl, 7 vols. (Freiburg: Herder, 1902–1922); Reinier R. Post, *The Modern Devotion: Confrontation with Reformation and Humanism* (Leiden: Brill, 1968).

Incipit prologus deuoti viri fratris Thome kempis presbiteri canonici regularis pfessi et defuncti in mōte beate agnetis prope zwollis. in sermones ad nouicios regulares

Dilectis in cristo fratribus innocentio simpliciano ac ceteris crucifixi discipulis: sacre religionis disciplinam diligentibus. Frater peregrinus in valle lacrimarum degens: orationum vestrarū iuuamina humiliter petens. Pax cristi in cordib3 vestris habūdet: et paciencia multiplex vobis et michi in cruce cristi cōdonetur. Sermones quos per modum dulcis collationis pro nouicijs nostris diuersis quidem temporibus in vnum collegi: vobis in caritate cōmunicare pium censui iustumqꝫ existimaui. Quāuis igitur incultus sit sermo. et materia nō ardua: tamen simplicibus placere cupiens. quod dominus inspirauit et dedit: libenter pijs et deuotis offero ad legendum. Quod si forte indiscretus sermo quēpiam offenderit. peto vt venia concedat exiguo: atqꝫ in melius reformetur. quod absurdum foris sonare videtur. Et quia exempla sepe plus mouent audientes ꝙ sola verba: idcirco more beati gregorij īstructus. in plerisqꝫ locis post finem sermonis pro maiori assertione exempla quedā sicut memorie occurrebant breuiter annotaui. Gratanter fratres accipite que vobis sicut dilectis amicis offero: oretis vt sint omnia ad honorem dei et multorum profectum. Sciendū itaqꝫ ꝙ liber iste continet sermones xxx et habet tres ptes Quarꝫ prima ps continet nouem sermones: ad designandū nouē choros angelorum. Secunda autem pars cōtinet sermones decem: ad designandum decalogum legis. secundum numerum decem preceptorum. Tercia vero pars continet sermones vndecim ad designandū statum religiosorum. in renunciatione seculi et baiulatione crucis: secundum consiliū nostri saluatoris dicentis. Qui vult venire post me abneget semetipsum et tollat crucem suam et sequatur me

Explicit prologus

b

A Louvain print as a guidebook for Columbus ~ 1483

Pierre d'Ailly
Ymago mundi
Leuven: Joannes de Westfalia, c. 1483
[172] f. · in 2°
P Inc SJH Q° R 37 U PETR 1483*

Pierre d'Ailly (Petrus ab Alliaco) (1351–1420), theologian, Bishop of Cambrai and later a cardinal, was very active in religious, political and scientific circles. His peers called him *Aquila Franciæ et aberrantium a veritate malleus indefessus* (the eagle of France and the indefatigable hammer of the heretics). Confessor of Charles VI and Chancellor of the Sorbonne, he sided with the Avignon popes during the Western Schism. He played an important role at the Council of Constance, which ended the schism with the election of Pope Martinus V in 1418. As a scholar, he wrote more than 170 manuscripts about philosophy, theology, asceticism, astrology, and astronomy. One of his most famous works is *Ymago Mundi*, a type of encyclopedia containing what was known, at that time, about geography and astronomy. As Aristotle, Pliny, and many scholars from his time had thought, he too assumed the earth was round and at the centre of the universe. On the globe reproduced here, besides indicating Europe, Africa and various rivers and seas, he showed that the road from Europe to India was shorter over the western seas than around Africa. This work was printed in Louvain for the first time in 1483.

Johannes de Westfalia was born in Paderborn in 1440/45. He left Paderborn for Cologne, followed by Mainz and then to Venice to learn the art of printing. In 1472, he ended up in Louvain, a city well known for its university as well as for its beer, where there was seen to be a future for competent printers. Johannes worked for a year with Dirk Martens in Aalst before starting his own business in Louvain.

Johannes de Westfalia cast his own letters, *litera vera modernata,* an easy to read gothic letter type as well as a new roman letter. From 1474 to 1496, he printed at least 190 books, gradually becoming the main printer from the Netherlands. Out of 16,299 incunabula (according to Hain), 1,250 originated in the Netherlands.

The book *Ymago Mundi* is best-known for Christopher Columbus having used one of its copies as a guidebook to sail to India from the west. Columbus annotated the book with more than 900 personal notes. This copy is kept in the Biblioteca Colombina of Seville that was founded in the 16th century by Fernando Columbus, the son of Christopher. In twenty-five years he collected more than 15,000 manuscripts and books. On the occasion of a trip to Louvain in 1532, he convinced Nicolaus Clenardus (1493/95–1542) from Diest and Johannes Vassæus (1511–1561) from Bruges, both associated with the Collegium Trilingue, to travel with him to Spain. Vassæus afterwards became the first librarian of the Biblioteca Colombina.

Literature:
Laura Ackerman Smolle, *History, Prophecy, and the Stars: The Christian Astrology of Pierre d'Ailly, 1350–1420* (Princeton, NJ: Princeton University Press, 1994).

Septima figura.

Hec figura seruit.xiiii. capitulo ⁊ pluribꝰ aliis pro diuisione terre in tres partes ⁊ similiter pro distinctione maris ac quorūdam fluminū ac regionū hic gr̄a exempli posito rum quia particularior distinctio maiorē figurā requirit. Mare mediterraneū exit ab oceano per strictum meatū circa hispaniā prope gades herculis. Mare vero rubrū exit ab oceano circa mediū oriētis ⁊ meridiei id est versus meridiē circa mediū oriētis ⁊ occidentis ā cuius litore vir in āno terminus indici oceani nauigatione attingitur.

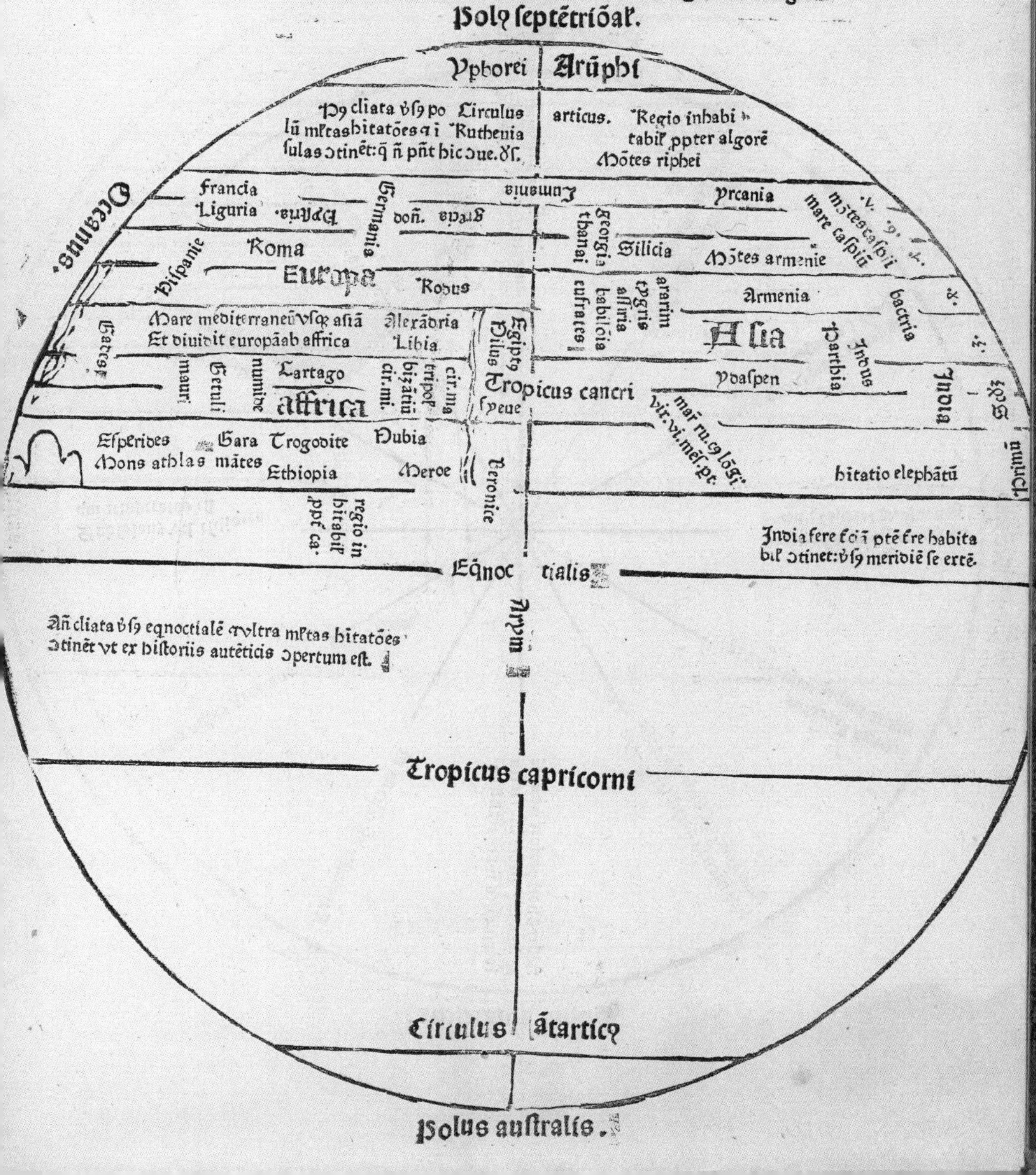

¢ A Venetian edition of an Arabic therapeutic guide ~ 1483

Kitab al-Mansouri (*Book on Medicine Dedicated to al-Mansur*) is one of the most renowned Arabic medical treatises from the Middle Ages. It was composed in the early 10th century by the famous Arab-Persian physician, polymath, philosopher, and alchemist Abu Bakr Muḥammad ibn Zakariya al-Razi (c. 865–925), also known by his latinized name Rhazes (or Rasis). Al-Razi was born in Rayy (south of present-day Tehran, Iran) and became a well-know physician and hospital director in Rayy and Baghdad. He was the author of an impressive number of medical, philosophical, and alchemical works. *Kitab al-Mansouri*, dedicated to Al-Mansur ibn Ishāq, the governor of the province of Rayy, was a general textbook on medicine, which became one of the most influential works in medical practice and education throughout the Middle Ages. In the late 12th century, it was translated into Latin by Gerard of Cremona (c. 1114–1187), a translator of Arabic scientific works, active in Toledo. This Latin translation was known as *Liber medicinalis ad Almansorem* or *Liber Almansoris.* The work is organised as follows: the first, mainly theoretical part, consists of six chapters dealing with diet, hygiene, anatomy, physiology, general pathology, and surgery; part two, with chapters seven to ten, is devoted to more practical issues, such as diagnosis, therapy, special pathology, and practical surgery.

The ninth chapter of the book frequently circulated by itself in Latin translations as the *Liber Nonus ad Almansorem* or *Liber Nonus Almansoris.* This popular treatise of medical pathologies, describing over hundred different complaints or diseases, was extensively copied and commented upon until the 17th century. The first distinct printed edition was published in Padua in 1476. The 1483 edition at hand, printed in Venice by Bernardinus de Tridino, includes the commentary by Sillanus de Nigris' (15th century), printed alternatively with sections of Rhazes' text, and also an additional work: the *Receptæ* of Pietro da Tossignano († c. 1401), a textbook of therapeutics and *materia medica* following the order of the *Liber Almansoris.*

On f. a2 recto (f. a1, which contains the register, is lacking in our copy, originating from the Friars Minor of Sint-Truiden), beneath the incipit, there is a nine-line initial 'T' illustrated in red and green, with red pen work extending into the inner margin. On top of the folio we see handwritten entries which refer to owners of the book. There are early marginal notes in brown ink throughout the copy.

Rhazes
Nonus liber Almansoris: cum expositione eiusdem clarissimi doctoris Sillani de Nigris de Papia
Venice: Bernardinus de Tridino, 1483
[136] f. · in 2°

Literature:
Plinio Prioreschi, *A History of Medicine, 4: Byzantine and Islamic Medicine* (Omaha, NE: Horatius Press, 2001, ²2004), 239–250; Heinrich Schipperges, 'Bemerkungen zu Rhazes und seinem Liber Nonus', *Sudhoffs Archiv für Geschichte der Medizin und der Naturwissenschaften* 47 (1963): 373–377.

Incipit nonus liber Almansoris: cum
expositione eiusdē clarissimi doctoris Sil
lani de nigris de Papia.

Motus timor
dei preueniat ꝛ prici
piat opa mea felicita
bitqꝫ ea: qꝛ omne qđ
mouetur ab alio mo
uetur. Ut Aristote. v.
phisycorū. Ideo cau
sa mouens me Silla
num de nigris de pa
pia ad scribendū super nono libro Almā
soris tractatu de oībus egritudinibus a ca
pite vsqꝫ ad pedes contingentibus est: vt
cōplacerē illustri principi ac etiā magnifi
co dn̄o dn̄o Galeacio vice comiti virtutuꝫ
impiali vicario comiti generali virtutibꝰ
preclarissimo. et ideo virtutū comes meri
to noīat et pcordialiter mihi dilectissime:
Quia ī libro Almansoris ponit modus sa
lutis satis breuis in oībus egritudinibus.
Ideo hunc librū salutis volo nuncupari
In quo ordo talis seruabit. Primo quid
sit dispositio explicabitur. Secūdo que ꝛ
quot sunt cause. Tertio que ꝛ quot sunt si
gna manifestabitur ꝛ de pronostico aliqđ
addetur. Quarto modus salutis in oībus
egritudinibus applicabitur quibus oībus
deus felicē terminuꝫ imponat.

De cephalea ꝛ emigranea. c. j.

In principio huius libri quatuor īqui
rantur. Primū que ꝛ quot sunt eius
cause. Secundū quis sit libri titulus.
Tertium cui parti phie supponatur.
Quartuꝫ quis sit ordo hꝰ libri ad alios libros
Ad primuꝫ dicendum ꝙ cause huius libri sunt
q̄tuor. s. efficiens materialis formalis ꝛ finalis.
Causa efficiens fuit Ras. zacharie filius pre
cepto regis almansoris filii ysaias uel ysias: ꝛ
sic patet qđ sit nomē auctoris. Causa material'
est subiectū huius libri. s. corpus humanū sana
bile ab oībus egritudinibꝰ a capite usqꝫ ad pe
des ꝛ egrotabile. ꝛ sic patꝫ que sit intentio libri:
qꝛ est determinare de oībus egritudinibꝰ a capi
te usqꝫ ad pedes. Causa finalis est duplex scilꝫ
operis ꝛ operatoris. Operis est perfecta cogni
tio eorū que tradūtur in hoc libro. Sed opera
toris cā est duplex. s. mediata ꝛ imediata. Causa
imediata est per cognitionē eoꝝ que tradūtur ī
hoc libro. Scire curare oēs egritudines cōtin
gentes a capite usqꝫ ad pedes. Causa mediata
ē multiplex. s. exercicii ꝓprii intellectꝰ. Remanē
tia eius post mortē in fama uiuentiū ꝑpter obli
uionē cōtingentē ī senectute. Acquisitō honoris
Copia amicorū: ꝛ sic pꝫ q̄ sit utilitas libri. Cau
sa formalis est duplex. s. forma tractatus ꝛ for
ma tractandi. Forma tractatus est modus quē
tenet auctor in libro. s. diffinitiuus diuisiuꝰ ꝛc.
Forma tractandi est diuisio libri in tot capitula
quot sunt passiones de q̄bus determināt. Ad se
cundū dicendū ꝙ titulus libri est. Incipit nona
pars libri almansoris: qꝛ fuit ille cuiꝰ p̄cepto fuit
factus: ꝛ sic pꝫ quid sit nomen libri. Ad tertium
dicendū ꝙ supponitur phie naturali. Ad quar
tū dicendū ꝙ iste liber est nonus in ordine. Hic
eni totus liber habet decem partes. In prima
determinat de anathomia corporis humani ꝛ
membroꝝ. In scđa parte determinat de signis
corporis humani ꝛ physonomie. In tertia de
uirtutibꝰ medicinarū simpliciū. In quarta de
cōseruatione sanitatis. In quinta de decoratio
ne. In sexta de preseruatione iter agentiū a no
cumētis extrinsecis. In septima de chyrurgia.
In octaua de cura uenenorū. In nona de om̄i
bus egritudinibus a capite usqꝫ ad pedes potē
tibus accidere. In decima de febribus.

Circa rubricā ē notādū p̄io ꝙ egritudo
ē duplex. s. generalis ul' ul'is ꝛ particula
ris. Uniuersalis dr̄ q̄tuor modis: uno mō
uia p̄dicatiōis ꝛ sic mala complexio ē egritudo
ul'is. Similr̄ dr̄ ul'is solutio ꝯtinuitatis: p̄dicatur
eni de morbo ꝛ de figura. Secūdo dr̄ egritudo
ul'is uia occupatiōis uel cōtinentie: ꝛ sic febris
dr̄ egritudo uniuersal'. Tertō dr̄ egritudo uni
uersal' uia indifferētie: ꝛ sic apostema dr̄ egritu
do vl'is: qꝛ lꝫ apostema sit in uno mēbro: pōt ta
men fieri in aliis. Quarto dicitur egritudo vni
uersalis uia uirtutis ꝛ inferens nocumentū toti
corpori: ꝛ sic sincopis tremor cordis ꝛ appople
xia dicuntur egritudines ul'es: qꝛ oēs uirtutes
cadunt sub eis. Sed egritudo particularis dici
tur p oppositū quatuor modis. Uno modo ra
tione predicatiōis qꝛ nō predicatur nisi de vno
ꝛ sic mala cōplexio simplex inducta dicitur egri
tudo particularis. Scđo egritudo dicitur par
ticularis via occupationis: qꝛ solū unā partem
corporis occupat. ꝛ sic appoplexia dicitur par
ticularis capitis egritudo. Tertio dicitur egri
tudo particularis uia indifferentie: qꝛ sic fit in
uno mēbro ꝙ nō in alio: ꝛ sic appoplexia ē egri
tudo capitis ꝙ nō alterius mēbri: ꝛ istis tribus
modis capitur ab Auicē. tertio tm̄ mō a Rasi.

¢ Breydenbach's *Peregrinatio* as a virtual journey ~ 1490

In 1486, Bernhard von Breydenbach published his *Peregrinatio in Terram Sanctam*. Breydenbach was dean of Mainz and in 1483 had joined a group that was travelling to Egypt and Palestine. He had his impressions of this journey printed in Latin and in German and provided the book with twenty-eight woodcuts. The *Peregrinatio* was the first illustrated account of a pilgrimage to Jerusalem in print. The book's contents fit with the genre of a travel diary, with Breydenbach taking notes of his personal experiences. He recounts different customs, clothing and dietary habits in Venice, Jerusalem, Sinai and Egypt. The *Peregrinatio* also fits the genre of a pilgrimage account, a genre that has existed in Europe since the 4th century.

The pilgrim experiences hope to bring the journey to a good end, satisfaction of finally seeing the holy places, and perhaps too disappointment about the bustle endured and the misery seen along the way. The pilgrim's narrative seeks to share all these emotions with the reader. With the art of printing democratising the genre of the pilgrim account – Breydenbach's *Peregrinatio* went through twelve editions between 1486 and 1522 – it gained the additional function of a 'virtual journey'. Those unable to undertake distant travels due to physical or financial limitations, could hold in their hands a tangible glimpse of faraway locations and make a mental journey over the waves of the Mediterranean to the holy places, experiencing the destination vicariously through the author's stories.

Images are particularly useful as 'virtual guides'. The *Peregrinatio* contains seven masterfully carved panoramic views, one of which is famous as the oldest printed map of Jerusalem and its environs. The map is so large that it had to be folded. The city itself is seen from the east. It is, after all, from the easterly Mount of Olives that pilgrims can look out over Jerusalem in all her glory. And the map in Bernhard von Breydenbach's *Peregrinatio* enables readers to imagine themselves in this stunning location. One can picture the sun coming up over the Holy Sepulchre; hear the birds singing in the fragrant pines; stand in the place where Jesus of Nazareth rested, taught, and ascended into Heaven.

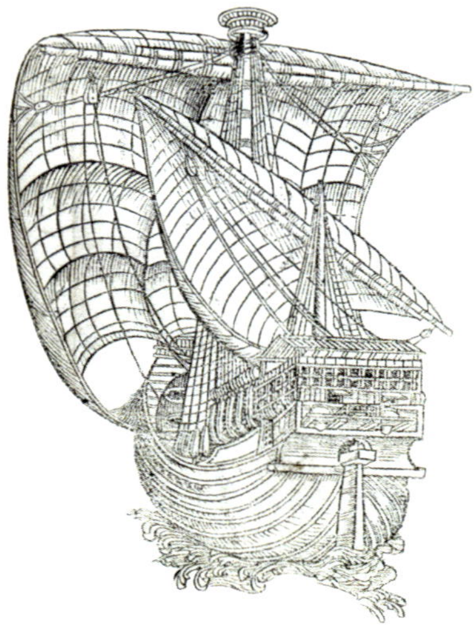

Bernhard von Breydenbach
Peregrinatio in Terram Sanctam
[Speyer]: Peter Drach, 1490
[120] f. · in 2°

Literature:
Frederike Timm, *Der Palästina-Pilgerbericht des Bernhard von Breidenbach und die Holzschnitte Erhard Reuwichs: Die* Peregrinatio in terram sanctam *(1486) als Propagandainstrument im Mantel der gelehrten Pilgerschrift* (Stuttgart: Dr. Ernst Hauswedell & Co., 2006); Bernhard von Breydenbach, *Die Reise ins Heilige Land: Ein Reisebericht aus dem Jahre 1483*, ed. Elisabeth Geck (Wiesbaden: Pressler, 1961, ²1977).

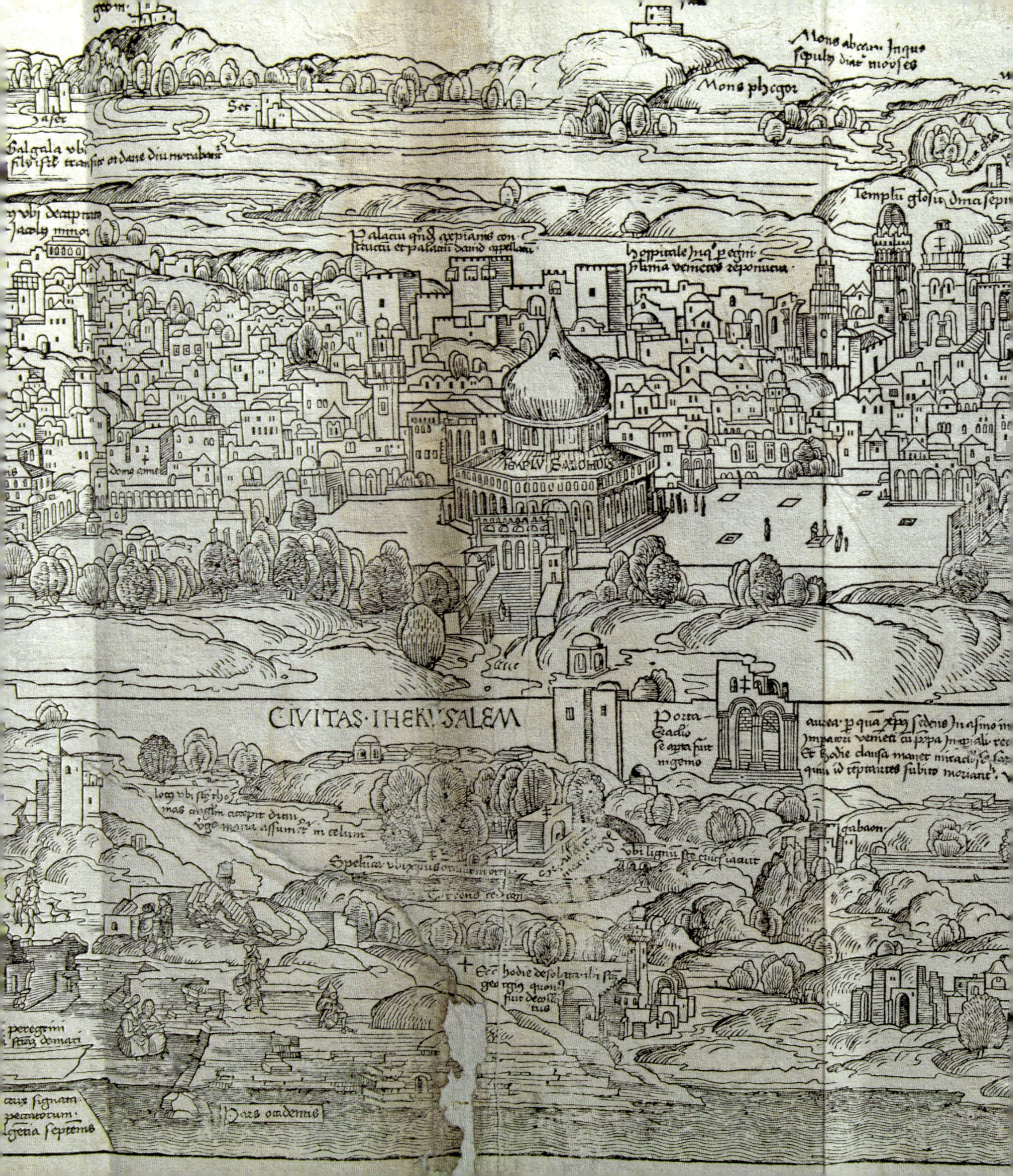
CIVITAS·IHERVSALEM
Mons phegor
Set
gabaon

¢ THE *BREVIARIUM ROMANUM* OF NICOLAS RUTERIUS ∾ C. 1500

A banderole with the motto *Equo Animo* in the lower part of the Ghent-Bruges style border decoration of this late 15th-century prayer book shows that it belonged to Nicolas Ruterius (1442–1509), Bishop of Arras and founder of the Arras College in Louvain. This famous bibliophile had excellent taste for luxuriously illuminated manuscripts: he was also probably the owner of the famous Neapolitan Bible of Anjou (see pp. 20–23 in this volume).

As commissioner of the two-volume breviary, written on the finest parchment, Ruterius left his motto and coat of arms, consisting of azure, three vine leaves, between flowers, insects, butterflies and birds. The decoration of the manuscript was carried out by one of the many thriving illuminators' workshops in Bruges.

The dark brown leather binding over wooden boards, decorated with panel stamps, testifies to the prestige of Ruterius's commission. Each cover has four impressions of the same panel stamp, representing a double row of three musician angels between branches. The six angels are playing the trumpet, the triangle, the tambourine, the lute, a hand organ and the harp. Around in gothic script is a citation of Psalm 137: *In conspectu angelorum / psallam tibi / domine et adorabo / ad templum sanctum / tuum et confitebor nomini tuo.* This remarkable panel stamp relates to those used by the De Gavere family of Bruges *boeckscrivers* (booksellers) and bookbinders, who were active at the end of the 15th and beginning of the 16th century. In the second half of the 15th century, blind-stamped book covers depicting a double row of mythical animals were particularly popular, but from c. 1500, compositions with music-making angels became more fashionable.

Later in the 16th century, the breviary was in the possession of Jacob van Pamele (Jacobus Pamelius, 1536–1587), a prominent bibliophile, who after his studies of philosophy and theology in Louvain and Paris, became a Canon of Saint Donatian's Church in Bruges and Archdeacon of Saint-Omer. This book lover left his gilded coat of arms on the front cover. At the end of the 18th century, during the upheavals of the French Revolution, the gilded coat of arms of Van Pamele was mercilessly scraped off with a small knife. Some gold fragments remain visible. In the mid-19th century, the breviary found a safe repository in the library of the Mechelen Seminary and was later transferred to the Maurits Sabbe Library.

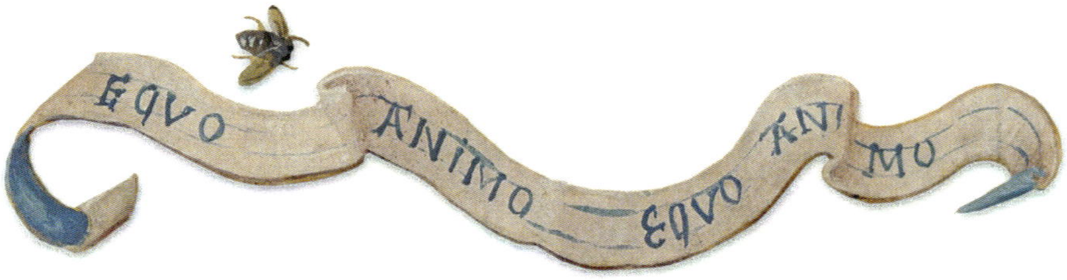

Breviarium Romanum
Flanders, c. 1500
348 f. · 198 × 140 mm
PM0010/V (Mechelen, Grootseminarie, codex 8)

Literature:
Carlo De Clercq, *Catalogue des manuscrits du Grand Séminaire de Malines* (Gembloux: J. Duculot; Paris: Les Belles Lettres, 1937), 31–33.

In vigilia pasche ad vš ā

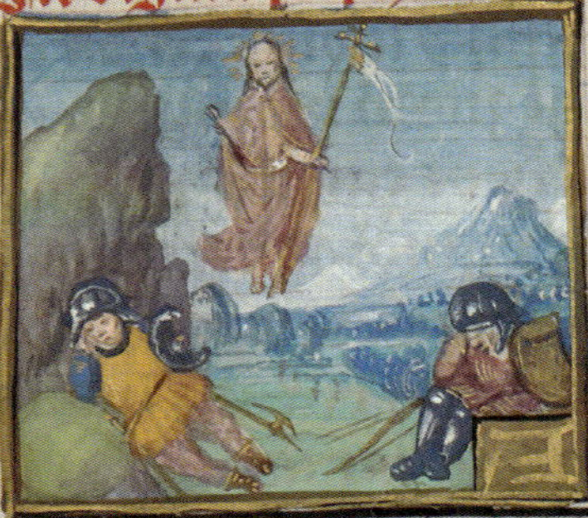

Alleluya alľa alľa Sub una
cātata cātatᷣ. ps Lauda
te dñm oēs gentes. cum
Glľa pri. Et reiteratᷣ ā.
Allľa Caplm. ẏmnus et vˀ
nō dñr. Ad aꝰ ā. Vespe
autē sabbati que luces
cit ī pma sabbi venit
maria magdalene ⁊ al
tera maria vidē sepul
chrū alľa post hoc dicat
sacerdos. Dñs vobiscū.
Spm nobis Dño
dñe tue caritatis
infunde. vt quos sacra
mētis paschalibus sa
asti. tua facias pietate
concordes. P eiusdem.
Dñs vobiscū postea dy

acon9 dicit. Ite missa ē.
cū duplici alľa. Sed nllo
alio tpe iūgitᷣ alľa cū Ite
missa ē. Ad cōplin. post
Iube dōpne. noctē qetā
et post lcōnē Fres sobri
i. et. Adiutoriū nrm In
cōfessione dicitᷣ vˀ. Cōn
te nos. Ds ī adiutoriū.
Deinde sn ā dicitᷣ ps con
sueti ī octauo tono. Cap
ẏm9 et vˀ nō dirˀ. Ad nūc
dittis ā. Vespe aūt sabbi.
orō. Visita qūs Ad ma
tutᷣ Inuitatoriū Sur
rexit dñs vere Alľa ps.
Venite Istē ẏm et capľa
nō dicitᷣ ī aliqua hora.
vsqȝ ad vš sabbi nec ṽsidi
ñ ad noctnū. In nº. aūt.
Ego sū qui sū et ꝯsili
ū meū nō ē cū īpns. ß
ī lege dñi volūtas mea
ē alľa p Btūs vir ā Pos
tulaui prēm meū alľa
dedit m̄ gentes alľa in
hereditatē alľa p Eruant

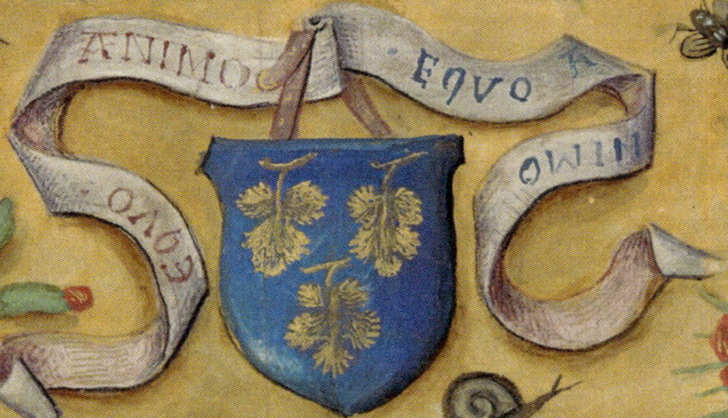

AN INFALLIBLE MANUSCRIPT? THE ADRIAN VI CODEX ~ 1499–1509

Collectanea Adriani
Leuven, 1499–1509
526 f. · 296 × 216 mm
PM0039/V (Mechelen, Grootseminarie, codex 17)

After Adrianus Florensz (Utrecht 2 March 1459–Rome 14 September 1523) had been enrolled as a student of Louvain University on 1 June 1476, he received his final degree as a Doctor of Divinity on 18 June 1491. As soon as 1490, he was teaching at the Faculty of Theology. Gradually he became one of the most influential men in the faculty, which found its expression in his two terms of office as rector of the university (1493 and 1500–1501) and as its vice-chancellor from the year 1497. His integrity and talent did not go unnoticed. In 1506, he became counsellor to Margaret of Austria and in 1507 he even tutored the young Charles V, who in 1515 sent Adrian to Spain in order to secure Charles's position as heir to the Spanish throne. Afterwards, Adrian remained in Spain as regent. At the same time, he rapidly rose in the ecclesiastical hierarchy: as Bishop of Tortosa, then inquisitor general, before becoming cardinal. On 9 January 1522, after Leo X's unexpected death, the conclave elected Pope Adrian VI in his absence. Only in August did the new pope arrive in Rome. Adrian tried to find an answer to the challenge put forward by Luther. His admission of abuses within the Church and his promised reforms, which were read at the Diet of Nuremberg in January 1523, remain well-known (and exemplary) up to the present day.

In his last will (dated 8 September 1523), Adrian founded a college for poor students of theology at his own house in Louvain, which still exists (Pope Adrian VI College). The volume now known as Maurits Sabbebibliotheek, MS 17, was preserved here until 1797, containing a series of autograph works by Adrian. This manuscript of 525 folios has his commentary on Proverbs (f. 2r–86v), his *Quæstiones quodlibeticæ* (f. 87r–222r) and his *Quæstiones in Quartum librum Sententiarum* (f. 223r–362r), as well as some orations for the promotions of former students of his, and sermons addressed to the Louvain clergy. Both *Quæstiones* were printed after Adrian left Louvain in 1515. New editions appeared after he had been elected pope. Central to these works is the reflection on the sacraments, first of all on that of confession. As this subject occupied a central position in Louvain theological thinking at that time, it is no wonder that among the theologians of the university originated the first reaction to Luther, culminating in the condemnation of some of Luther's theses in 1520 by the Louvain faculty.

Literature:
Michiel Verweij, *Adrianus VI (1459–1523): De tragische paus uit de Nederlanden* (Antwerp and Apeldoorn: Garant, 2011); R. Macken, 'The Hadrian VI Codex: A New Codicological Description', *Ephemerides Theologicæ Lovanienses* 59 (1983): 99–113; Michiel Verweij, ed., *De paus uit de Lage Landen: Adrianus VI 1459–1523. Catalogus bij de tentoonstelling ter gelegenheid van het 550ste geboortejaar van Adriaan van Utrecht* (Leuven: Leuven University Press, 2009), 146–150, no. 1.

De arbore affinitatis [illegible]

[illegible]

¢ Foresti's world chronicle ~ c. 1503

Jacobus Philippus Foresti
Novissimæ hystoriarum omnium repercussiones . . . quæ Supplementum supplementi Cronicarum nuncupantur
Venice: Albertino da Lissona, 1503
452 f. · in 2°

Jacobus Philippus Foresti (1434–1520) was an Augustinian friar who lived for a large part of his life in the convent of Bergamo where he took care of its library. He was the author of a *Supplementum Chronicarum*, which was published for the first time in 1483, and which was provided with rich illustrations in 1486, before being revised and extended by the author himself and printed in 1503 under the title *Novissimæ hystoriarum omnium repercussiones*. Between 1483 and 1547, at least eleven editions of the Latin version were published in Italy, as well as, between 1488 and 1581, eleven editions of the Italian translation; and a vernacular version was further published in Spain in 1510. The book's success was due to its self-identification as a 'supplement' to the various world chronicles and other chronographic works that were immensely popular among an early modern readership; Werner Rolevinck's *Fasciculus Temporum* being one of the most famous of such examples. Foresti had conceived his work to be an encyclopedic and universal chronicle, which arranged biblical, mythological, and historical figures and their acts, as well as the most important towns and geographic places connected to them, in fourteen chronologically arranged books (fifteen since 1503). One of its aims was also to show an example to those who had power over the course of history, so that they might act in a morally and responsible way in the interest of the Christian community. This task was, in Foresti's eyes, the more urgent, given the advance of the Ottoman Turks.

The Maurits Sabbe Library preserves a copy of the 1503 Latin edition, the last one that was reworked by Foresti and that was printed by Albertino da Lissona (Vercellensis) in Venice. It was illustrated with six large wood cuts with the coat-of-arms of Cardinal Antoniotto Palavicini (on the title page), a map of the world (f. a7r) and four biblical scenes, viz. the creation of Eve (f. a2v), the Fall and the expulsion of Adam and Eve (f. a8v), Cain and Abel (f. b2r), and the tower of Babel (f. b8r). It has an additional ninety small woodcuts with towns' sights. One of the peculiarities of the copy in the Maurits Sabbe Library is its being lavishly and beautifully coloured. It belongs to the historic Jesuit collection, and was preserved in the college of Halle, which was established in 1621. The first owner, however, was Joannes vander Schueren, parish priest of Saint Jacob's in Antwerp. After his death, the convent of Septem Fontes (Sevenborren or Seven springs), in the Sonian Forest near Alsemberg, came into possession of the book. As one of the former owners of the copy, also a certain Elisabeth Huyse is mentioned.

Literature:
Achim Krümmel, *Das "Supplementum Chronicarum" des Augustinermönches Jacobus Philippus Foresti von Bergamo* (Herzberg: Bautz, 1992); Frans Gistelinck and Maurits Sabbe, eds., *Early Sixteenth Century Printed Books 1501–1540 in the Library of the Leuven Faculty of Theology* (Leuven: Bibliotheek Godgeleerdheid and Peeters, 1994), 3, 6, 9, 11–12, 334 no. 380.

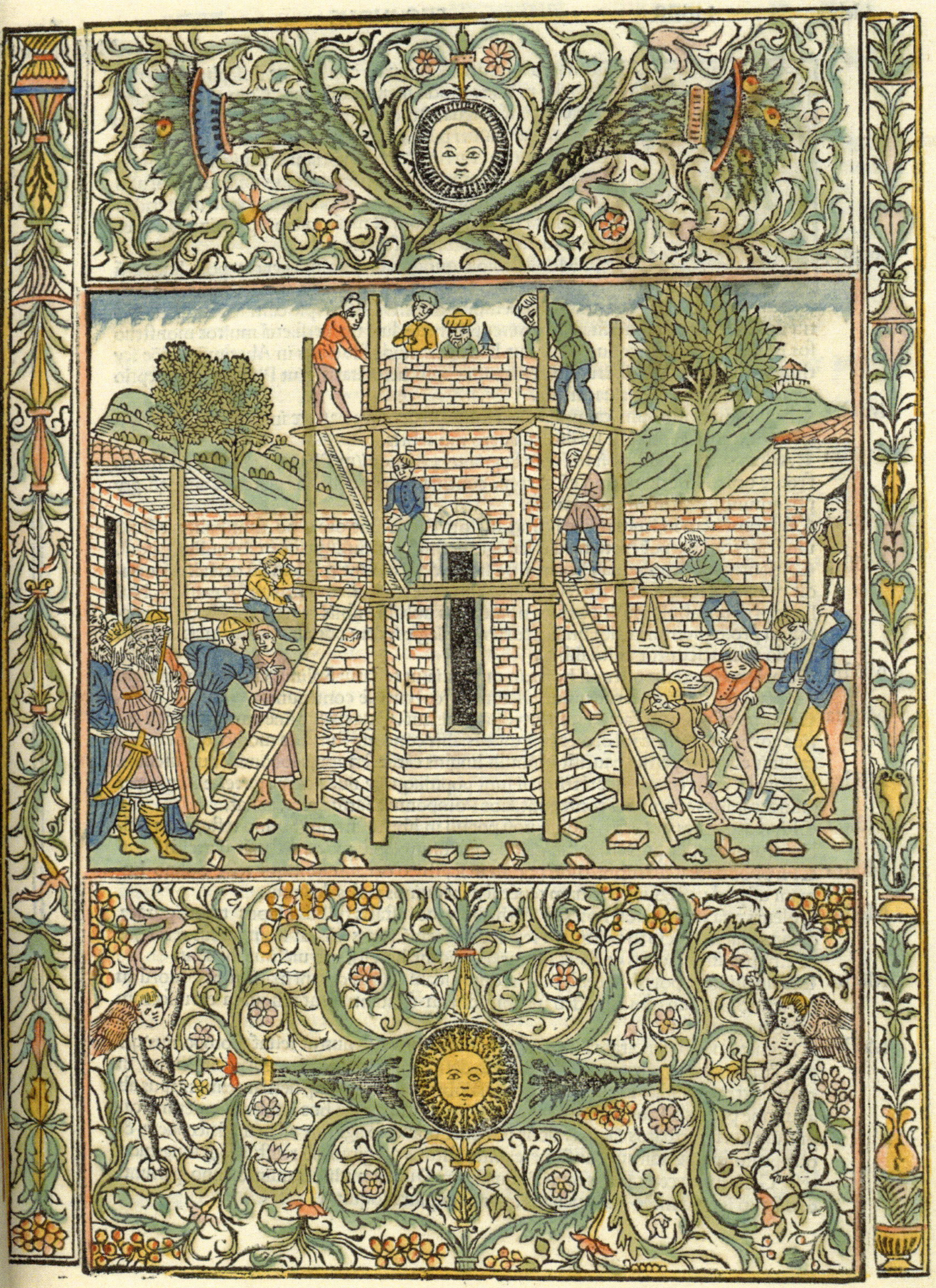

A choir psalter for Saint Barbara in Culemborg ~ 1521

Psalterium
South Holland, 1521
246 f. · 335 × 270 mm
PM0034/V (Nijmegen, Berchmanianum, 5000 FA 1)

The Psalter was made in 1521 for use by the choir of the Church of Saint Barbara in Culemborg in the Diocese of Utrecht. The small town of Culemborg is situated on the river Lek, on the border between the counties of Holland and Gelre (Guelders). The church became an independent parish church in 1420, when it was separated from Beusichem (Saint John the Baptist's Church), and a chapter was founded in 1421–1422. The buildings were extended in the 15th and 16th centuries.

The production of the manuscript was most probably supported by the last sovereign lady and lord of the fiefdom of Culemborg, Elisabeth of Culemborg (1475–1555) and her second husband, Antoine de Lalaing (†1540). Elisabeth was a patron of art, music and architecture and established a seminary in Culemborg in 1520. She was *dame d'honneur* to her second cousin Archduchess Margaret of Austria and was an influential figure at the court.

The choir psalter is decorated with large initials in red and blue, using South Holland penwork in the so called 'aubergine' style. High quality pen drawings with human faces and cats in different positions are added in between. The subtle pen drawings of cats integrated in the large initials, where they sing, play the horn or the bagpipes and catch mice, would entertain the singers during their vocal praying. Drawings of female figures in profile with well worked out headdresses decorate the music staves. The date of 1521 is inscribed in four initials (f. 49r, 58v, 83v, 159r).

The manuscript belongs to the collections of the Dutch Jesuits. Before arriving in the Maurits Sabbe Library, it was housed in the Library of the Aloysius College in The Hague, the Library of the Canisianum in Maastricht, and the Library of the Berchmanianum in Nijmegen.

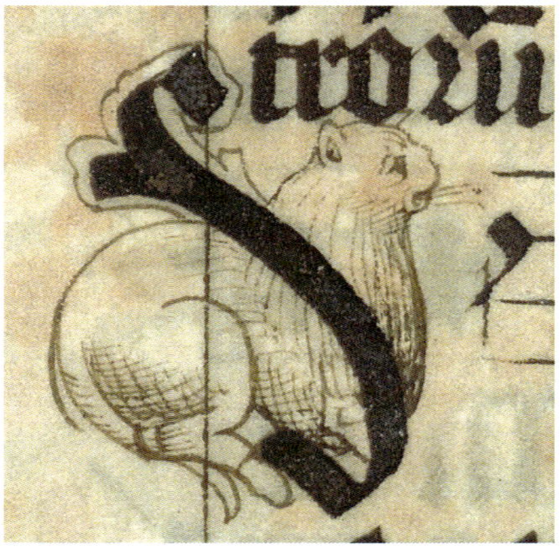

Literature:
J. Lauwerys, 'Elisabeth van Culemborg: Losse studiën bij de 400ste verjaardag van haar overlijden', *Jaarboek van Koninklijke Hoogstraten's Oudheidkundige Kring* 24 (1956): 20–21.

mea in domino
A custodia matutina
usqz ad noctē: speret is
rahel in dño
Quia apd dñm mīa:
et copiosa apd eū redēp
Et ipse redimet isrl: ex
õibz iniqtatibz ei9
Gl'a pri et aāt
De pfundis clamaui
ad te domine ā Speret
Ps cxxx.
Domine Euouae
nō est exaltatū cor meū:
neqz elati st oculi mei
Neqz ambulaui i mag
nis: neqz in mirabilibz
super me
Si nō humiliter sen
tiebā: sed exaltaui ani
mam meam

Sicut ablactatus su
per matrē suā: ita retri
butio in aīa mea
Speret isrl in dño: ex
hoc nūc et usqz in sclm
Gl'a pri et fi aāt
Speret israhel in domi
no Feria quinta Ad vs aāt.
Et
omnis Euouae
ps cxxxi.
Memēto dñe da
uid: et õnis
māsuetudīs ei9
Sicut iurauit
dño: votū vouit deo iacob
Si itroiero
in tabernaculū domus
mee: si ascendero in lec
tū strati mei
Si dedero sōpnū ocu
lis meis: et palpebris

Jacobus Latomus versus Martin Luther ∾ 1521

Jacobus Latomus (c. 1475–1544) was one of Louvain's leading theologians of the first decades of the 16th century and one of Martin Luther's most formidable adversaries. The Reformer, after he had been condemned by the universities of Cologne and Louvain in August and November 1519 respectively, had formulated his reply in May 1520. Latomus, in turn, brought together the text of the courses that he had taught in the summer of 1520 about the controversy regarding Luther's positions, with the Antwerp printer Michiel Hillen van Hoochstraten eventually publishing the text in May 1521, under the title *Articulorum doctrinæ fratris Martini Lutheri … damnatorum ratio* (*Foundation from Sacred Scriptures and Ancient Writers of the Condemnation of the Doctrinal Sentences of Friar Martin Luther Done by the Louvain Theologians*). Latomus wanted to provide a more elaborate doctrinal justification for Louvain's condemnation, especially of one of Luther's central positions, viz. that every 'good' work is in essence sinful, even those performed by saints. While admitting that all children are born stained by original sin, Latomus argued that, in baptism, the human person receives sanctifying grace, by which his sins are forgiven, both original sin and personal sins, and his nature is recreated from the inside with Christ's love. Nevertheless, the baptised continue to give in to the allures of sin, but when they show real repentance, they receive remission in the sacrament of confession. Doing good works and performing acts of penance is pleasing to God and is meritorious with a view to salvation.

The title of Latomus' work also refers to the two foremost sources he appealed to in his refutation of Luther's theses. Latomus confirmed the prime value of Scripture in theological argumentation, as an answer to Luther's criticism that his (and the Louvain) condemnation was insufficiently based upon scriptural foundations. At the same time, the Louvain theologian underscored that Scripture was obscure and should be understood in light of the *regula fidei*, as it was developed by the Church fathers – with Augustine taking pride of place – as well as the more recent scholastic theologians, and doctrinally defined by the pope and councils. Latomus' *Articulorum doctrinæ fratris Martini Lutheri … damnatorum ratio* was the very first anti-Lutheran work printed and published in the Low Countries.

Jacobus Latomus
Articulorum doctrinæ fratris Martini Lutheri per theologos Louanienses damnatorum ratio
Antwerp: Michael Hillenius Hoochstratanus, 1521
[102] f. · in 4°

Literature:
Hannegreth Grundmann, *Gratia Christi: Die theologische Begründung des Ablasses durch Jacobus Latomus in der Kontroverse mit Martin Luther* (Münster: LIT, 2012); Jos. E. Vercruysse, 'Jacobus Latomus und Martin Luther: Einführendes zu einer Kontroverse', *Gregorianum* 64 (1983): 515–538; Anna Vind, *Latomus and Luther: The Debate: Is Every Good Deed a Sin?* (Göttingen: Vandenhoeck & Ruprecht, 2019).

ARTICV-
LORVM DOCTRINAE FRA
tris Martini Lutheri per theologos
Louanienses damnatorꝝ Ratio
ex sacris literis, & veteribus
tractatoribus, per Iacobum
Latomū sacrę theologię
professorem.

Antwerpiae. 1521
Michaël Hillenius

¢ Johannes Lichtenberger's *Prognosticatio* in print ∾ 1526

Johannes Lichtenberger
Prognosticatio
Cologne: Peter Quentel, 1526
[60] f. · in 4°

Prognosticatio (1488) by the astrologer Johannes Lichtenberger, which forecasts the future, was avidly read until well into the 16th century. Proof of this is Peter Quentel's 1526 edition, printed in Cologne (fig. 1). Lichtenberger's *Prognosticatio* should be read against the background of the intermingling of Christian redemption literature and classical astronomy, typical of the 15th century. In his introduction, he delimits the indispensable qualities for an astrologer to possess: mature age, insight into human nature, the study of ancient astronomers (in particular of Aristotle, Plato, and Ptolemy), and, most importantly, attention for God's revelation in messages from angels, and hagiography. The *Prognosticatio*, therefore, made its ideological contribution in the defence of the perennially threatened Christian empire.

Apart from the illustrated title page, the first illustration in the *Prognosticatio* is a representation of Ptolemy, Aristotle, a Sibyl, Bridget, and Reynaerd under the Pantocrator, who was seen as the architect of planetary movements in Lichtenberger's time (fig. 2). The woodcut divulges Lichtenberger's most important sources of inspiration and clarifies their subservience to the Christian God. Claudius Ptolemy (Greek, Ptolemaîos) wrote his *Megistē* – *Almagest* in Arabic – in the 2nd century. The tract reduced astronomy to rules and laws, making it the primary source for all subsequent astrologers.

Aristotle had also devoted his seminal study *Physica* to the planetary system. He describes the planets as consisting of the four known elements, with a fifth unknown. Like Plato, Aristotle was convinced that the planets are gifted with a soul and intelligence. They are placed hierarchically right under the 'immovable mover', the organizing divine principle.

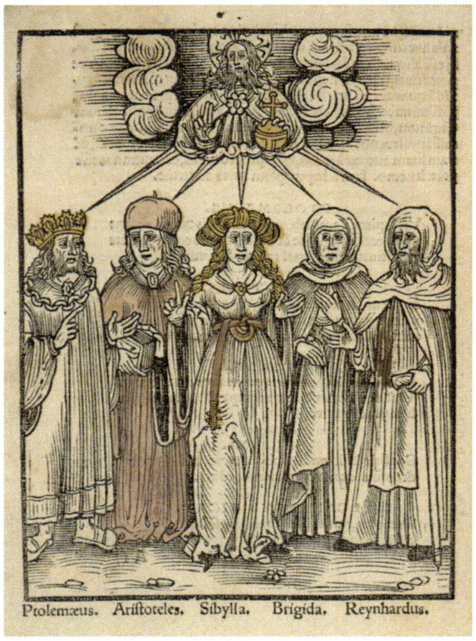

[fig. 2]

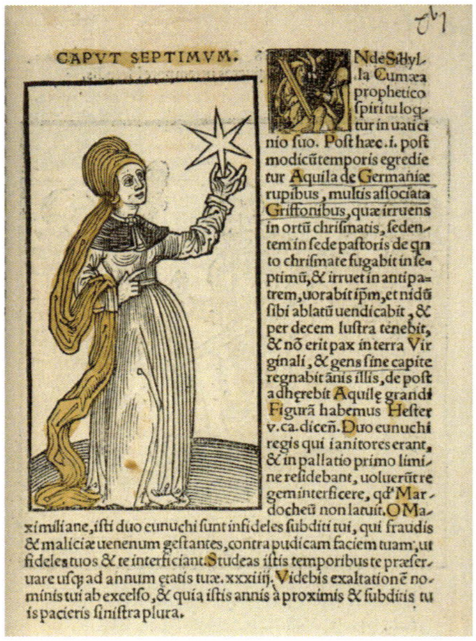
CAPVT SEPTIMVM.

Nde Sibylla Cumæa prophetico ſpiritu loqtur in uaticinio ſuo. Poſt hæc .i. poſt modicũ temporis egredietur Aquila de Germaniæ rupibus, multis aſſociata Griffonibus, quæ irruens in ortũ chriſmatis, ſedentem in ſede paſtoris de qnto chriſmate fugabit in ſeptimũ, & irruet in antipatrem, uorabit ip̃m, et nidũ ſibi ablatũ uendicabit, & per decem luſtra tenebit, & nõ erit pax in terra Virginali, & gens ſine capite regnabit ãnis illis, de poſt adhęrebit Aquilę grandi Figurã habemus Heſter v. ca. diceñ. Duo eunuchi regis qui ianitores erant, & in pallatio primo limine reſidebant, uoluerũt regem interficere, qđ Mardocheũ non latuit. O Maximiliane, iſti duo eunuchi ſunt infideles ſubditi tui, qui fraudis & maliciæ uenenum geſtantes, contra pudicam faciem tuam, ut fideles tuos & te interficiant. Studeas iſtis temporibus te præſeruare uſq; ad annum ętatis tuæ. xxxiiij. Videbis exaltationẽ nominis tui ab excelſo, & quia iſtis annis à proximis & ſubditis tuis pacieris ſiniſtra plura.

[fig. 3]

The presence of a Sibyl is no less surprising (fig. 3. The Sibyl Cumæa). The twelve mythological prophetesses from classical Antiquity were respected well into the Middle Ages. While in ancient Greece they delivered bad tidings, in the Roman tradition their utterances were oriented towards reconciliation. The Judeo-Christian *Oracula Sibyllina* (compiled between the 2nd century BC and the 3rd or 4th century AD), assigns them oracles related to Christian eschatology. Patristic authors derived apologetic arguments from these *Oracula*. Moreover, they canonized the oracles' pagan origin by considering Moses the prototypical source of these wise sayings and predictions.

[fig. 1] ▸

PROGNOSTICATIO IOHANNIS LIECHTENBERGERS,

QVAM olim scripsit super magna illa Saturni ac Iouis cõiunctione, quæ fuit Anno M. CCCC. LXXXIIII. præterea ad eclypsim Solis anni sequẽtis uidelicet LXXXV. durans in annum usq; M. D. LXVII. iam iterum, sublatis mendis quibus scatebat pluribus, quandiligentissime excussa.

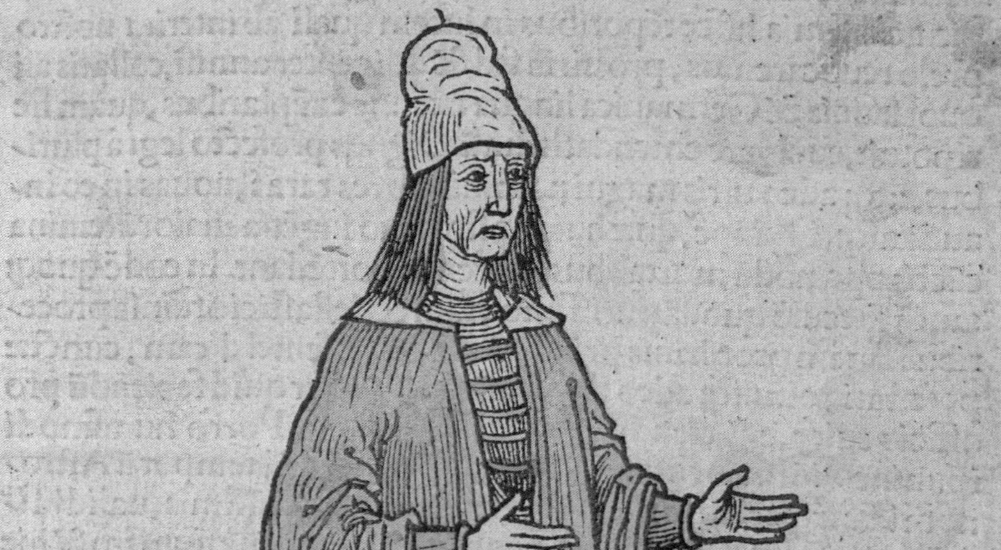

Qualitas, locus, et tempus mirabilis constellationis narratur

HOMO DECREPITVS, BARBATVS, CLAVDIcans & sustentans se baculo cū sinistra, habens falcem in dextra, iacēs supra hominem habentem bouem cum cornubus in dextra ac si uellet opprimere eum. Signum Scorpionis in medio eorum Saturnus.

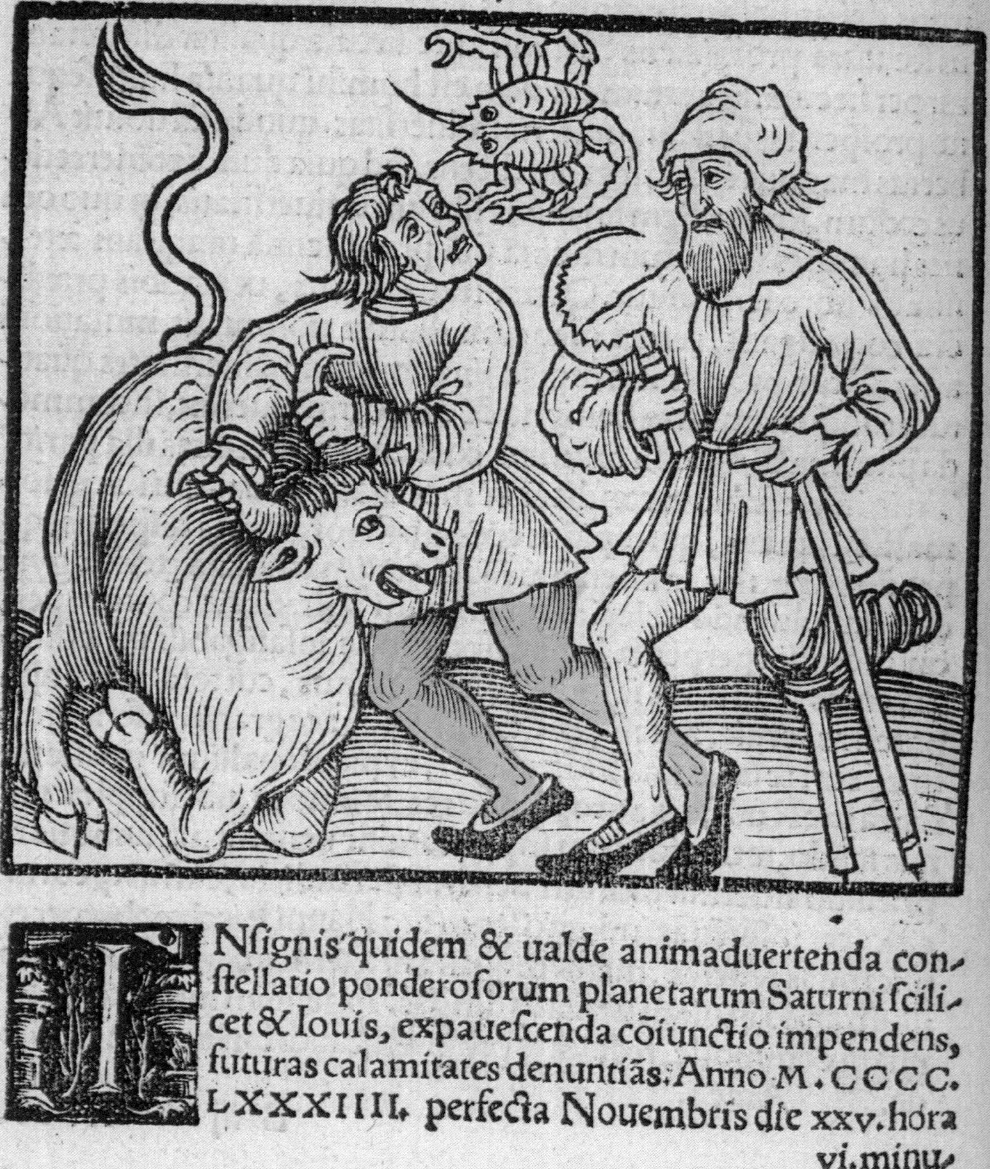

Coniunctio planetarum.

INsignis quidem & ualde animaduertenda constellatio ponderosorum planetarum Saturni scilicet & Iouis, expauescenda cōiunctio impendens, futuras calamitates denuntiās. Anno M. CCCC. LXXXIIII. perfecta Nouembris die xxv. hora vi. minu-

The group of Sibyls was not always clearly delineated. Contaminations arose, which often resulted in the incorrect attribution of their gifts to one woman, either Sibyl (classification becomes personal name) or to the queen of Sheba. A German translation of a Sibylline book appeared around 1369 near Thüringen. It was passed down in numerous manuscript and print editions until the late 16th century. Lichtenberger was presumably familiar with this German variant.

'Brigida' refers to the mystic Bridget of Sweden (c. 1303–1373), canonized in 1391 (fig. 4). It is through her *Revelationes* that such motifs as Mary's prayer at birth, Judas' small size, the flogging with fifty thousand lashes, the crown of thorns, and the preparation for the crucifixion, have entered into literary and artistic realms. It is remarkable that Lichtenberger still attributed prophetic value to these visions.

Although the figure of the unknown 'Reynhardus Lollardus' is hardly remembered in history, Lichtenberger praises him for a wisdom compatible with the Apocalypse of John. Presumably, he is the author of the now lost *Liber Multarum Tribulationum*, because Lichtenberger connects the name of Reynhardus Lollardus at least once directly to this book. Reynaerd is presented as an old man with a cane and a monk's habit. Lichtenberger consulted him for his remarkable combination of animal symbols and eschatological forecasts. This illustration thanks its iconographical relevance solely to the introductory text of the *Prognosticatio*. The depiction of great philosophers alongside mythological and unimportant figures shows that Lichtenberger did not want to make a qualitative distinction, nor did he intend to apply rules of historical criticism. All are given prophetic value, whether technically (Ptolemy), metaphysically (Aristotle), mystically (the Sibyl and Bridget), or symbolically and apocalyptically (Reynaerd) founded (*calculatio* versus *divinatio*); and whether directed to an intellectual or a more popular audience (theology versus popular devotion). Christian astrology is mainly interested in eschatologically-oriented predictions, expressed with symbolic embellishment. The book also has to be interesting to read and exciting to look at. Therefore, the *Prognosticatio* reverts to principles and sources that are not so much conservative or anti-humanistic, as they are timeless and universal (fig. 5. Astrological image of Saturn, Jupiter and the scorpion).

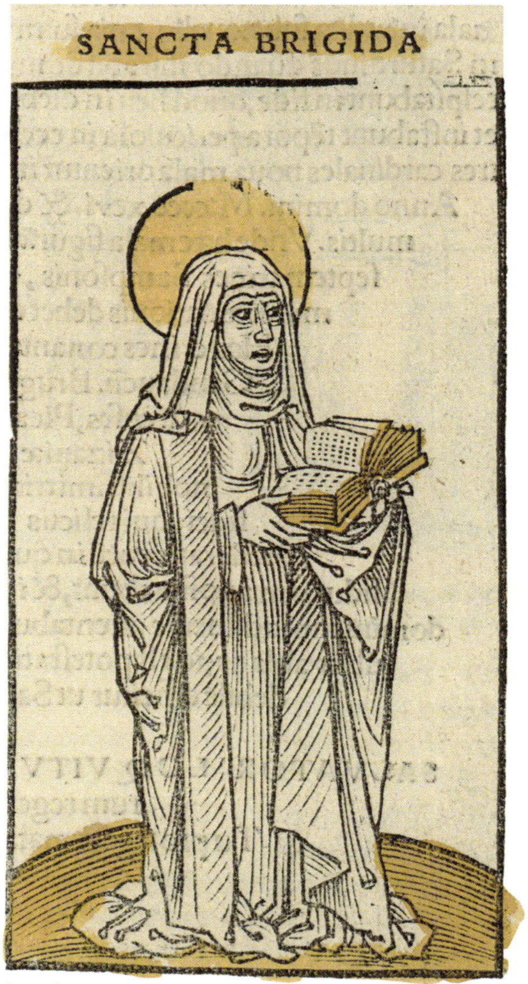

[fig. 4]

Literature:
Dietrich Kurze, *Johannes Lichtenberger (†1503): Eine Studie zur Geschichte der Prophetie und Astrologie* (Lübeck: Matthiesen, 1960); Dietrich Kurze, 'Prophecy and History: Lichtenberger's Forecast of Events to Come (From the Fifteenth to the Twentieth Century): Their Reception and Diffusion', *Journal of the Warburg and Courtauld Institutes* 21 (1958): 63–85.

¢ Woodcuts in a missal for Cambrai ~ 1527

Missale Cameracense completissimum novissime impressum et emendatum una cum multis missis devotissimis nusquam antea impressis
Paris: Pierre Roffet, Nicole Vostre, Simon Hadrot and Nicolas Prévost
[8], CXLIIII, [82], XL f. · in 2°
P264.12/F° MISS Came 1527

This missal, printed in Paris in 1527 for the use of Cambrai, is a reworked and enlarged edition of the first printed *Missale Cameracense* of 1503 and the edition of 1507, also printed in Paris. The brother of Nicole Vostre (†1537?), the libraire-relieur Simon Vostre (†1521) printed the 1503 missal for use of Cambrai together with Henri Estienne for Wolfgand Hopyl (active 1489–1522), and for the 1507 edition Vostre and Estienne collaborated again.

The edition of 1527, as seen in the copy preserved in the Maurits Sabbe Library, repeated the numerous small woodcuts of the two previous editions. In 1527 the woodblocks probably belonged to Simon Hadrot, who in July 1523 had bought a part of the type and woodblocks inherited by the widow of Simon Vostre. To produce the *Missale Cameracense,* Simon Hadrot and Nicole Vostre collaborated with Nicolas Prévost (son-in-law of Henri Estienne) and Pierre Roffet (known as *Le Faucheur*), both printer-bookdealers in Paris, specializing in liturgical works.

The missal is printed in two columns in red and black throughout, with woodcut lombard initials, numerous illustrations and printed musical notation on staves. The Canon of the Mass starts with beautiful full-page coloured representations: on the left, Christ on the Cross with Saint John and the Virgin and, on the right, God the Father enthroned, surrounded by the symbols of the four evangelists and by angels. The insertion of full-page woodcuts, printed on a double folio of thick parchment, reveals the importance of the visual image at the most significant point in the liturgy. The two large woodcuts on parchment are printed with text on the reverses so that they are completely integrated into the paper text block of the missal. In a missal for the use of Sarum, printed in Antwerp in the same year by Christoffel van Ruremund (1475?–1531) for Franz Birckman (in London), 28 March 1527, the same large Calvary woodcut appears. In this publication the woodcut stayed uncoloured.

Stylistically the two full-page woodcuts are inspired by German models and relate closely to illuminated manuscripts. These kind of large woodblocks were first used by the Paris printer Philippe Pigouchet (active 1488–1518) in collaboration with Simon Vostre at the beginning of the 16th century.

Literature:
W. H. J. Weale and H. Bohatta, *Bibliographia liturgica: Catalogus missalium ritus Latini ab anno 1474 impressorum* (London: Quaritch, 1928), 229.

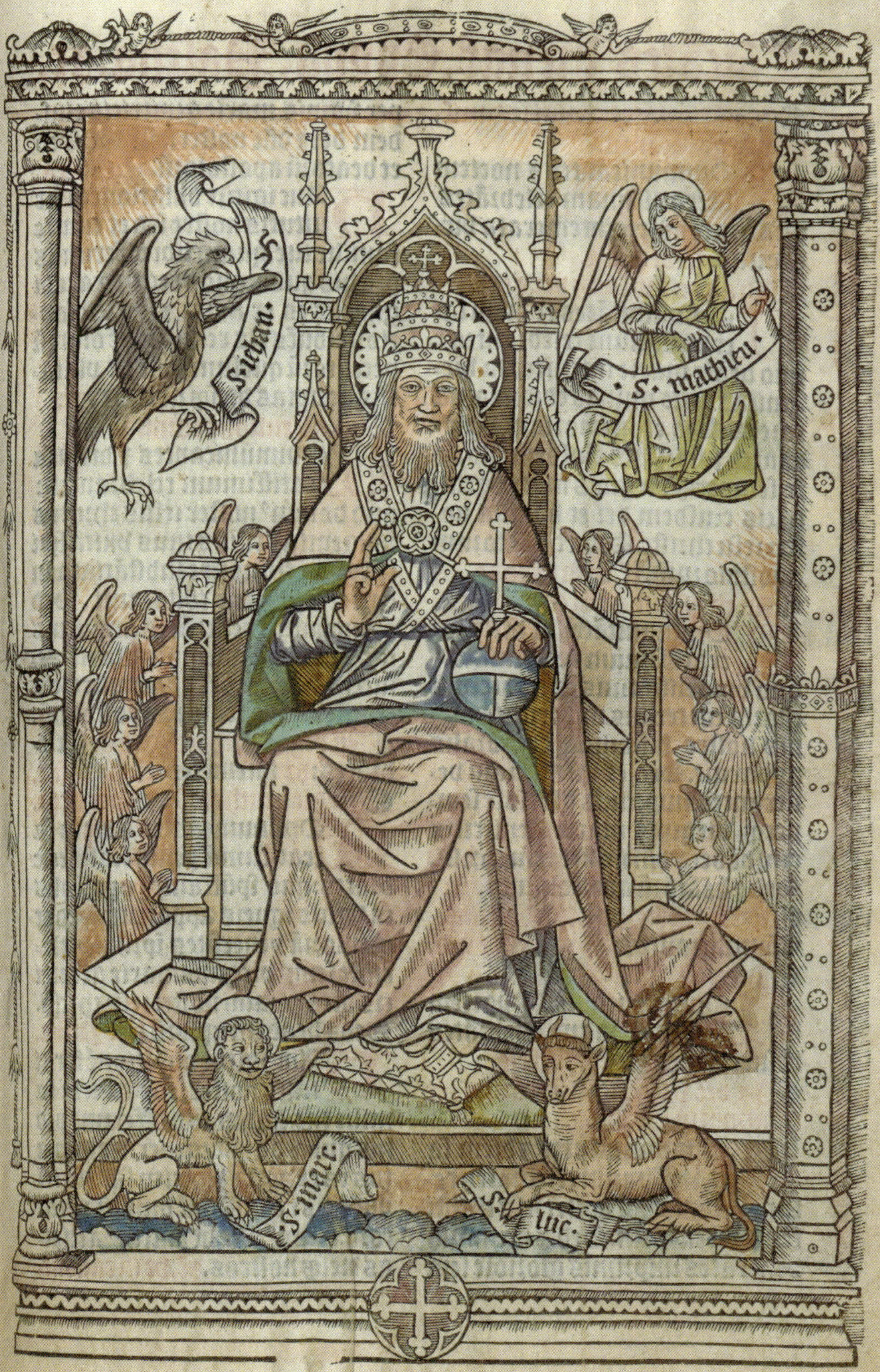
S·iehan·
·S· mathieu·
S·marc·
S·luc·

¢ An annotated Vorsterman Bible ∾ 1534

Den Bibel. Tgeheele Oude ende Nieuwe Testament, met grooter naersticheyt na den Latijnschen text gecorrigeert . . .
Antwerp: Willem Vorsterman, 1533–1534
[14], CXCVI, CLXVII, CII f. · in 2°
P22.055.1/F° BIJB 1533 C

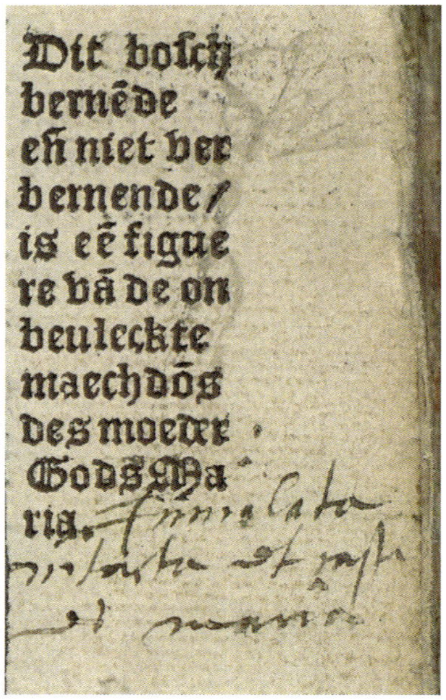

The time span between 1526 and 1546 is sometimes called the twenty golden years of Dutch Bible production. True showpieces of this era are the large Bibles in folio by the Antwerp printers and publishers Jacob van Liesvelt and Willem Vorsterman. Both printers took turns publishing innovative editions, Liesvelt mainly 'protestantising' and Vorsterman 'catholicising' ones. Willem Vorsterman was the first to add a Dutch thematic index in his Bible with glosses of 1533–1534. As eye-catching as the historical glosses are the typological glosses that were printed alongside the biblical text or the images and that interpret biblical events in the Old Testament as typological prefigurations of events in the New Testament.

Moreover, it was not unusual for readers or users to add handwritten annotations to such Bible copies. Based on these annotated Bibles, it becomes possible to discover how historical readers interacted with certain editions. The Maurits Sabbe Library preserves a heavily annotated copy of the 1533–1534 Vorsterman edition, which the Franciscans (or Recollects) of Ghent kept during the 19th and 20th century until the dissolution of their monastery in 2004. The annotations however are from the 16th century and are presumably written by a cleric from the town who was not completely insensitive to the new religious ideas.

It is notable that certain annotations by this contemporary reader are at the same level as some typological printed glosses. A good example is Exodus 3, which shows an image of Moses and the Burning Bush. Alongside there is a marginal gloss, which elucidates the Burning Bush as a prefiguration of Mary remaining a virgin: "Dit bosch bernende ende niet verbernende is een figuere van de onbeuleckte maechdoms des moeder Gods Maria" ("This bush on fire and not being burned is a figure of the immaculate virginity of the mother of God Mary"). The annotator observed: "Inuiolata intacta et casta es Maria" ("Inviolate, untouched and pure art thou Mary"). The *Inviolata* is also the title of a song in honour of Mary, more specifically a 'prose' or 'sequence' that was sung during the high feasts of Mary, amongst other feasts.

This annotation is an example of the many relicts of historical Bible reading that are still discovered in extant Bible copies. However, this particular annotation is remarkable: it is a striking illustration of linking the vernacular text of the Old Testament, the image, the printed marginal gloss with its typological explanation, and finally the handwritten marginal gloss. This and other annotations give us, in the present day, insight into the living environment of biblical readers that have remained (largely) anonymous through the ages.

Literature:
Wim François, 'Typology – Back with a Vengeance! Text, Images, and Marginal Glosses in Vorsterman's 1534 Dutch Bible', in *Imago Exegetica: Visual Images as Exegetical Instruments, 1400–1700*, ed. Walter S. Melion, James Clifton, and Michel Weemaes (Leiden: Brill, 2014), 89–136; Bert Tops, 'Users and Types of Use of the Dutch Vorsterman Bible of 1533–1534', *The Journal of Early Modern Christianity* 6, no. 2 (2019): forthcoming; Louis Vermeulen, 'Die alder beste maniere van ouer te setten: Een andere visie op het gebruik van bronnen in het Oude Testament van de Vorstermanbijbel', *Trajecta* 27 (2018): 57–126.

Nde daer ghinc een man vandē huy-
se Leui/ eñ nam een * huysvrouwe vā
sinē geslachte) eñ dat wijf ontfinck eñ
baerde eenē sone/ Eñ doen si sach dat
tet een fijn kindeken was/ verborch si
hē drie maendē/ Eñ als si hem niet langher verber-
ghen en conde/ nam si een kiste van biesen/ eñ si be-
streecse/ met lijme/ eñ pecke/ eñ leyde thint daer in-
ne/ ende steldet int lisch/ aenden oeuer des vloets/
Maer sijn suster stont vā verre/ dat si beuinden wil
de hoe dattet met hem vergaen soude.

Eñ siet Pharaos dochter quā neder om haer te
wasschē in de vloet/ eñ haer ioncwiuē ghinghē lanex
den hooghē kant der dieptē/ eñ als si die kiste in dye
leege kant sach: sant si een vā haer dienst ioncwijuē
eñ lietet halen. Alst ghehaelt was/ dedet si open eñ
siende daer in een kindekē schreyende/ heeft si sijns
ontfermt/ ende sprack tis een vanden Hebreeuschen
kinderkens. Doen sprack sijn suster/ tot Pharaos
dochter/ Wildy dat ick gae eñ roepe een vandē He-
breeuschen wiuē/ die daer sooget/ dat si v dat kinde
ken sooghe? Pharaos dochter sprac tot haer/ gaet/
die maecht ghinck/ eñ riep des kints moeder. Doen
sprack Pharaos dochter tot haer/ neemt dat kinde-
ken ende sooghet mi/ ick salt v loonen: dat wijf nam
dat kint ende soochdet.

Eñ doe dat kint groot ghewordē was bracht sijt
Pharaos dochtere/ Si nam hē door verkiesinghe in
een plaetse vā haerē sone/ eñ ghaf hē den naē Moy
ses: segghende. Ick heb hē wt den water ghetrockē.

In dien tijdē als Moyses groot gheworden was
ghinc wt tot sinē broederē/ eñ sach haere verdrucke
nis/ eñ wert gewaer dat een Egyptenaer sloech si-
nen broeder/ een vandē Hebreeuschē: eñ als hy ront
ōme herwaert eñ ghinswaert gesien hadde/ eñ sach
datter nyemāt bi en was/ versloech hy dē Egypte-
naer/ eñ groef hem in dat sant/ Des ander daechs
ghinc hi oock wt eñ sach twee Hebreeusche mannen
kiuen eñ sprac totten ghenē die den anderē onrecht
dede/ Waer om slady uwē naesten? Maer hi sprac/
Wie heeft v een rechter oft ouerste ouer ons geset?
Wildy mi oock verslaen/ ghelijck ghi den Egypte-
naer ghisterē versleghē hebt? Moyses vreesde doen
eñ sprack/ Hoe is * dit woort) openbaer ghewordē?
* Eñ Pharao hoorde dese reden) eñ Pharao sochte
Moysen om te dooden/ Maer Moyses vloot voor
Pharaos ghesichte/ eñ onthielt hem int landt Ma-
dian/ eñ hi sadt neuen een fonteyne.

Eñ die priester vā Madian hadde seuē dochterē
die quamē om water te scheppē eñ vuldē die goten/
eñ begheerdē haers vaders kuddē te drenckē. Doen
quamē die herderē eñ stietense daer af. Maer Moy
ses stont op eñ beschermde die maechdē/ eñ drencte
haer schapen. Ende als si tot haeren vader * Raguel)
quamē/ sprack hy/ Hoe sidy huyden so volcken ghe-
comen? Sy spraken/ een Egyptisch mā verloste ons
vandē herderē/ eñ daer en bouen schepte hy ons wa-
ter/ eñ drencte die schapē/ Hy sprack tot sinē dochte
ren/ Waer is hi? Waer om hebt ghi den man laten
gaen? * roept hē dat hy met ons broot ete) * daer ō
swoer Moyses) dat hi met hem woonē soude/ eñ nā
Sephorā sijn dochter/ dye baerde hē eenen sone/ eñ
hiet hem Gerson/ wāt hy sprack/ ick ben een vrem-
delinc gewordē in vremdē landē. Eñ si baerde noch
eenen sone/ dien hiet hi Eliezer/ eñ sprack. Die God
mijns vaders is mijn hulper/ eñ heeft mi van Pha-
raos handē verlost. * Na veel tijts sterf) die coninck

Gerson et Eliezer filii Moisi

vā Egyptē/ eñ dye kinderē vā Israel suchtedē ouer
haerē arbeyt/ eñ riepē/ eñ haerē roep haers arbeyts
quā voor God/ eñ God hoorde haer suchtē/ eñ ghe-
dachte aen sijn verbont/ dat hi met Abrahā/ Ysaac/
eñ Jacob gemaeckt hadde/ eñ die HEERE aensach
die kinderen vā Israel/ eñ * verlostse.)

een huytē lantsche
Eliezer heet God mijn hulper.
H. Na sommige dagē th. bekenden.

Hoe Moyses die schapen wachte/ ende God sprac van-
den brandenden eñ niet verbrandendē doorne/ ende seynt
Moysen tot die kinderen van Israel/ ende tot Pharaonem
den verdruckere.

Dat.iij.Capitel.

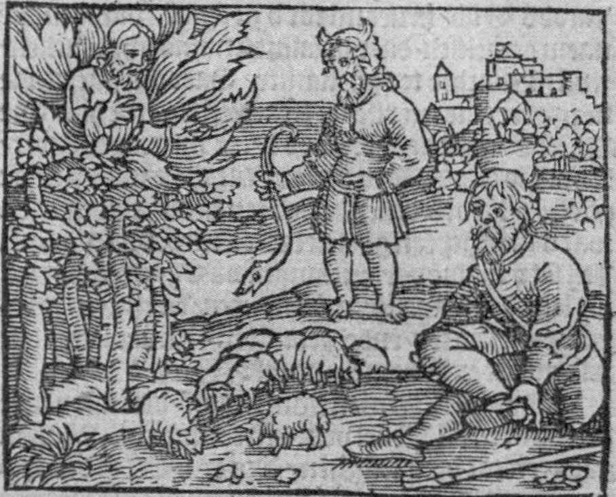

Dit bosch bernēde eñ niet verbernende/ is eē figure vā de onbevleckte maechdōs des moeder Gods Maria.

Oyses huede dye schapen Jetro sijns
sweers des priesters/ vā Madian/ eñ
als hi ghedreuen hadde die schapē bin
nen in die woestijne: quam hy aenden
berch Gods Oreb/ ende die * HEE
RE) openbaerde hem in een vierighe vlāme/ wt den
bosch/ eñ hi sach dat doornen bosch met viere bernē/
ende dattet niet verbernt en wert/ Ende Moyses
sprac/ Ic wil daer henen/ eñ besien dit grote visioen
waer om dat bosch niet en verbernt.

M the. die engel des Heren.

Als die HEERE sach dat Moyses ghincom te
sien/ riep hē God wt dē middē des boschs/ eñ sprac
Moyses Moyses/ hi antwoorde/ hier ben ick. Eñ
die HEERE sprac: En comt hier niet naerder: treck
v schoenē wt vā uwē voeten/ want die plaetse daer
ghi op staet is een heylich lant/ Eñ sprac noch. Ic bē
die God ws vaders/ Abrahās God/ Ysaacs God/
eñ Jacobs God. Ende Moyses decte sijn aensicht/
want hi en dorste teghen God niet sien.

Eñ die HEERE sprack tot hē/ Ick heb be ghesien
die allende mijns volcx in Egyptē/ eñ ick heb huer
geroep ghehoort ouer * die herdicheyt der ghenē die
ouer haer werc gestelt sijn) eñ wetende haer smerte
eñ leet/ ben ick weder ghecomē dat ic hen verlossen
soude wt dē gheweldigē handē der Egyptinarē/ eñ
salse leydē wt desen lande/ in een goet eñ breet lāt/
in een lant dat vā melcke eñ honich vloeyt/ te wetē:
totter plaetsen der Cananitē/ Hethitē/ Amoriten/
Pheritē/ Heuiten/ ende Jebusiten. Daer omme
wāt dat gheroep der kinderē vā Israel voor mi ghe-
comen is: ende ick ghesien hebbe huere verdruckin-
ghe daer si mede verdruct wordē vandē Egyptina-
ren/ Soo coemt/ Ick sal v seynden tot Pharaonem
dat ghi mijn volck dye kinderen van Israel wt E-
gypten leydet.

C theb. dieses drijuen.

Eñ Moyses sprack tot God/ wie ben ick dat ic
tot Pharao gaen soude/ ende leyden die kinderē vā
Israel wt Egypten? Die HEERE sprac. Ick sal met
v sijn/ eñ dat al uwe teekē sijn/ dat ic v gesondē heb-
be/ als ghi mijn volc wt Egyptē ghelept hebt/ suldi

C Mer der ritter zů dem knecht sprach/vnd ob der beck sprech alß er vor gsprochē
hat/ich schick dich nitt zů ihm vmb wein/so frag ihn wa ich dich hien oder zů
wem ich dich schick/der knecht wider zů dem becken kam/vnd sprach/fürwar
glaub mir Cisti/mein herr schickt mich zů dir vmb wein/fürwar sun neyn er/
du solt nit recht vernum̃en haben/ghe wider heym vnd heyß dich baß vnder/
richten. Nun wa schickt er mich dañ hien sprach der knecht? Dem Cisti bald
antwurt vnd sprach/Zů dem bach vnnd grossen wasser. Diese antwurt der
knecht dem ritter widerbracht/zů jm sprach/Herr der beck spricht/jr schicket
mich vmb wein zů dem bach. Der Ritter balt Cisti meynũg vernumen hett/
zům knecht sprach/Laß sehen die fläschen die du jm bracht hast/vnd da er die
gesehen hett/zů dem knecht sprach/Cisti sagt war vnd hat recht/das er dich
zům bach weißt/du thetst vnrecht mitt solcher grossen vnzüchtigen flaschen/
in eyns handtwercks hauß on gelt vmb wein zůghen. Ghe hin vnd nīme eyn
kleyns fläschlin vnd sag ihm das er dir es vol seins gůten weissen weins geb.
Vnd da Cisti den knecht mit dem züchtigen kleinen fläschlin kumen sahe/zů
ihm sprach: Nu sih ich wol das dich dein herr zů mir schickt/jm balt dz fläsch
lin fült/vnd zůhand es dem ritter also vol heymschickt vnnd jm nachfolget/
Zů dem Ritter sprach/herr ich wolt nit das jr glaubtē dz mich die groß fläsch
auff diesen morgen erschreckt hett/sunder mich beduncken ließ/wie euch ver/
gessen wer/was ich euch mit meinem brüglin in diesen vergangen tagen be/
weiset hett/vnd das was dz mich bedaucht/wie mein wein nit wer knechten
zůtrincken zů geben/das hab ich euch sagen wöllen. Vnd damit ich deß ew/
wer hůter nitt lenger bedürff sein/hab ich jn euch allen herbringē thun/thůt
D damit hin für ewer gefallen. Doch eyns bitt ich euch/jr sehet nitt an die
kleynen gab/sunder den gůten willen ewers Cisti. Der Ritter Cisti
gab vnd schanckung nit außschlůg/sunder die wirdigklich em/
pfienge/jm deß dancksaget/alß dañ solche gab wirdig wz/
vnnd hinfür alle zeit für seinen grossen freundt hielte.

Wie fraw Nanna mit eyner schnellē züchtigē antwurt in schimpffs iij
form/eynen Bischoff seiner vnzüchtigen rede stillet vnnd schweigen machet.

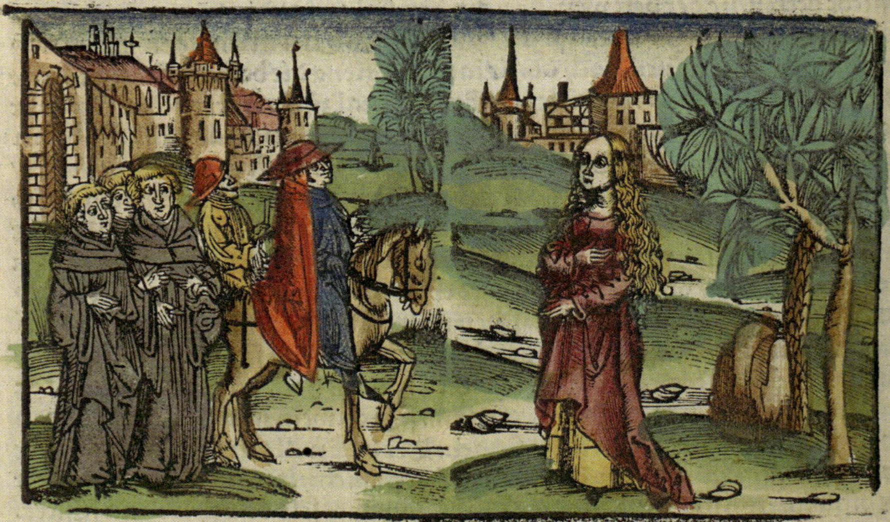

Nun

¢ Frivolous sin in Boccaccio's *Decamerone* ∾ 1537

Giovanni Boccaccio
Centum nouella Iohannis Boccatij. Hundert neuwer historien ...
Strasbourg: Johann Albrecht – Jakob Cammerlander, 1535
[4], CCXVIIJ f. · in 2°
P940.224.1/F°VERG Erfy

Boccaccio's hilarious stories are a spicy reminder of sin. This fine German translation with 67 lavish hand-coloured woodcuts is a visually stunning celebration of its humour. Giovanni Boccaccio (1313–1375) invented stories that groups of youngsters would tell to while away idle hours when they had fled pest-infected Florence to the safety of the countryside hills. The amorous dreams of the youths turn into digressions about the immorality of the world, illustrated by humorous incidents of tricks and deceit. As of today, no commentator is quite sure whether Boccaccio aims to warn us or indulges in funny stories for the sake of recreation.

Take the third story of the sixth day, in which Antonio d'Orso, Bishop of Florence, receives the handsome Catalan nobleman Diego della Ratta. Diego pays the parsimonious husband of the bishop's niece to have sex with her, to the husband's humiliation and the wife's disgust. The bishop pretends not to know about it. On the feast of Saint John the Baptist, on the 24 June, the bishop and the nobleman ride past Saint Peter's gate. Nonna de'Pulci, a fresh and beautiful young woman (who later dies during the pestilence) stands waiting there for her husband. The bishop approaches her, puts his hand on her shoulder and asks her if she thinks she can conquer the nobleman. She swiftly replies: "perhaps he can win, but I will not ask him for corrupting money." This serves to dishonour both men and they keep silent for the rest of the day. Boccaccio praises the young woman for her candid and quick reply as she was asked an impertinent question. In this edition, the story is illustrated with a depiction of a shining and fleshy coloured 'fraw Nanna' standing upright opposite the bishop and nobleman and their followers on horseback.

The German translator, Heinrich Steinhöwel (1411/12–1479) was skilled in comic literature, having also produced a marvellous Esop translation, published in 1476–1477, with vibrantly coloured woodcuts comparable to the ones in this edition. Boccaccio's stories revolve around the lust for sex of monks, priests and bishops and their devious ways of hiding their dalliances. Books such as these sharpen the reader's wit about recognizing sin in very witty ways.

Literature:
Decameron von Heinrich Steinhöwel, ed. Heinrich Adelbert von Keller (Stuttgart: Litterarischer Verein, 1860); Elisabeth Arend-Schwarz and Volker Kapp, eds., *Übersetzungsgeschichte als Rezeptionsgeschichte: Wege und Formen der Rezeption italienischer Literatur im deutschen Sprachraum vom 15. bis 20. Jahrhundert* (Marburg an der Lahn: Hitzeroth, 1993); Elisabeth Arend, *Lachen und Komik in Giovanni Boccaccio's Decameron* (Frankfurt am Main: Vittorio Klostermann, 2004).

¢ A CENSURED DUTCH VULGATE VERSION BY ALEXANDER BLANCKART ~ 1548

Die Bibel, wederom met grooter nersticheit oversien ende gecorrigeert . . .
Duer B. Alexander Blanckart, Carmelit
Cologne: Jaspar von Gennep, 1548
[7], CCCCLXIIII, [1], CIX, [1 blank] f. · in 2°
P22.055.1/F° BIJB 1548

After the Council of Trent had proclaimed the Latin Vulgate to be the authentic Bible version of the Catholic Church (1546), efforts were made to publish vernacular versions. In the Dutch speaking language area, the most important initiative was the Bible translated in Louvain by the Augustinian canon regular Nicholas van Winghe, under the supervision of the Louvain theologians. But several months before the 'Louvain Bible' was published in 1548, a 'competing' Dutch version, translated by the Carmelite Alexander Blanckart († 1555), was published in Cologne by Jaspar van Gennep (1547–1548). The Maurits Sabbe Library preserves a copy of this Bible, which has a vividly-coloured title page displaying a variation of a well-renowned picture by Anton Woensam, called 'of Worms' († 1541). Above the page border we find a variation of the famous staircase of grace. Jesus is showing the wounds on his hands and his side to the Father, who sits enthroned as a severe judge (see the accompanying passages from Zacharias 1:15: "And I am angry with a great anger with the nations" and Deuteronomy 32:23: "I will spend my arrows among them." Jesus' act should be seen as an act of intercession on behalf of a condemned humankind. Just as God created Eve from Adam's rib – depicted below on the page border –, Jesus has opened the possibility for humankind to be restored and saved through the open wounds in his hands and his side. On the other side of Jesus, Mary is also involved in this act of intercession before God's throne.

The presence of an inkblot just along the length of Jesus' figure is striking. This inkblot is no accident, but instead has most probably been applied as a deliberate censure of the image. The reason is that Jesus is not at the place where He should be, namely enthroned at the right hand of God, but is depicted on a lower step, kneeling before the Father, and even on the same level as Mary. The hypothesis of a deliberate censorship is supported by the fate of other images of the same kind, the most famous example being the painting of the staircase of grace by Abraham Bloemaert (1564/66–1551), which is currently still in Saint John's Cathedral in 's-Hertogenbosch. Immediately after its arrival there c. 1615, the painting evoked the discontentment of Antonius Bruynincx, a member of the cathedral chapter. At the behest of the bishop, Bloemaert made a pen drawing of the painting, which was sent to the Louvain theologians for further examination. The theologians did not hesitate to issue a negative assessment, for the reasons explained above, and the bishop forbade the exposition of the painting.

Literature:
Wim François, 'The Early Modern Bible between Material Book and Immaterial Word', in *The Agency of Things in Medieval and Early Modern Art: Materials, Power and Manipulation*, ed. Grażyna Jurkowlaniec, Ika Matyjaszkiewicz, and Zuzanna Sarnecka (New York and London: Routledge, 2018), 137–139.

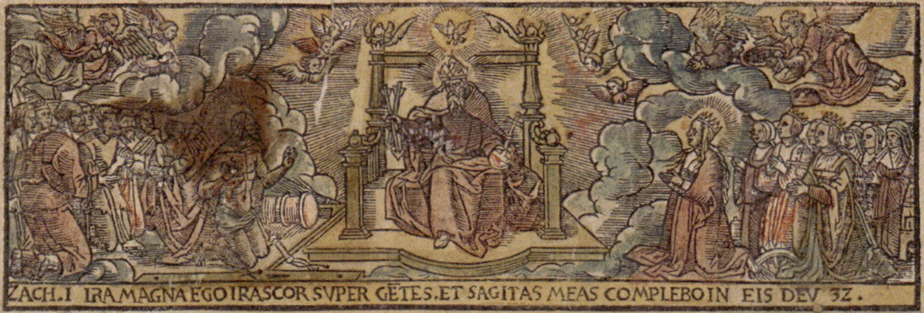

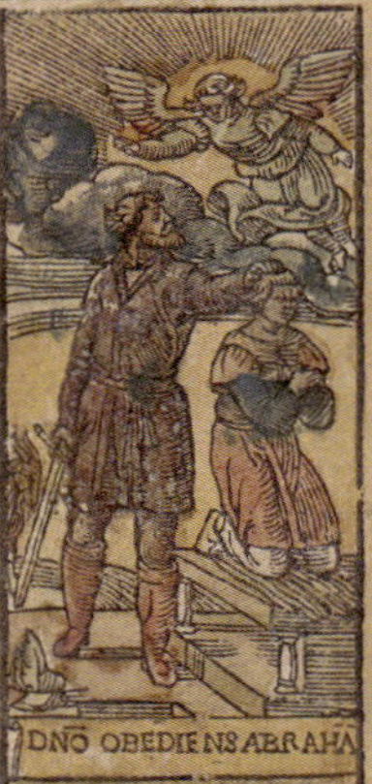

Die Bibel/ werom met grooter nerstiheit ouersien ende gecorrigeert/ meer dan in ses hōdert plaetzen/ ende Collacioneert met dē oudē Latinschē/ ongefalstē Biblie.

Duer B. Alexander Blanckart/ Carmelit.

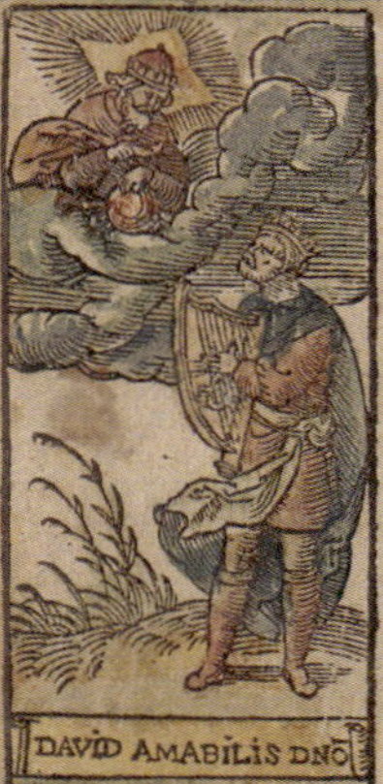

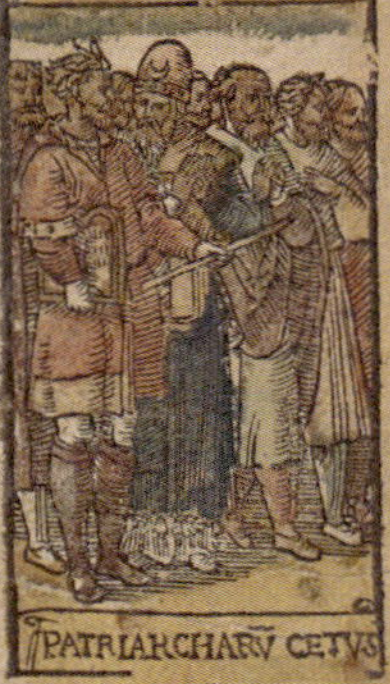

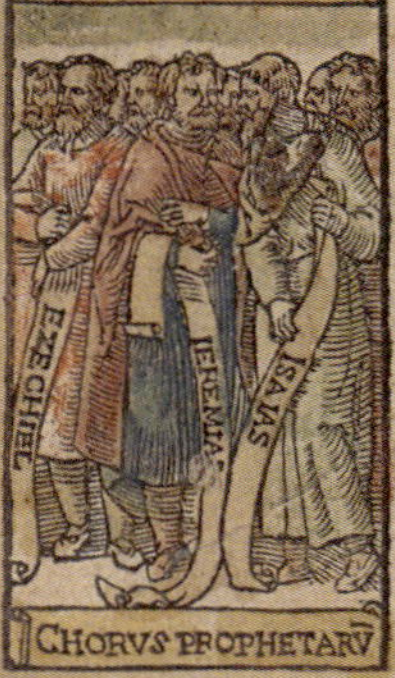

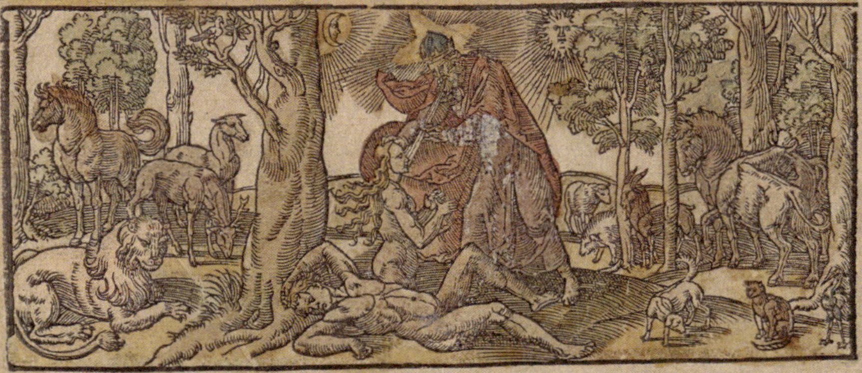

Gheprent toe Coelen by Jaspar van Gennep/ met Keyserlyker Genade ende Priuilegien/ Int Jaer ons Heerē Jesu Christi/ M.D.XLVIII.

¢ Noble bishops and Catholic reform in the Netherlands ~ 1551

Acta & decreta Synodi diœcesanæ Cameracensis
Paris: Matthieu David, 1551
[24], 209, [3] p. · in 4°

Traditionally, early-16th-century bishops within the Low Countries did not maintain a good reputation. As the story goes, their noble mind set and elitist behaviour would cause them to forfeit their pastoral duties and, consequently, leave them ill-equipped to halt the Reformation in these crucial parts of north-western Europe. Also, the new strict prescriptions of the Council of Trent (1545–1563) on the tasks of bishops reinforced this negative image of contemporary officeholders. Nonetheless, the differences between pre- and post-Tridentine bishops were not always as great as most assume. This is evidenced by a 1551 Parisian edition of the statutes concluded at a diocesan synod of Cambrai, a border diocese that stretched from the imperial enclaves of the Cambrésis and some French territories across Habsburg lands, even including the city of Antwerp in the duchy of Brabant.

The then installed Bishop of Cambrai, Robert de Croÿ (c. 1502/6–1556) descended from a noble family who held vast possessions in the borderlands between the Low Countries and France, and had amassed an impressive array of titles and offices, including several episcopal honours. As both a Duke of Cambrai and a Prince of the Holy Roman Empire, the Bishop of Cambrai would likely have acted not only as a spiritual leader, but also as a powerful secular ruler. On this particular imprint, he accentuated both his aristocratic origin – *à jamais Croÿ* – and kinship with prestigious noble houses, by having the coats of arms of Croÿ, Lorraine, Luxemburg, Estouteville, Bar... printed before the text of the synod's statutes. An initial glimpse would thus confirm that the bishop made the publication of reformatory statutes foremost as an act of noble self-fashioning.

On closer inspection, however, it appears that Robert de Croÿ was willing to help implement Catholic Reform in Cambrai and the Low Countries. He had attended the Council of Trent's first period and participated in the debate on the interpretation of episcopal duties. Upon his return from Trent, he summoned the aforementioned synod, describing the assembly "as a good remedy against the heresy of Luther." As a result, the synod made important changes to the diocese's old statutes in response to this "disaster of their own time." In addition, it accepted the *Formula Reformationis,* a far-reaching reform program that Emperor Charles V wanted to implement throughout his Empire from 1548 onwards. Robert de Croÿ also carried out visitations to follow up this reformatory program. Hence, this rare pamphlet shows that noble bishops, such as de Croÿ, facilitated Catholic Reform more than a decade before the promulgation of the Tridentine decrees in the Low Countries.

Literature:
Hans Cools, 'Bishops in the Habsburg Netherlands on the Eve of the Catholic Renewal, 1515–1559', in *Episcopal Reform and Politics in Early Modern Europe,* ed. Jennifer Mara DeSilva (Kirksville, MO: Truman State University Press, 2012), 46–62; Violet Soen and Aurelie Van de Meulebroucke, 'Vanguard Tridentine Reform in the Habsburg Netherlands: The Episcopacy of Robert de Croÿ, Bishop of Cambrai (1519–56)', in *Church, Censorship and Reform in the Early Modern Habsburg Netherlands,* ed. Violet Soen, Dries Vanysacker, and Wim François (Turnhout: Brepols, 2017), 125–144; Alexander Soetaert, 'Printing at the Frontier: The Emergence of a Transregional Book Production in the Ecclesiastical Province of Cambrai (c. 1560–1659)', *De Gulden Passer: Journal for Book History* 94 (2016): 137–163.

Acta & decreta Synodi diœcesanae Cameracensis, præsidente Reuerendissimo in Christo patre, ac Illustrissimo Principe Domino, D. ROBERTO DE CROY, Episcopo & Duce Cameracensi, Sacri Imperii Principe, Comite Cameracesii, &c. celebratæ anno Redemptoris nostri Iesu Christi, M. D. L. mense Octob.

ITEM,

Antiqua statuta synodalia Cameracensis diœcesis ab eadem synodo recognita, adiectisque moderationibus, correctionibus, & additionibus reformata.

His adiuncta est formula reformationis per Cæsaream maiestatē statibus Ecclesiasticis, in Comitiis Augustanis, ad deliberandū proposita, & ab eisdem recepta & probata.

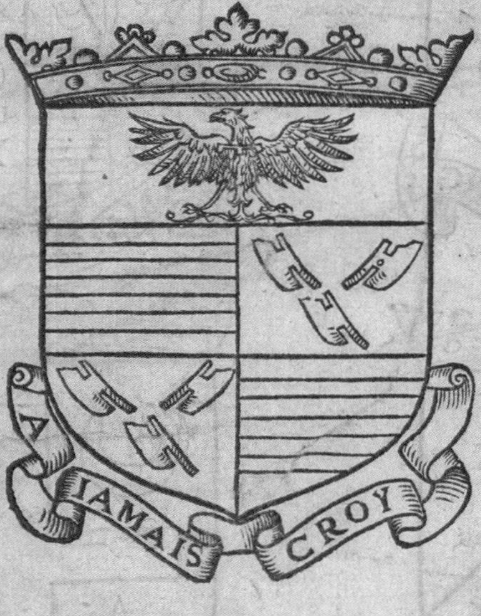

PARISIIS,
Ex typographia Matthæi Dauîdis.
1 5 5 1.

A botanist's tool: Rembert Dodoens' *Cruydeboeck* ~ 1554

Rembert Dodoens (1517–1585), the famous Mechelen-born 16th-century botanist, began his studies in medicine, cosmography and geography at the University of Louvain. He became court physician of the Holy Roman Emperor Maximilian II and Austrian Emperor Rudolph II, and in 1582 he was appointed professor of medicine and botany at the University of Leiden. Dodoens is most known for his *Cruydeboeck*. In this Dutch herbal book, first published in Antwerp in 1554 by Jan van der Loe, 715 woodblocks from the works of Leonart Fuchs (1501–1566) were reused.

In the early 16th century, botanists began to apply a scientific approach of observation, documentation and experimentation to the study of plants. Dodoens copied these methods from some German botanists and started by adding some two hundred descriptions of plants to Fuchs's work based on his own observations. He was able to construct a kind of botanical systematics, where he divided and ordered 980 plants in groups, based on their (medical) properties and physical similarities. Peter van der Borcht (1535/40–1608) and Arnoud Nicolai were appointed with the task of producing new illustrations of the two-hundred supplemented plants in Dodoens' work.

The *Cruydeboeck* was revised and translated numerous times. There is, for example, a special and very precious 1583 edition from Christopher Plantin (1520–1589), with new illustrations from Van der Borcht and Nicolai: *Remberti Dodonæi [...] Stirpium historiæ pemptades sex. Sive libri* XXX. If we take into account all later editions and translations, Dodoens' herbal book can be considered as the ultimate textbook for future generations of physicians and apothecaries up until the beginning of the 19th century. Furthermore, Dodoens was able to make his scientific work accessible for a broader audience (horticulturists, farmers, traders...), by adding, for instance, some of the plants' common names in the vernacular and their local usages in his descriptions.

This particular copy of Dodoens' *Cruydeboeck* is property of the Canons Regular of the Holy Cross of Coimbra of Diest. The book shows signs of it having been used in more ways than one. Some members of the *Ordo Crucis* saw the book as a perfect tool, considering its size and weight, for making their own personal herbarium. Between certain pages, you will find dried plant-specimens, which have probably been preserved there for several centuries.

Rembert Dodoens
Cruydeboeck, in den welcken die gheheele historie ... begrepen ende verclaert es ...
Antwerp: Jan vander Loe, 1554
[39, 1 blank], CCCCCCCCXVIII, [20] p · in 2°
PN000141/F°

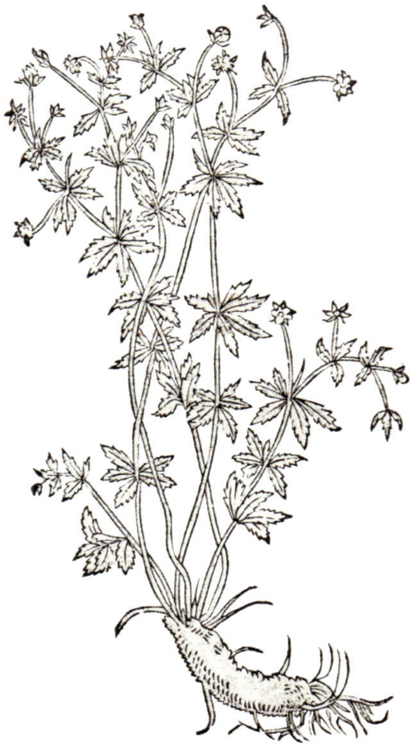

Literature:
Guy Gilias, Cornelis van Tilburg, and Vincent Van Roy, *Rembert Dodoens: Een zestiende-eeuwse kruidenwetenschapper, zijn tijd- en vakgenoten en zijn betekenis* (Antwerp: Garant, 2016); M. Thiery, 'Rembert Dodoens (1517–1585) en "Dodonaea"', *Tijdschrift voor Geneeskunde* 61, no. 8 (2005): 654–656.

groot dick ende lanckworpich/en van den eenen gheslachte bruyn gruen/veel ribbē heb-
bende/ende seer herde scellen/ende van den anderen gheslachte wit/met saechten dun-
nen scellen bedeckt. In die vruchten wast dat saet dat breet ende wit es/ ende veel meer
der dan Concommer saet.

2 Dat tweede gheslacht met den ronden vruchten heeft oock rouwe stekende stelen en-
de bladeren/maer die stelen sijn minder/ende cruypen meest lancx der eerden. Die bla-
deren sijn oock cleynder ende niet zoo diep ghesneden. Die bloemē sijn geel den bloemen
van anderen Pepoenen van fatsoene gelijck. Die vrucht es ront ende platachtich/ van
den eenen oock gruen/ende van den anderen wit/ende daer in groeyet oock dat saet/dat
minder es dan tsaet van anderen Pepoenen/ nochtans noch meerder dan tsaet van
Concommeren.

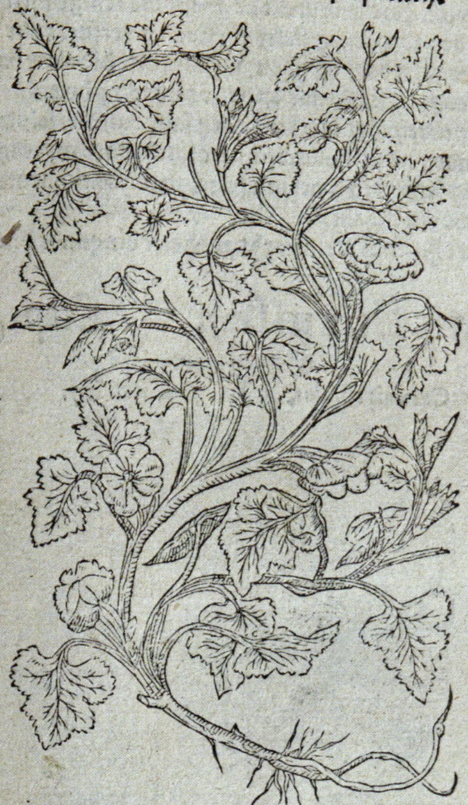
Pepones lati. Breede Pepoenen.

3 Tderde gheslacht van Pepoenen/es den tweeden van cruypende stelen bladeren en-
de bloemen seer ghelijck/maer die stelen en sijn niet zoo rouw. Die vrucht es plat breet
ende ront/met een saechte dunne scelle becleet/rontsomme die canten ghecronckelt en-
de ghefroncelt eenen buekelaer schier gelijckende/ ende daer in leyt dat saet/ dat wit es
ende den Concommer sade oock ghelijck maer meerder.

¶ Plaetse.

Dese gheslachte van Pepoenen worden oock in die hoven ghesaeyet/ ende worden in
die spijse ghebruyckt.

¶ Tijt.

Dese vruchten worden in Oghstmaent rijp ende bequaem om eten/oft somtijts eer
alst vroech werm weer es.

¶ Naem.

Dese vruchten worden gheheeten in Griecx ende Latijn *Pepones*/vā Galenus oock
Sicyopepones/dat es/*Pepones cucumerales*.

Unbuilt architecture by Jacques Androuet du Cerceau ∾ 1559/1561

Du Cerceau is known in French architectural history as a family business. The Du Cerceau sons were involved in the construction of the Louvre, the Tuileries and Fontainebleau and contributed to the realisation of 'the State as a Work of Art', political architecture that allows history of art to be placed in relation to successive rulers, with the royal styles of Louis XIII to Louis XVI and their derivatives, from the 'Pompadour style' to 'Pompidou style'.

The designs by father Jacques often did not get much further than the drawing board but they did end up on the printing press and gained a much wider reputation as a result. As an architect, if you have your sights set on the eternal, it is better to publish than build. It is still true today but was all the more true in the Renaissance when the contemporary discovery of perspective and printing caused a boom in architectural theory. Du Cerceau designed ideal castles and complete model cities with a free hand. All these paper palaces have become part of the collective memory and architectural phantasmagoria.

Du Cerceau did not restrict himself to castles in the air. In his *Livre d'architecture,* he gives a typology of living space, with buildings with possible modular extension depending on the financial resources of the owner. In a second part he provides a sample of fireplaces, roof windows, wells with nymphs and satyrs and concludes with a dozen tombs. Through his engravings Du Cerceau gained a reputation as a pioneer of French Renaissance architecture. He is no stranger to mannerism as is clear from the bizarre combination of a mantelpiece with a window ornamentation in it.

The volume belonged to the Jesuit college in Bruges – a Father provided the three graces with loincloths – and came from the library of Charles de Croy, the avid bibliophile, who had it from his father Philip de Croy (1526–1595). *Ce Livre est à moy Phles Sire de Croy … 1565,* the latter had written in the book, accompanied by his family motto *j'y parviendrai.* The work was intended for his architect: *Ad usum architecti.* However, Philip was too busy with politics and had little time for architecture, while Charles had even more building plans. His project for the courtyard with galleries at Heverlee Castle was never realised and equally remained a paper palace, *un chateau en Espagne,* 'in the Brabant style'.

Jacques Androuet du Cerceau
Livre d'architecture
Paris: Benoît Prévost, 1559
2°, [16] f.
Second Livre d'architecture
Paris: Andreas Wechel, 1561
[68] f. · in 2°
P72/F° ANDR Libr 1559

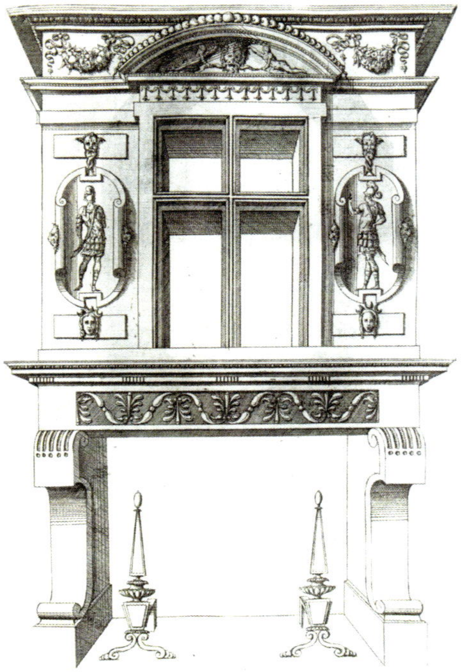

Literature:
Royal Institute of British Architects, *Early Printed Books 1478–1840: Catalogue of the British Architectural Library Early Imprints Collection,* vol. 1 (London: Bowker, 1994); Vaughan Hart and Peter Hicks, eds., *Paper Palaces: The Rise of the Renaissance Architectural Treatise* (New Haven, CT: Yale University Press, 1998); K. de Jonge, '*Up die manier van Brabant*: Brabant en de adelsarchitectuur van de Lage landen (1450–1530)', *Bijdragen tot de Geschiedenis* 86 (2003): 409–423; Alexandre Cojannot and Alexandre Gady, *Dessiner pour bâtir: Le métier d'architecte au XVIIe siècle* (Paris: Le Passage, 2017).

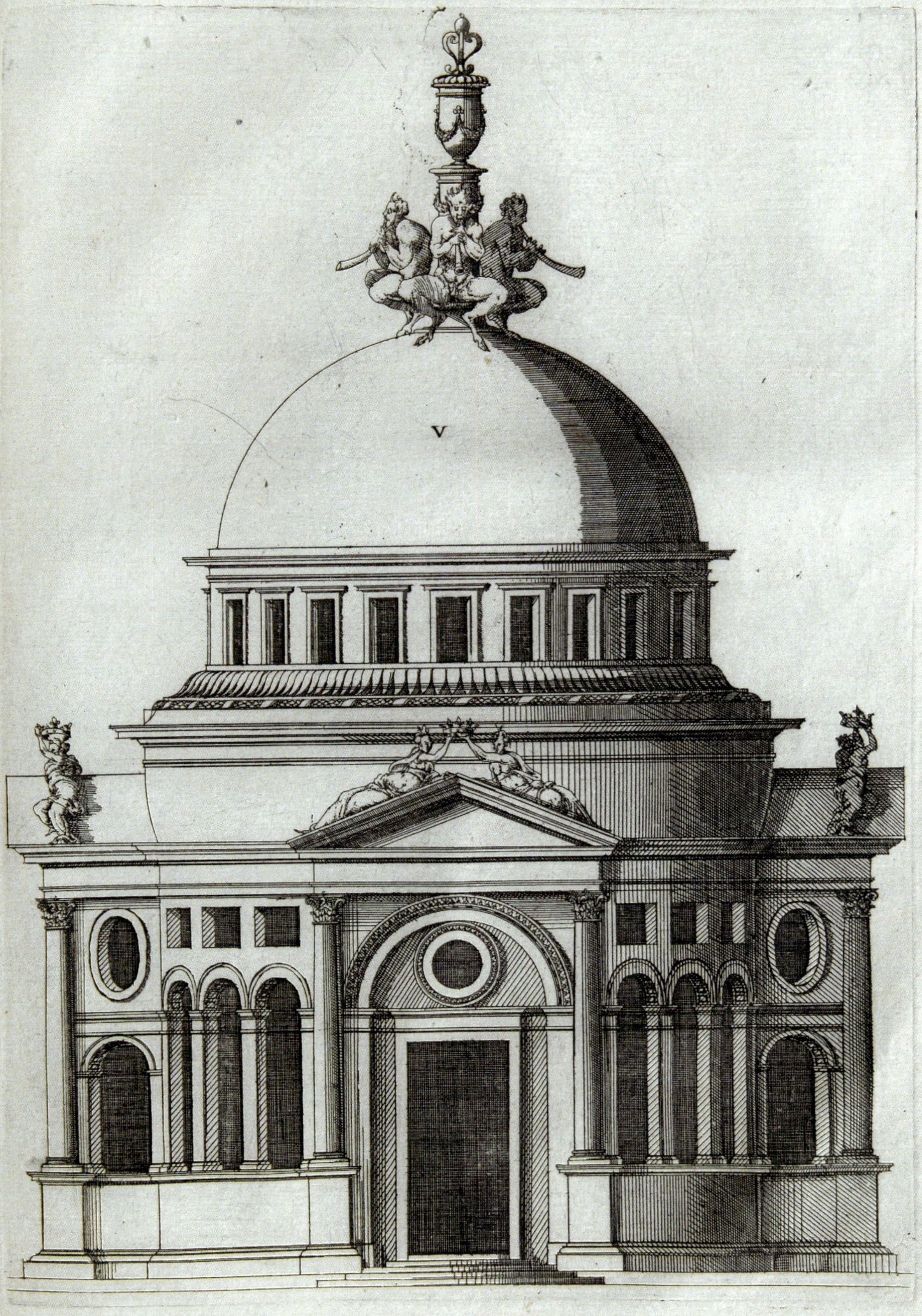
V

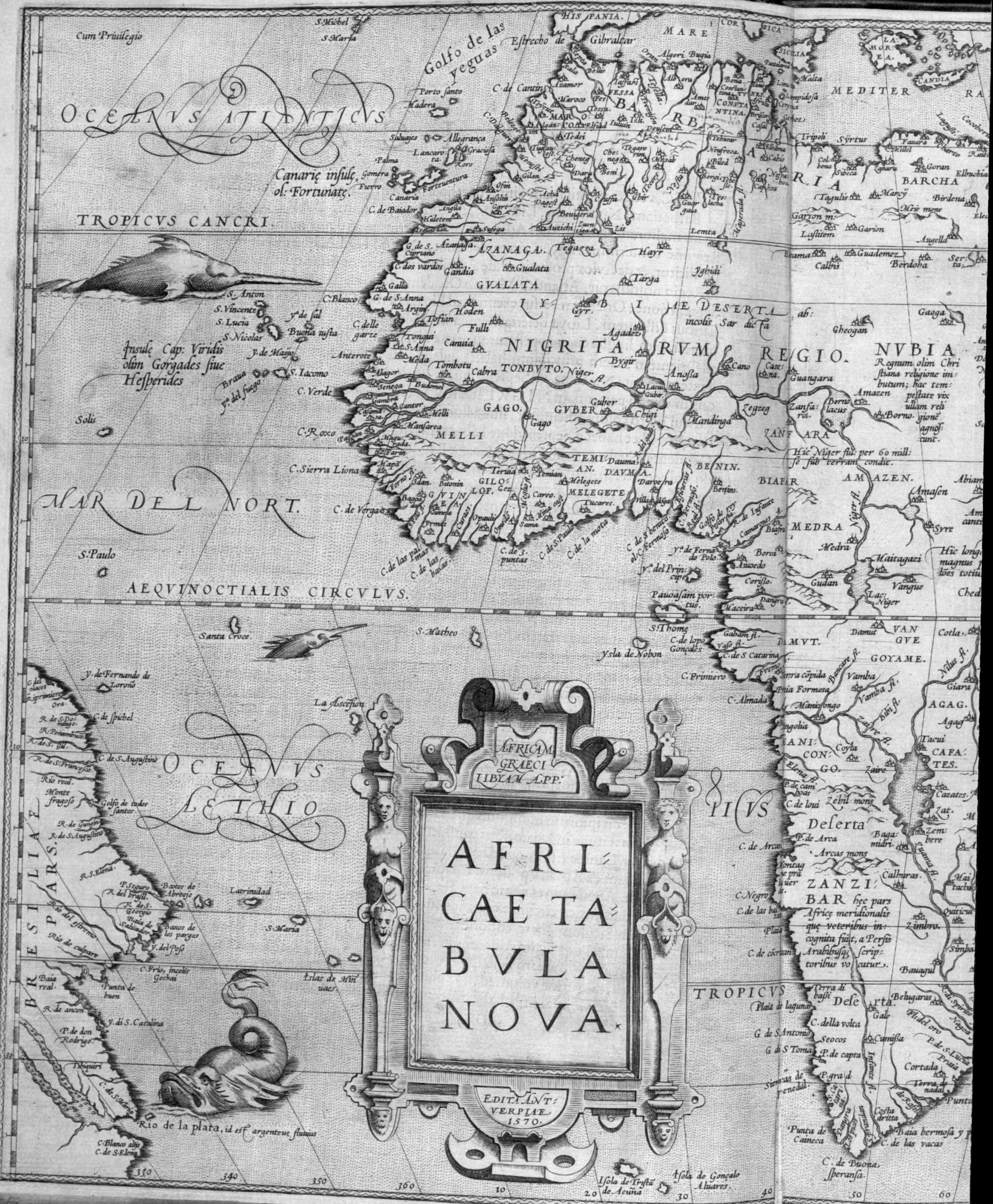

AFRICAE TABVLA NOVA.
AFRICAM GRAECI LIBYAM APP.
EDITA ANTVERPIAE 1570.
Cum Priuilegio
OCEANVS ATLANTICVS
Golfo de las yeguas
Estrecho de Gibraltar
HISPANIA
MARE
MEDITER
Canarię insulę, ol: Fortunatę.
TROPICVS CANCRI
AZANAGA
GVALATA
LYBIAE DESERTA
NIGRITARVM REGIO.
NVBIA
insulę Cap: Viridis olim Gorgades siue Hesperides
C. Verde
C. Blanco
GAGO
GVBER
MELLI
ZANFARA
BIAFAR
MEDRA
AMAZEN
C. Sierra Liona
MAR DEL NORT.
AEQVINOCTIALIS CIRCVLVS.
Santa Croce
S. Matheo
Ysla de Nobon
S. Thome
C. de lopo Gonçales
La Ascension
OCEANVS AETHIOPICVS
BRESILIAE PARS.
Latrinidad
S. Maria
Islas de Miniuaes
Rio de la plata, id est argenteus fluuius
C. Blanco alijs C. de S. Elena
TROPICVS
MANICONGO
Deserta
ZANZIBAR hec pars Africę meridionalis quę veteribus incognita fuit, a Persis Arabibusq; scriptoribus vocatur.
Isola de Trista de Acuña
Isola de Gonçalo Aluares.
C. de Buona speransa.
Punta de Caineca
Baia hermosa
C. de las vacas
330
340
350
360
10
20
30
40
50
60

¢ Tombotu and Ortelius' *Africæ tabula nova* ∾ 1570

The *Africæ tabula nova* (*New map of Africa*) appeared in the first edition (1570) of *Theatrum orbis terrarum* (*Theatre of the world*). In this atlas, the cartographer and geographer Abraham Ortelius (1527–1598), assembled the most reliable maps of his time into one volume, publishing all the maps in the same style and from copper plates of the same size, arranged by continent, region and state. All Western European knowledge of the world was brought together. For the map of Africa, Ortelius relied on the work of the Italian cartographer, engineer, and astronomer Giacomo Gastaldi (c. 1500–1566). Gastaldi had published an eight-sheet wall map of Africa in 1564 that was the first to reflect accurately the knowledge of African geography gained by Europeans from the explorations of the previous century. For the verbal descriptions of the western African regions, Ortelius used the 1526 publication *Della descrittione dell'Africa et delle cose notabili che iui sono* by El Hasan am Muhammed el-Wazzan-ez-Zayyati, better known as Leo Africanus (c. 1494–c. 1554?), a diplomat and one of the earliest 16th-century travellers to Africa. The *Descrittione dell'Africa* was translated from Italian to Latin by Johannes Blommaerts in 1556 and published that same year by Jan de Laet in Antwerp.

The first Western European mention of 'Tombotu' is on the *New map of Africa*. The description of the flourishing West African city of Timbuktu is detailed: during the prosperous Shonghay empire (15th–16th centuries) the city was a very important trading centre on the trans-Saharan caravan route. It was a wealthy commercial and intellectual centre connecting Saharan, tropical and Mediterranean Africa. Leo Africanus writes: "The city was inhabited by doctors, judges, priests and scholars, all appointed by the king. There are manuscripts and written books from the Barbary coast [modern Morocco, Algeria, and Tunisia] to be bought here, and they are sold for more money than any other merchandise." Through Africanus, the fame of Timbuktu as a rich and erudite intellectual centre reached Europe: without doubt it could be compared favourably with Paris for excellence of scholarship, intellectual culture and collective knowledge.

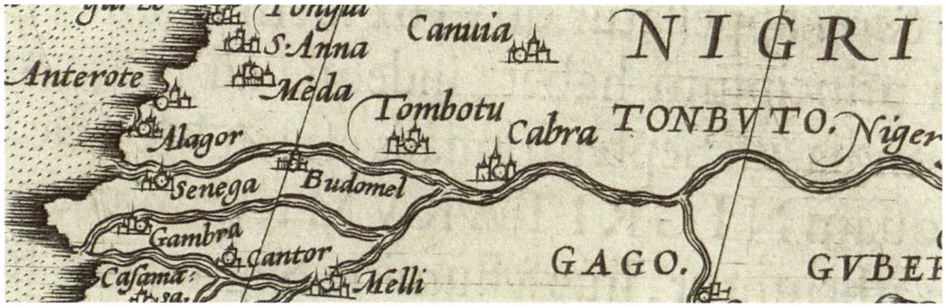

Abraham Ortelius
Theatrum orbis terrarum
Antwerp: Gillis Coppens van Diest, 1570
[142] f. · in 2°

Literature:
Rome, Biblioteca Nazionale Vittorio Emmanuele, MS 953: Leo Africanus, *Della descrittione dell'Africa;* Giovanni Battista Ramusio, *Primo volume delle navigationi et viaggi* (Venice: heirs of Lucantonio Giunta, 1550).

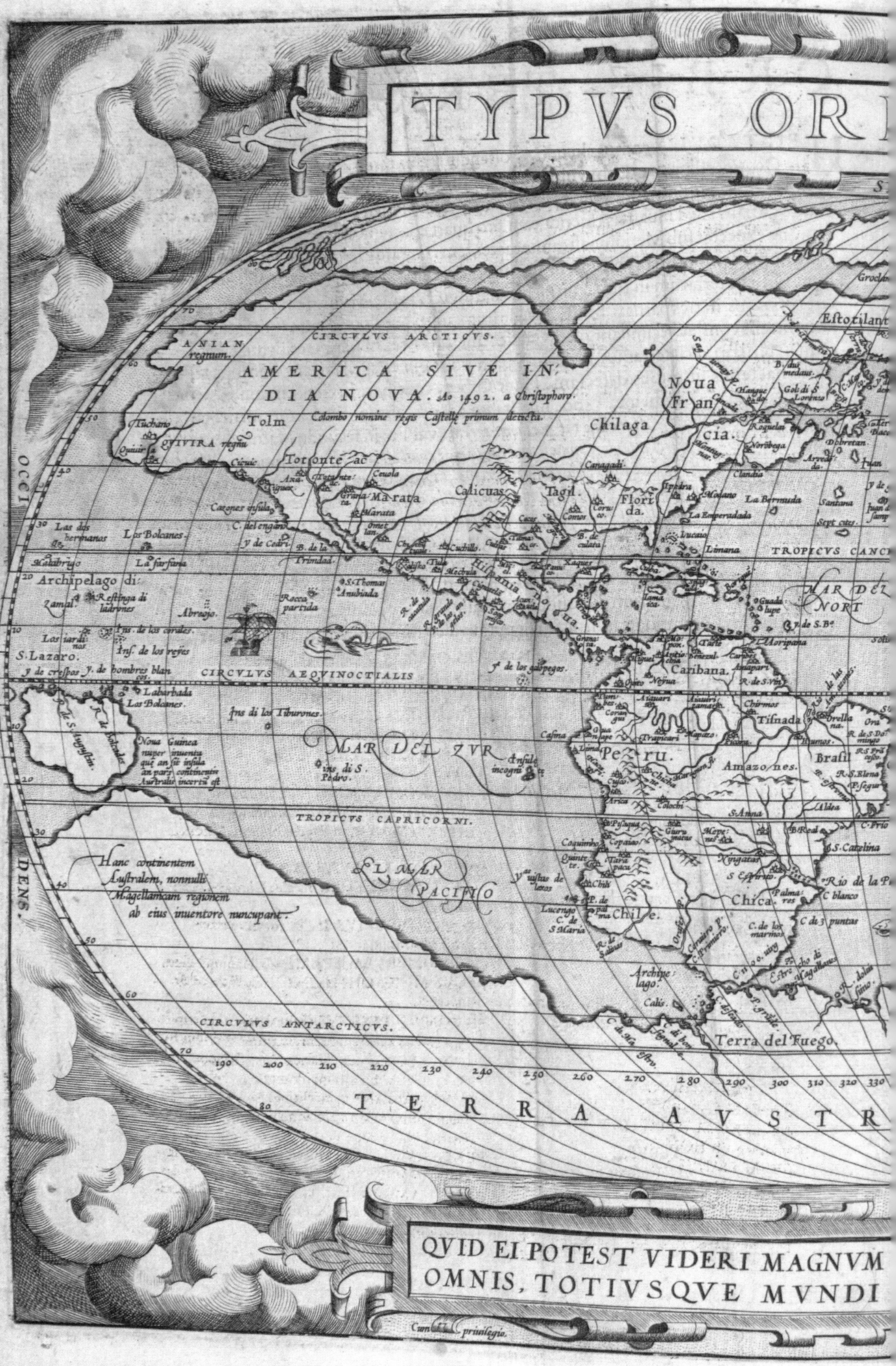
TYPVS ORB
AMERICA SIVE INDIA NOVA. Ao 1492. a Christophoro Colombo nomine regis Castellę primum detecta.
ANIAN regnum.
CIRCVLVS ARCTICVS.
QVIVIRA regnu
Tolm
Totonteac
Marata
Chilaga
Noua Francia.
Calicuas
Tagil
Florida.
Estotilant
TROPICVS CANC
Archipelago di Zamal.
Restinga di ladrones
Los Bolcanes
La farfana
S. Lazaro.
CIRCVLVS AEQVINOCTIALIS
Nova Guinea nuper inuenta quę an sit insula an pars continentis Australis incertu est
MAR DEL ZVR
MAR DEL NORT
Caribana.
Peru.
Amazones.
Brasil
TROPICVS CAPRICORNI.
Hanc continentem Australem, nonnulli Magellanicam regionem ab eius inuentore nuncupant.
EL MAR PACIFICO
Chile.
Chica.
Rio de la P
Terra del Fuego.
CIRCVLVS ANTARCTICVS.
TERRA AVSTR
OCCIDENS.
190 200 210 220 230 240 250 260 270 280 290 300 310 320 330
QVID EI POTEST VIDERI MAGNVM
OMNIS, TOTIVSQVE MVNDI
Cum privilegio.

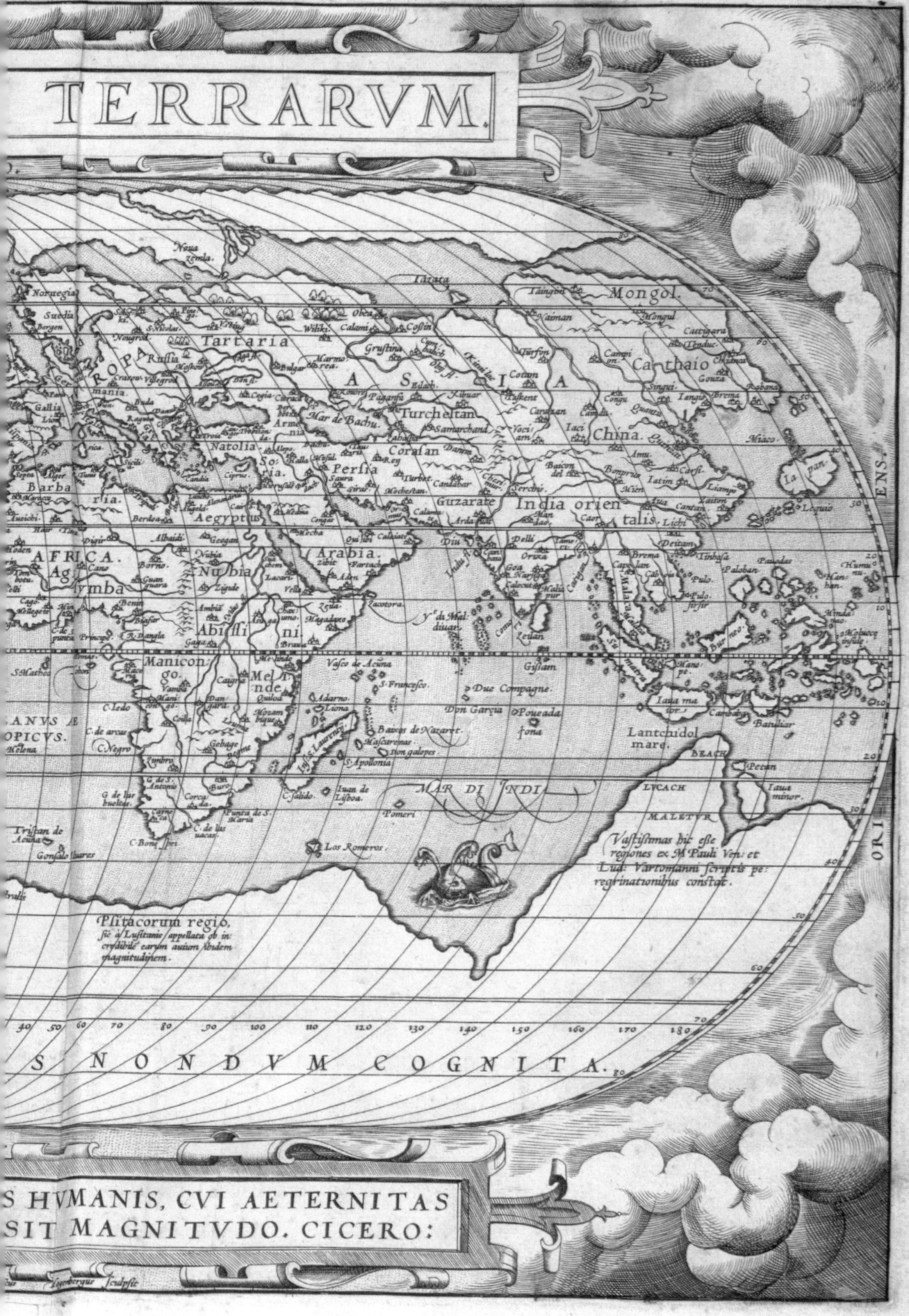
TERRARUM
Noua Zemla
Norwegia
Suedia
Tartaria
ASIA
Mongol
Cathaio
Turcheſtan
Mar de Bachu
Natolia
Soria
Perſia
Coraſan
China
Iapan
India orientalis
Guzarate
Arabia
Aegyptus
AFRICA
Nubia
Abiſſini
Manicongo
Melinde
Barbaria
Mar di Indi
Lantchidol mare
BEACH
LUCACH
MALETUR
Petan
Iaua minor
Iaua major
Sumatra
Burneo
Moluccæ insulæ
Zeilan
Isla de S. Lorenzo
Mascarenas
Don Garcia
Due Compagne
Vasco de Acuna
S. Francisco
Los Romeros
Pomeri
C. Bone ſpei
Tristan de Acuna
Gonsalo Aluares
Vaſtiſsimas hic eſse regiones ex M. Pauli Ven: et Lud: Vartomanni ſcriptis peregrinationibus constat.
Pſitacorum regio, ſic à Luſitanis appellata ob incredibile earum auium ibidem magnitudinem.
ORIENS
S NONDVM COGNITA.
S HVMANIS, CVI AETERNITAS
SIT MAGNITVDO. CICERO:
Hogenbergus ſculpsit

¢ THE POLYGLOT BIBLE BY CHRISTOPHER PLANTIN ~ 1568–1572

Biblia sacra hebraice, chaldaice, græce, & latine [**Benedictus Arias Montanus ... recensuit et probavit**]
Antwerp: Christopher Plantin, 1568–1572
8 v. · in 2°
P22.04/F° BIJB

The *Biblia regia* published by Christopher Plantin (1520–1589) is often described as the greatest achievement in book production in the 16th century. Financed by the Spanish King Philip II, and comprising eight large folio volumes, it took five years to print all 1,200 copies of this edition. When we page through the Bible, we see several columns of text in different languages. In the volumes with the Old Testament, the Hebrew text with the Latin translation by Saint Jerome is on the left; the Greek text with its Latin translation is on the right, and beneath, spread over the left and right pages, the Chaldean or Aramaic text, printed with Hebrew type, and accompanied with Latin paraphrasing. In the New Testament, which is the fifth volume of the Bible, the Hebrew is replaced by Syriac, a language in which the text of the New Testament was written in the early centuries. Designing and maintaining this well-balanced arrangement of the text over so many pages could only be done by highly skilled compositors at an expert printing press. These five volumes of the text of the Bible were supplemented with the so-called *Apparatus*. This comprised the 'Pagnini Bible', in which the Hebrew Old Testament and the Greek New Testament texts were printed with a line-by-line Latin translation, whereby the reader could follow both languages almost word by word. The last two volumes contained several grammar sections and dictionaries for the languages in which the texts were printed, as well as historical and philological treatises on several related topics.

In Plantin's *Biblia regia*, this stunning typographic accomplishment highlights a remarkably esteemed scholarly achievement. The Spanish theologian Benito Arias Montano supervised the scholarly work for this project. In addition, Plantin was helped by his son-in-law Franciscus Raphelengius, Andreas Masius, and the brothers Le Fevre de la Boderie, whilst several theologians at the University of Louvain assisted by comparing numerous manuscripts and printed editions to determine what the correct text for the Bible was. Augustinus Hunnæus was one such theologian, who had, for example, published Thomas Aquinas' *Summa* and various other theological and philosophical works at the Plantin Press. Plantin gave a free copy of the *Biblia regia* to each of the scholars who assisted with this immense project, in appreciation of their work. We can still admire Hunnæus's copy in the Maurits Sabbe Library.

Literature:
Leon Voet, *The Plantin Press (1555–1589): A Bibliography of the Works Printed and Published by Christopher Plantin at Antwerp and Leiden* (Amsterdam: Van Hoeve, 1980–1983), vol. I, 280–315, no. 644; Baldomero Macías Rosendo, *La Biblia políglota de Amberes en la correspondencia de Benito Arias Montano* (Huelva: Universidad de Huelva, 1998); Julianne Simpson, 'Selling the Biblia Regia: The Marketing and Distribution Methods for Christopher Plantin's Polyglot Bible', in *Books for Sale: The Advertising and Promotion of Print Since the Fifteenth Century*, ed. Robin Myers, Michael Harris, and Giles Mandelbrote (New Castle, DE: Oak Knoll Press, 2009), 27–55.

PROFESSOR LOVANII FIERI F·D·AVGVSTINVS

א

1 חזוֹן יְשַׁעְיָהוּ בֶן־אָמוֹץ אֲשֶׁר חָזָה עַל־
יְהוּדָה וִירוּשָׁלָ͏ִם בִּימֵי עֻזִּיָּהוּ יוֹתָם
אָחָז יְחִזְקִיָּהוּ מַלְכֵי יְהוּדָה׃
2 * שִׁמְעוּ שָׁמַיִם וְהַאֲזִינִי אֶרֶץ כִּי
יְהוָה דִּבֵּר בָּנִים גִּדַּלְתִּי וְרוֹמַמְתִּי וְהֵם פָּשְׁעוּ בִי׃
3 * יָדַע שׁוֹר קֹנֵהוּ וַחֲמוֹר אֵבוּס בְּעָלָיו יִשְׂרָאֵל לֹא
יָדַע עַמִּי לֹא הִתְבּוֹנָן׃
4 * הוֹי גּוֹי חֹטֵא עַם כֶּבֶד עָוֺן זֶרַע מְרֵעִים בָּנִים
מַשְׁחִיתִים עָזְבוּ אֶת־יְהוָה נִאֲצוּ אֶת־קְדוֹשׁ יִשְׂרָאֵל
נָזֹרוּ אָחוֹר׃
5 * עַל־מֶה תֻכּוּ עוֹד תּוֹסִיפוּ סָרָה כָּל־רֹאשׁ לָחֳלִי
6 וְכָל־לֵבָב דַּוָּי׃ * מִכַּף־רֶגֶל וְעַד־רֹאשׁ אֵין־
בּוֹ מְתֹם פֶּצַע וְחַבּוּרָה וּמַכָּה טְרִיָּה לֹא־זֹרוּ וְלֹא
חֻבָּשׁוּ וְלֹא רֻכְּכָה בַּשָּׁמֶן׃
7 * אַרְצְכֶם שְׁמָמָה עָרֵיכֶם שְׂרֻפוֹת אֵשׁ אַדְמַתְכֶם
לְנֶגְדְּכֶם זָרִים אֹכְלִים אֹתָהּ וּשְׁמָמָה כְּמַהְפֵּכַת זָרִים׃
8 * וְנוֹתְרָה בַת־צִיּוֹן כְּסֻכָּה בְכָרֶם כִּמְלוּנָה
בְמִקְשָׁה כְּעִיר נְצוּרָה׃
9 * לוּלֵי יְהוָה צְבָאוֹת הוֹתִיר לָנוּ שָׂרִיד כִּמְעָט
10 כִּסְדֹם הָיִינוּ לַעֲמֹרָה דָּמִינוּ׃ * שִׁמְעוּ דְבַר־יְהוָה
קְצִינֵי סְדֹם הַאֲזִינוּ תּוֹרַת אֱלֹהֵינוּ עַם עֲמֹרָה׃
11 * לָמָּה־לִּי רֹב־זִבְחֵיכֶם יֹאמַר יְהוָה שָׂבַעְתִּי עֹלוֹת
אֵילִים וְחֵלֶב מְרִיאִים וְדַם פָּרִים וּכְבָשִׂים וְעַתּוּדִים
12 לֹא חָפָצְתִּי׃ * כִּי תָבֹאוּ לֵרָאוֹת פָּנָי מִי־בִקֵּשׁ זֹאת
13 מִיֶּדְכֶם רְמֹס חֲצֵרָי׃ * לֹא תוֹסִיפוּ הָבִיא מִנְחַת־
שָׁוְא קְטֹרֶת תּוֹעֵבָה הִיא לִי חֹדֶשׁ וְשַׁבָּת קְרֹא מִקְרָא
לֹא־אוּכַל אָוֶן וַעֲצָרָה׃

ESAIAS PROPHETA.

CAPVT I.

1 VISIO Esaiæ filij Amos,quã
vidit super Iudam & Hie-
rusalem, in diebus Oziæ,
Ioatham, Achaz, & Eze-
chiæ regum Iuda.
2 * Audite cæli, & auribus
percipe terra, quoniam Dominus locutus
est:Filios enutriui & exaltaui, ipsi autẽ spre
3 uerunt me. * Cognouit bos possessorem
suum, & asinus præsepe dñi sui; Israel autẽ
me non cognouit, & populus meus nõ in-
4 tellexit. * Væ genti peccatrici,populo graui
iniquitate, semini nequam, filiis sceleratis.
dereliquerunt Dñm, blasphemauerũt san-
ctum Israel:abalienati sunt retrorsum.
5 * Super quo percutiam vos vltrà addẽtes
præuaricationem? Omne caput languidũ,
6 & omne cor mœrens. * A planta pe-
dis vsque ad verticem non est in eo sanitas.
Vulnus & liuor & plaga tumens, non est
circũligata nec curata medicamine, neque
7 fota oleo. * Terra vestra deserta, ciuitates
vestræ succensæ igni: regionẽ vestram corã
vobis alieni deuorant, & desolabitur sicut
8 in vastitate hostili. * Et derelinquetur filia
Sion vt vmbraculũ in vinea, & sicut tugu-
rium in cucumerario, sicut ciuitas quæ va-
9 statur. * Nisi Dñs exercituũ reliquisset no-
bis semẽ, quasi Sodoma fuissemus, & quasi
10 Gomorra similes essemus. * Audite verbũ
Dñi principes Sodomorum:percipite auri-
bus legem Dei nostri populus Gomorræ.
11 * Quo mihi multitudinẽ victimarum ve-
strarum,dicit Dñs?Plenus sum. holocausta
arietũ & adipẽ pinguium, & sanguinẽ vitu
12 lorũ & agnorũ & hircorũ nolui. * Cùm ve-
neritis ante conspectũ meũ, quis quæsiuit
hæc de manibus vestris, vt ambularetis in
atriis meis?
13 * Ne offeratis vltrà sacrificium frustra.
Incensum abominatio est mihi. Neome-
niam & sabbatum & festiuitates alias non
feram. iniqui sunt cœtus vestri.

תרגום יונתן

א

1 נְבוּאַת יְשַׁעְיָהוּ בַר אָמוֹץ דְּאִתְנַבִּי עַל אֱנָשׁ יְהוּדָה וְיָתְבֵי יְרוּשְׁלֶם בְּיוֹמֵי עֻזִּיָּה יוֹתָם אָחָז יְחִזְקִיָּהוּ מַלְכַיָּא דְבֵית יְהוּדָה׃
2 שְׁמַעוּ שְׁמַיָּא דְזָעוּ כַּד יַהֲבַת אוֹרַיְתִי לְעַמִּי וְאַצִּיתִי אַרְעָא דְאִתְרְגִיפַת מִן קֳדָם פִּתְגָמֵי אֲרֵי יְיָ מַלֵּל עַמִּי בֵּית יִשְׂרָאֵל
קְרֵיתִי לְהוֹן בְּנִין וְחַבֵּבְתִּנוּן וִיקַרְתִּנוּן וְאִנּוּן מְרַדוּ בְמֵימְרִי׃ 3 יְדַע תּוֹרָא זְבָנֵהּ וַחֲמָרָא אוּרְיָא דְמָרוֹהִי יִשְׂרָאֵל לָא אֲלִיף לְמִדַּע דַּחַלְתִּי עַמִּי לָא
אִסְתַּכַּל לְמֵתַב לְדַחַלְתִּי׃ 4 וַוי עַל דְּאִתְקְרִיו עַם קַדִּישׁ וַחֲטוֹ כְּנִישָׁא בְחִירָא וְאַסְגִּיו חוֹבִין אִתְכְּנִיו בְּזַרְעָא רְחִימָא וְאַבְאִשׁוּ וְאִתְאַמַּר לְהוֹן
בְּנִין חַבִּיבִין וְחַבִּלוּ אָרְחַתְהוֹן שְׁבַקוּ יַת פָּלְחָנָא דַייָ קְצוּ בְּדַחַלְתָא קַדִּישָׁא דְיִשְׂרָאֵל וּבְדִיל עוֹבָדֵיהוֹן בִּישַׁיָּא אִסְתְּחַרוּ וַהֲווֹ לַאֲחוֹרָא׃ 5 לָא
מִסְתַּכְּלִין לְמֵימַר עַל מָה לְקִינָא עוֹד מוֹסְפִין לְמֶחְטֵי וְלָא אָמְרִין מְדֵין כָּל רֵישׁ מְרַע וְכָל לֵב דְּוֵי׃ 6 מִשְּׁאָר עַמָּא וְעַד רֵישָׁא לֵית בְּהוֹן דִּשְׁלִים
בְּדַחַלְתִּי כּוּלְּהוֹן סָרְבִין וּמָרְדִין אִתְגְּעָלוּ בְּחוֹבֵיהוֹן כְּמַחָא מַרְסְסָא לָא שָׁבְקִין מִזְּדוֹנֵיהוֹן וְלָא מְחַמְרִין לְתְיוּבְתָּא וְאַף לָא זַכְיָן לְהוֹן לְאַגְנָא
עֲלֵיהוֹן׃ 7 אַרְעֲכוֹן צַדְיָא וְקִרְוֵיכוֹן יְקִידַת נוּרָא אַרְעֲכוֹן לְקֳבְלֵיכוֹן עַמְמַיָּא מַחְסְנִין יָתַהּ וּבְחוֹבֵיכוֹן צְדִיַּת אַרְעָא מִנְּכוֹן וְאִתְחַלְּפַת לְנָכְרָאִין׃
8 וְאִשְׁתְּאָרַת כְּנִשְׁתָּא דְצִיּוֹן כְּמִטַּלַּלְתָּא בְכַרְמָא בָּתַר דְּקַטְפוּהִי כְּעַרְסִיל מְבִיתוּתָא בְּמַקְטַיָּא בָּתַר דְּאַבְעִיוּהִי כְּקַרְתָּא דְצָיְרִין עֲלַהּ׃
9 אִלּוּלֵפוֹן מוֹתַר טוּבֵהּ דַייָ צְבָאוֹת אַשְׁאַר לָנָא שֵׁיזָבָא בְּרַחֲמוֹהִי אִית עַמָּנָא חוֹבִין דִּכְאֱנָשׁ סְדוֹם פּוֹן אֲבַדְנָא וּכְיָתְבֵי עֲמוֹרָה אִשְׁתֵּיצֵינָא׃
10 קַבִּלוּ פִּתְגָמָא דַייָ שִׁלְטוֹנַיָּא דְעוֹבָדֵיהוֹן בִּישִׁין כְּשִׁלְטוֹנֵי סְדוֹם אֲצִיתוּ לְאוֹרַיְתָא דֶאֱלָהָנָא עַמָּא דְעוֹבָדֵיהוֹן דָּמְיָן לְעַם עֲמוֹרָה׃ 11 לָא
רַעֲוָא קֳדָמַי בְּסְגִיאוּת נִכְסַת קֻדְשֵׁיכוֹן אֲמַר יְיָ שְׂבִיעָה מֵימְרִי עֲלָוָת דִּכְרִין וְתָרַב פַּטִּימִין וְדַם תּוֹרִין וְאִימְּרִין וְגַדְיָן דִּכְאִלֵּין לָא רַעֲוָא קֳדָמַי בְּהוֹן׃
12 כַּד אַתְיָן אַתּוּן לְאִתְחֲזָאָה קֳדָמַי מַן תְּבַע דָּא מִידְכוֹן לְמֵיתֵי לְאִדְּרוּשׁוּן עֲזָרָתִי׃ 13 לָא תוֹסְפוּן לְאַיְתָאָה מִנְחַת אֲנִיסָא קֻרְבַּן מְרַחַק
הוּא קֳדָמַי יַרְחִין וְשַׁבְּיָן כְּנִישָׁא אַתּוּן מִתְכַּנְשִׁין לָא שָׁבְקִין חוֹבֵיכוֹן לְקַבָּלָא צְלוֹתְכוֹן בְּעִדָּן כְּנִישַׁתְכוֹן׃

ESAIAS. CAPVT I.

VISIO quã vidit Esaias fi- 1
lius Amos, quam vidit con-
tra Judæam & contra Jeru-
salem in regno Oziæ, et Joa-
tham, Achaz et Ezechiæ, qui
regnauerunt in Judæa.
* Audi cælum, et auribus percipe terra, quia 2
Dominus locutus est: Filios genui & exaltaui;
ipsi autẽ me spreuerunt. * Cognouit bos possessorẽ, 3
& asinus præsepe domini sui; Jsrael autem me
non cognouit, & populus me non intellexit.
* Væ gens peccatrix, popule plene peccatis, se- 4
men nequam, filij iniqui dereliquistis Dominũ,
& ad iracundiam concitastis sanctum Jsrael:
alienati sunt in retro.
* Quid vltrà percutiemini addentes iniqui- 5
tatem? Omne caput in laborem, & omne cor in
tristitiam. * A pedibus vsque ad caput non
est in eo sanitas: vulnus, liuor, plaga tumens; non
est malagma imponere, neque oleum neque alli-
gaturas. * Terra vestra deserta, ciuitates 6
vestræ succensæ igni: regionem vestram coram
vobis alieni deuorant eam: & desolata est sub- 7
uersa à populis alienis.
* Derelinquetur filia Sion sicut tentorium 8
in vinea, et sicut pomorum custodia in cucume-
rario, sicut ciuitas obsessa. * Et nisi Dominus
Sabaoth reliquisset nobis semen, quasi Sodoma 9
vtique facti fuissemus, & quasi Gomorra vtiq;
assimilati essemus. * Audite verbum Domini 10
principes Sodomorum, attendite legẽ Dei nostri
populus Gomorræ. * Quid mihi multitudo vi- 11
ctimarum vestrarum, dicit Dominus? plenus
sum holocaustis arietum, et adipem agnorum, &
sanguinem taurorum & hircorum non volo.
* Neque veneritis apparere mihi. quis enim 12
quæsiuit hæc de manibus vestris? calcare atrium
meum, * Non apponetis. si obtuleritis siliginem; 13
vanum: incensum abominatio mihi est. Neome-
nias vestras & sabbata, & diem magnum non
feram: ieiunium & ocium,

ΗΣΑΙΑΣ. κεφ. α΄.

1 Ὅρασις ἣν εἶδεν ἠσαΐας υἱὸς ἀμὼς, ἣν εἶδεν
κατὰ τῆς ἰουδαίας, καὶ κατὰ ἱερουσαλὴμ ἐν
βασιλείᾳ ὀζίου καὶ ἰωάθαμ καὶ ἄχαζ
καὶ ἐζεκίου, οἳ ἐβασίλευσαν τῆς ἰουδαίας.
2 * ἄκουε οὐρανὲ καὶ ἐνωτίζου γῆ, ὅτι κύ-
ριος ἐλάλησεν. υἱοὺς ἐγέννησα καὶ ὕψωσα, αὐτοὶ δέ με
3 ἠθέτησαν. * ἔγνω βοῦς τὸν κτησάμενον, καὶ ὄνος τὴν
φάτνην τοῦ κυρίου αὐτοῦ, ἰσραὴλ δέ με οὐκ ἔγνω, καὶ ὁ
4 λαός με οὐ συνῆκεν. * οὐαὶ ἔθνος ἁμαρτωλὸν, λαὸς
πλήρης ἁμαρτιῶν, σπέρμα πονηρὸν, υἱοὶ ἄνομοι ἐγκατε-
λίπετε τὸν κύριον, καὶ παρωργίσατε τὸν ἅγιον τοῦ ἰσραὴλ,
ἀπηλλοτριώθησαν εἰς τὰ ὀπίσω.
5 * τί ἔτι πληγῆτε προστιθέντες ἀνομίαν; πᾶσα κεφα-
λὴ εἰς πόνον, καὶ πᾶσα καρδία εἰς λύπην·
6 * ἀπὸ ποδῶν ἕως κεφαλῆς οὐκ ἔστιν ἐν αὐτῷ ὁλοκληρία,
τραῦμα μώλωψ πληγὴ φλεγμαίνουσα, οὐκ ἔστι μά-
λαγμα ἐπιθεῖναι οὔτε ἔλαιον οὔτε καταδέσμους.
7 * ἡ γῆ ὑμῶν ἔρημος, αἱ πόλεις ὑμῶν πυρίκαυστοι, τὴν
χώραν ὑμῶν ἐνώπιον ὑμῶν ἀλλότριοι κατεσθίουσιν αὐτὴν.
καὶ ἠρήμωται κατεστραμμένη ὑπὸ λαῶν ἀλλοτρίων.
8 * ἐγκαταλειφθήσεται ἡ θυγάτηρ σιὼν ὡς σκηνὴ ἐν ἀμ-
πελῶνι· καὶ ὡς ὀπωροφυλάκιον ἐν σικυηράτῳ, ὡς πόλις
9 πολιορκουμένη. * καὶ εἰ μὴ κύριος σαβαὼθ ἐγκατέλιπεν
ἡμῖν σπέρμα, ὡς σόδομα ἂν ἐγενήθημεν, καὶ ὡς γό-
μορρα ἂν ὡμοιώθημεν.
10 * ἀκούσατε λόγον κυρίου ἄρχοντες σοδόμων, προσέχε-
τε νόμον θεοῦ ὑμῶν λαὸς γομόρρας.
11 * τί μοι πλῆθος τῶν θυσιῶν ὑμῶν, λέγει κύριος; πλή-
ρης εἰμὶ ὁλοκαυτωμάτων κριῶν, καὶ στέαρ ἀρνῶν, καὶ αἷμα
ταύρων καὶ τράγων οὐ βούλομαι.
12 * οὐδ᾽ ἂν ἔρχησθε ὀφθῆναί μοι· τίς γὰρ ἐξεζήτησε ταῦτα
ἐκ τῶν χειρῶν ὑμῶν, πατεῖν τὴν αὐλήν μου.
13 * οὐ προσθήσεσθε. ἐὰν φέρητε σεμίδαλιν, μάταιον
θυμίαμα βδέλυγμά μοί ἐστι. τὰς νεομηνίας ὑμῶν καὶ
τὰ σάββατα καὶ ἡμέραν μεγάλην οὐκ ἀνέξομαι. νηστείαν
καὶ ἀργίαν·

INTERPRETATIO LATINA TRANSLATIONIS CHALDAICAE IN ESAIAM;

Ex Complutensi Bibliotheca, ad Hebraicam & Chaldaicam veritatem à B. Aria Montano correcta.

PROPHETIA Esaiæ filij Amos, quam prophetauit super viros Iuda, & habitatores Ierusalẽ in diebus Oziæ, Iotham, Achaz, Eze-
chiæ, regum domus Iuda. [2] Audite cæli, qui commoti estis, quando dedi legem meam populo meo; & ausculta terra, quæ contre-
muisti à facie Verbi mei, quoniã Dñs locutus est. Populus meus domus Israel, quos vocaui filios, & dilexi eos, & honorificaui eos,
& ipsi rebellauerunt in verbum meum. [3] Cognouit bos emptorem suum, & asinus præsepe domini sui; Israel autem non didicit
vt sciret timorem mei: populus meus non intellexit vt conuerteretur ad timorem mei. [4] Væ eis qui vocati sunt populus san-
ctus, & peccauerunt; congregatio electa, & multiplicauerunt delicta. cognominati sunt semen electum, & malè egerunt; & dicti sunt filij
dilecti; & corruperunt vias suas; dereliquerunt cultum Domini; detestati sunt timorem Sancti Israel, & propter opera eorum praua auersi
sunt, & facti sunt retrorsum. [5] Non animaduerterunt, dicentes: Propter quid percussi sumus? adhuc addunt peccare, nec dicunt: Quare
omne caput languidũ; & omne cor mœrens? [6] A reliquo populo vsque ad principes, non est in eis qui perfectus sit in timore mei: omnes
sunt cõtumaces, & rebelles; coinquinati sunt in peccatis suis, sicut plaga vlcerosa; nõ dimittunt superbias suas, nec desiderant agere pœniten-
tiam, neque sunt in eis iustitiæ quibus protegantur. [7] Terra vestra deserta, ciuitates vestræ succensæ igni: terrã vestram coram vobis populi
possident eam, & propter peccata vestra deserta est terra, & translata est ad alienos. [8] Et relinquetur cœtus Sion, sicut vmbraculũ in vinea,
postquam vindemiarunt eam; sicut tugurium manens in cucumerario postquam legerunt cucumeres ab eo; sicut ciuitas quæ obsidetur.
[9] Nisi superexcedens bonitas Domini exercituum reliquisset nobis redemptionem in miserationibus suis; peccata sunt in nobis propter
quæ quasi viri Sodomæ perissemus, & quasi habitatores Gomorræ consumpti essemus. [10] Suscipite verbum Domini principes, quorũ ope-
ra sunt mala, sicut principum Sodomæ; auscultate legem Dei nostri populi quorum opera similia sunt populo Gomorræ. [11] Non est bene-
placitum coram me in multitudine victimarum vestrarum, dicit Dominus: satiatus sum abundantia holocaustorum arietum, & adipe pin-
guium, & sanguine taurorum, & agnorum, & hircorum: quia in eis non est beneplacitum coram me. [12] Cùm venitis vt appareatis in con-
spectu meo, quis quæsiuit hoc de manibus vestris, vt veniatis ad conculcanda atria mea? [13] Non addatis vltrà offerre oblationem ex rapi-
na; sacrificium abominabile est coram me, & neomeniæ & sabbatha cœtus congregationis vestræ, quoniam non relinquitis peccata vestra,
vt exaudiatur oratio vestra in tempore congregationis vestræ.

THE LOUVAIN THEOLOGIANS' EDITION OF AUGUSTINE ~ 1577

In 1570, with the financial support of Plantin, the Louvain theological faculty started on a new edition of the works of Augustine. This Louvain edition was intended to replace previous editions undertaken by Amerbach and Erasmus. The edition was reflective of the faculty's enduring interest in Augustine. It could profit from the work by the canons regular of Saint Martin's Valley in Louvain, who were known for their tireless search for manuscripts.

The promoter of the project was Thomas Gozæus (1515–1571). Thanks to the support of the vicar general of Mechelen, Maximilian Morillon (1557–1586), and with the help of an inventory made by the canons of Saint Martin, two hundred manuscripts had been collected for this new edition, which also contained unpublished sermons and letters. The manuscripts not only came from Louvain (Saint Martin's; the Holy Spirit College; the houses of the Jesuits and the Carthusians; Park Abbey), but also from abbeys such as Gembloux, Cambron, Aulne, Saint-Amand, and even from Rome. However, owing to situation of war in these years, manuscripts present in neighbouring countries could not be consulted.

The edition was a collective enterprise. For each volume, of ten in total, a team leader was appointed to oversee it. Thus, Henricus Gravius (1536–1591) was in charge of the anti-Donatist and anti-Pelagian works, William Estius (1542–1613) of Augustine's commentaries on New Testament texts, Jacobus Baius (1545–1614) of Augustine's letters and Henricus Cuyckius (1546–1609) of the first part of the *didactica*. The tenth volume, dealing with the complex edition of the sermons, was entrusted to the canons of Saint Martin's. First Gozæus supervised this edition, and after his death in 1571, Johannes Molanus (1533–1588) continued his work. The edition, consisting of ten volumes and a detailed index, was completed in 1577. Thousand copies were printed. The publication costs were more than 13,000 florins. The work was dedicated to Cardinals Cristophoro and Ludovico Madruzzo, successive Prince-Bishops of Trent. The frontispiece was decorated with a beautiful engraving by Crispin Van den Broeck, an associate of Plantin. The edition was sold for 25 florins. This edition of Augustine's work would be the standard edition for more than a century, and was often reprinted in Venice, Paris, Geneva, Cologne and Lyon, among other places.

Aurelius Augustinus
Opera ... tomis decem comprehensa. Per theologos Lovanienses ... emendata et ... vindicata ...
Antwerp: Christopher Plantin, 1576–1577
10 v. · in 2°

Literature:
Arnoud Visser, 'How Catholic Was Augustine? Confessional Patristics and the Survival of Erasmus in the Counter-Reformation', *Journal of Ecclesiastical History* 61 (2010): 86–106; Lucien Ceyssens, 'Le "Saint Augustin" du XVIIe siècle: L'édition de Louvain (1577)', *XVIIe Siècle* 34 (1982): 103–120; Leon Voet, *The Plantin Press (1555–1589)* (Amsterdam: Van Hoeve, 1980), vol. 1, 205–218.

OPERA

D. AVRELII

AVGVSTINI

HIPPONENSIS EPISCOPI
ET DOCTORIS PRÆCIPVI,
TOMIS DECEM COMPREHENSA:

PER

THEOLOGOS LOVANIENSES EX MAnuscriptis codicibus multo labore emendata, & ab innumeris erroribus vindicata:
Illustrata pręterea eruditis censuris, & locupletata multis homiliis & aliquot epistolis eiusdem B. AVGVSTINI, antea non editis.

Cum Indice tripartito.

Ex Libris jois [illegible] 1722
[illegible] 1829.

ANTVERPIAE

EX OFFICINA CHRISTOPHORI PLANTINI,
ARCHITYPOGRAPHI REGII.
cIↄ. Iↄ. LXXVII.

LABORE ET CONSTANTIA

¢ The *Rhetorica christiana* by Diego Valadés ~ 1579

Diego Valadés
Rhetorica christiana ad concionandi, et orandi usum accommodata, utriusque facultatis exemplis suo loco insertis; quæ quidem, ex Indorum maximè deprompta sunt historiis. Unde præter doctrinam, summa quoque delectatio comparabitur
Perugia: Pietro Giacomo Petrucci, 1579
[20], 378, [16], [2 blank] p. · in 4°

How do you communicate with utterly strange Amerindians speaking an utterly strange language? Christopher Columbus tackled the problem effortlessly without any previous linguistic or 'intercultural' training. As soon as he had disembarked in America, he started to converse with the natives he met. His message to his European readers was clear and reassuring: converting the local population would be very easy.

Far less naïve was the Franciscan friar Diego Valadés (1533–1582?). According to him, conversion presupposed education, which in turn implied thorough knowledge of the language and customs of the Amerindians. This is precisely what he taught future missionaries in his *Rhetorica christiana* from 1579, which was based on his yearlong experience as a preacher in Mexico.

Valadés was a mestizo, the son of a Spanish conquistador and an Indian mother. The Franciscan friar Pedro de Gante sent him at an early age to the Latin school he had established for gifted Amerindian children. After having entered the Franciscan order, Valadés attended the college at Tlaltecoleo, where he became deeply immersed in classical literature and culture; he was thoroughly educated, successfully 'westernized'. No wonder, then, that in his *Rhetorica,* he invariably presents himself as a European missionary whose lofty task it is to civilise and Christianise strange, exotic Amerindians.

According to Valadés such an ambitious project can only succeed if the teacher/preacher lends the natives a helping hand. He should learn to speak the local language and use it actively. Furthermore, he has to acquaint himself thoroughly with the specific nature of the native population. Hence the intimate connection between rhetoric, linguistics and ethnography in his work. Hence, too, his strong emphasis on the lavish use of visual aids which, in his opinion, perfectly suit the Amerindians who have a strong visual disposition.

The engraving shown, devised by Valadés himself, shows a priest wearing a habit and giving a sermon on the suffering of Jesus Christ. He uses a stick to point out one of the large illustrated canvasses (*lienzos*) which have been hung on the church's walls in order to lend visual support to his sermon. The flock consists of Amerindians who do not really look like Indians. Wearing a toga, they rather look like ancient Romans. A nice illustration of the kind of Europeanisation which Valadés had in mind while composing his rhetorical manual.

Literature:
Martha Elena Venier, 'La *Rhetorica christiana* de Diego Valadés', *Caravelle: Cahiers du monde hispanique et luso-brésilien* 76–77 (2001): 437–442; Don Paul Abbott, 'Diego Valadés and the Origins of Humanistic Rhetoric in the Americas', in *Rhetoric and Pedagogy: Its History, Philosophy, and Practice. Essays in Honor of James J. Murphy*, ed. Winifred Bryan Horner and Michael Leff (New York and London: Routledge, 2013), 227–242.

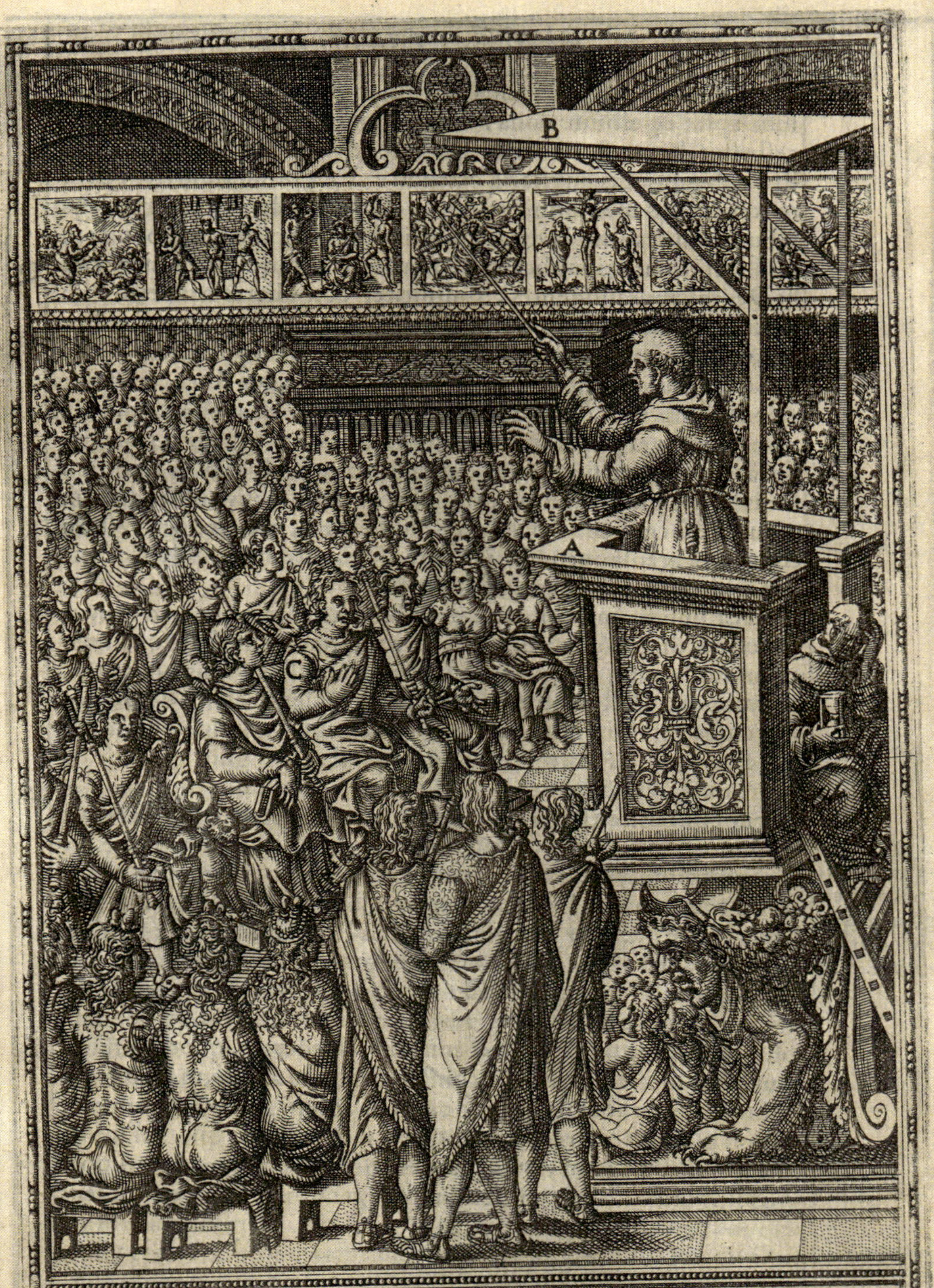

Ad sensus aptat coelestia dona magister,
Aridaq; eloquij pectora fonte rigat.

An English Catholic Bible for a Dutch whisky distiller ~ 1582

The New Testament of Iesus Christ, translated faithfully into English, ...
Reims: Jean Foigny, 1582
745 p. · in 4°
PN00073/Q°

We see here the *editio princeps* of the Catholic English translation of the New Testament by Gregory Martin (1542–1582), with corrections and paratexts by William Allen, Richard Bristow, William Rainolds and Thomas Worthington. William (later Cardinal) Allen was the first president of the English College of the University of Douai (founded in 1568 and during the period 1578–1593 temporarily transferred to Reims). Bristow was study prefect there and Martin (from Saint John's College Oxford, who in 1576–1578 was Allen's assistant in Rome) taught Hebrew and Bible exegesis. The Bible text itself was translated by Martin, whilst the controversialist introduction, commentaries and notes are mainly Bristow's work. Allen was responsible for the publication as a whole. The translation, known as the 'Douay-Rheims Version', faithfully follows the Latin text of the Vulgate but also shows signs of a meticulous comparison with the Greek text. Martin extensively used previous English translations, in particular Miles Coverdale's bilingual text (Latin-English) of 1538. Martin's translation, with its many Latinisms, had a significant impact on the much discussed ('protestantising') King James Bible of 1611 with words such as 'acquisition', 'advent', 'allegory', 'character', 'holocaust' (= 'burnt offering'), 'resuscitate', 'victim' being traced back to his version. His other publications include *A discovery of the manifold corruptions of the holy scriptures by the heretikes of our daies* (Reims 1582).

Jean Foigny was active in Reims 1561–1688 and printed another three English books there (by William Allen in 1582 and 1583, and Martin's *Discovery* in 1582). This edition of the New Testament was reprinted in Antwerp (1600, 1621, 1630) and Rouen (1633). Its publication immediately provoked reactions by English Protestants such as William Fulke (1583), William Whitaker (1583, 1585), Edward Bulkeley (1588), George Wither (1588), and Thomas Cartwright (1602, 1618).

Soon after publication, this copy was ruled in French style with brown-reddish ink. It is bound in 18th-century sheepskin, with a gilt spine. According to three inscriptions (dated 1745, 1746, 1752), it belonged to Henricus van Wyngaerden, a Dutch business man in Edinburgh, who was involved in the development of whisky distilling there. The book also features later English names and notes, as well as provenance inscriptions by the libraries of the Crosiers in Maaseik and Diest. Two gilded religious ornaments from an older binding are pasted on the flyleaves.

Literature:
A. W. Pollard and G. R. Redgrave eds., *A Short-Title Catalogue of Books Printed in England, Scotland and Ireland, and of English Books Printed Abroad 1475–1640*, 2nd ed. (London: The Bibliographical Society, 1976–1991), 2884; A. S. Herbert, *Historical Catalogue of Printed Editions of the English Bible: 1525–1961* (London: British and Foreign Bible Society, 1968), 177.

THE

NEVV TESTAMENT

OF IESVS CHRIST, TRANSLATED FAITHFVLLY INTO ENGLISH,

out of the authentical Latin, according to the best corrected copies of the same, diligently conferred vvith the Greeke and other editions in diuers languages: Vvith ARGVMENTS of bookes and chapters, ANNOTATIONS, and other necessarie helpes, for the better vnderstanding of the text, and specially for the discouerie of the CORRVPTIONS of diuers late translations, and for cleering the CONTROVERSIES in religion, of these daies:

IN THE ENGLISH COLLEGE OF RHEMES.

Psal. 118.

Da mihi intellectum, & scrutabor legem tuam, & custodiam illam in toto corde meo.

That is,

Giue me vnderstanding, and I vvil searche thy lavv, and vvil keepe it vvith my vvhole hart.

S. Aug. tract. 2. in Epist. Ioan.

Omnia quæ leguntur in Scripturis sanctis, ad instructionem & salutem nostram intentè oportet audire: maximè tamen memoriæ commendanda sunt, quæ aduersus Hæreticos valent plurimum: quorum insidiæ, infirmiores quosque & negligentiores circumuenire non cessant.

That is,

Al things that are readde in holy Scriptures, vve must heare vvith great attention, to our instruction and saluation: but those things specially must be commended to memorie, vvhich make most against Heretikes: vvhose deceites cease not to circumuent and beguile al the vveaker sort and the more negligent persons.

PRINTED AT RHEMES,
by Iohn Fogny.

1582.

CVM PRIVILEGIO.

¢ To teach with images: Jan David's *Veridicus Christianus* ~ 1601

Jan David
Veridicus Christianus
Antwerp: Jan Moretus I, 1601
[16], 374, [33], [1 blank], [8] p. · in 4°

The *Veridicus Christianus,* a work by the Jesuit Jan David, is presented in the form of a collection of one hundred engravings by Theodoor Galle, each one beginning a chapter in which the author develops the theme that is illustrated. The preface gives a justification for the presence of images by attributing to them an essentially didactic value, with the inevitable reference to Gregory the Great's *liber idiotarum:* the image is aimed at the *rudiores,* who will be able to discover through looking what they cannot otherwise understand, while those who can read will be able to consider through sight what they have learned through reading. David's undertaking is part of the continuation of his pedagogical project, closely linked to his militant action in the field of the defence of the faith. With this book, he wishes to offer a 'shield' to protect the readers from the lies of the heretics and to lavishly dispense pious advice so that they might lead a virtuous Christian life. We may see in such a project not only the pragmatic dimension of Jesuit pastoral practice, entirely dedicated to the teaching of precepts guiding a Christian life in conformity to the divine will and to the Tridentine directives, but also the distinctive brand of the actions by the Jesuits of the Flandro-Belgian province, constantly coming up against religious adversaries who had to be countered in every way possible.

At the end of the *Veridicus Christianus,* an ingenious mechanism has given its title to the second part of the work: *Orbita probitatis* or 'wheel of probity'. It consists of a moving circle fixed by a string to the back of a page that is pierced by four windows, each one corresponding to one of the four Evangelists. It is accompanied by its instructions for use: when turning the circle, figures appear in each window; the reader chooses a number, which refers him to a list of one hundred maxims chosen from classic authors. Having found and read the sentence corresponding to the number, the reader must then find in the body of the work the single image, out of a hundred others, that applies to the sentence; an image he must thus 'contemplate' so as to, then, consider the explanations of David's commentary. Explicitly conceived in order to fight back against the fashion of the lottery at the time, a playful invention of this kind testifies to the Jesuits' determination to inculcate in a pleasant way the truths of the Faith and the lessons of Wisdom, so as to win over those souls most resistant to this kind of teaching.

Literature:
Ralph Dekoninck, *Ad Imaginem: Statuts, fonctions et usages de l'image dans la littérature spirituelle jésuite du XVIIe siècle* (Geneva: Droz, 2005); Walter S. Melion, *Imago veridica: The Visual Form, Function, and Argument of Joannes David, S.J.'s Four Latin Emblem Books* (Leiden: Brill, forthcoming).

QVÆRITE ET INVENIETIS.

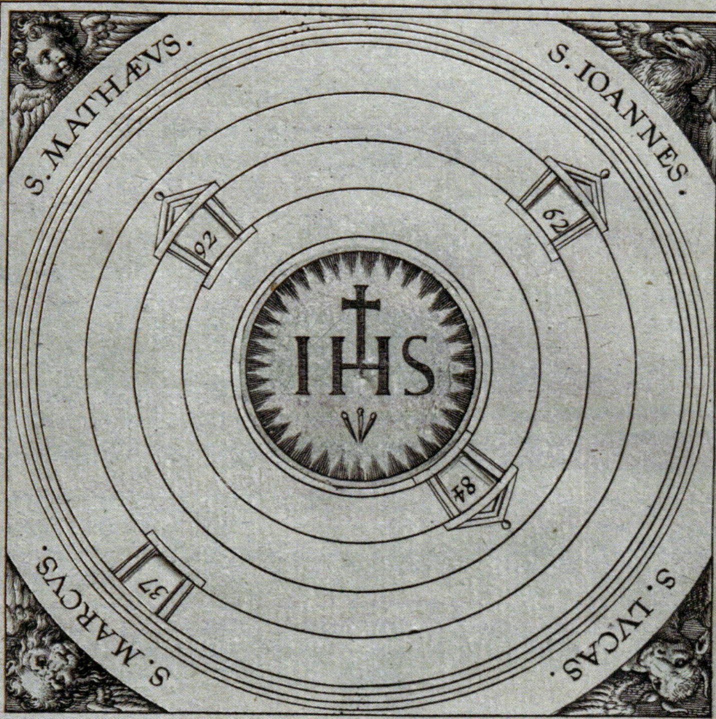

1. *Delige, quamcunque voles, ex quatuor fenestellis vnam.*
2. *Tum, verso parumper chartaceo orbiculo, siste.*
3. *Vide, quem delecta tibi fenestella suppeditet numerum.*
4. *Illum eundem in subiecto Indiculo require: ac Sententiam legito.*
5. *Quęre tunc in Veridico folium, quò te Sententia remittit.*
6. *Illic, et imaginem contemplare; et eius explicationem considera.*

Reuela oculos meos: Et considerabo mirabilia de Lege tua. Ps. 118.

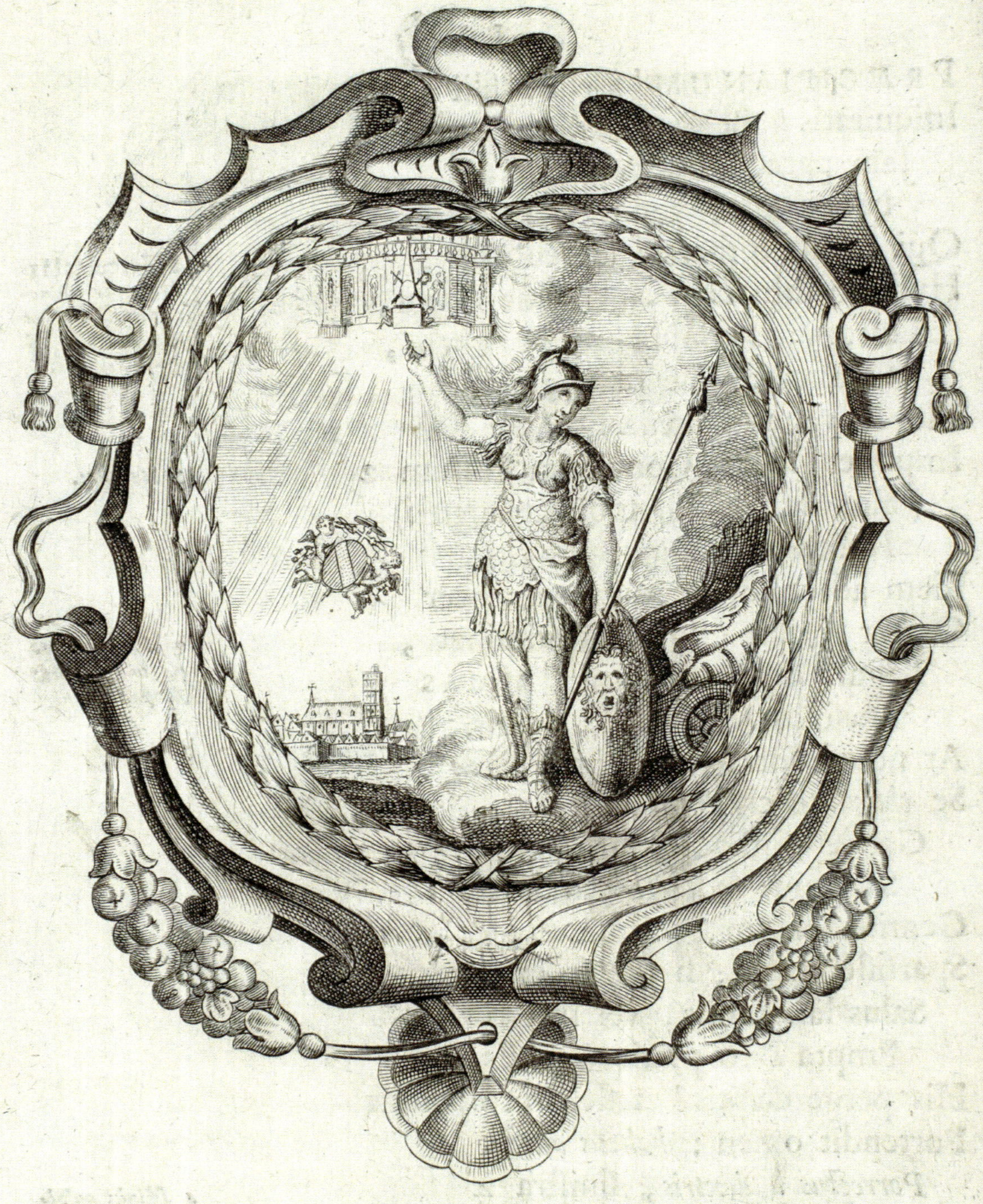

SE QUANTIS ATTOLLET GLORIA REBUS!

Virg. l. 4. Æn.

¢ A UNIQUE COLLECTION OF IGNATIANA AND JESUITICA ~ 1610 · 1622

Vita beati patris Ignatii Loyolæ
Antwerp: s.n., 1610.
in 2° oblong · 16 plates
Vita sancti patris Ignatii Loyolæ
Antwerp: Joannes Galle, [1622]
in 2° oblong · 16 plates
P Plano 136 RIBA Vita | P Plano 137 RIBA Vita

The Society of Jesus' founder, Ignatius of Loyola, was beatified in 1609 and later on canonised in 1622. During the beatification and canonisation processes, the Jesuits, spearheaded by Spanish Jesuit Pedro de Ribadeneira, commissioned several publications on Ignatius' life. While the 1610 edition of the *Vita* commemorates the founder's elevation to the status of *beatus*, the 1622 edition celebrates his canonisation. Both editions, as part of a worldwide campaign to promote this new blessed/saint, feature fifteen engraved plates, respectively by the hand of Cornelis Galle the Elder and Jan Galle, most of them depicting key events in Ignatius' life.

Pedro de Ribadeneira quickly became known as a hagiologist, paving the way, in fact, for the later Bollandists. Less known is that he also took up the task to write the first book on Jesuit books, *Illustrium scriptorium religionis Societatis Jesu catalogus* (1608), positioning himself as 'founder' of what would become a renowned Jesuit tradition in bibliography. Since then, Jesuits and books would always form a unique and intense bond. Not only did the Jesuits produce enormous amounts of publications concerning every subject imaginable, they also took special interest in constructing their own libraries, with collections of exceptional quality, quantity, and unique content.

This makes the event that took place on March 19th, 1969, of historic significance. On that day, the University of Louvain and the Flemish Jesuits signed a contract which stated that the Jesuits would transport their collections to the library of the Faculty of Theology, which at that time still needed to be built. In the following months and years, this theological collection of 400,000 volumes moved in its entirety to the library that would later on be named Maurits Sabbe Library. During the last five decades, more Jesuit books gradually found their home at the Maurits Sabbe Library. The most important additions should be mentioned: the Flemish Jesuits' Ignatiana and Jesuitica collections (2003); the Dutch Jesuit Province's Jesuitica and Preciosa collections (2006); the Jesuitica and Jansenistica collections from Maastricht University (2013).

All Jesuit/Jesuitica collections contain precious incunabula, post-incunabula and other rare books, a selection of which has been published in *Jesuit Books in the Low Countries 1540–1773* (2009). Now, the Maurits Sabbe Library is the proud guardian of one of the largest and richest Jesuit/Jesuitica book collections in the world, thus ensuring the important Jesuit library tradition and documentary heritage for generations to come.

Literature:
Walter S. Melion, 'Pedro de Ribadeneira S.J., *Vita beati/ sancti patris Ignatii Loyolae* (1610, n.d.)', in *Jesuit Books in the Low Countries 1540–1773: A Selection from the Maurits Sabbe Library*, ed. Paul Begheyn et al. (Leuven: Peeters, 2009), 13–17.

¢ A Costerus Bible, *with* images ~ 1614ff.

In 1614, the Jesuit Frans de Coster or Costerus, nicknamed the 'hammer of heretics', had a New Testament published by Joachim Trognæsius in Antwerp. It contained a slightly revised version of the 'Moerentorf Bible' (1599), which used the text of the 'Louvain Bible', the official Dutch Catholic Bible translation, adapted to the Sixto-Clementine Vulgate. In a dedicatory letter, addressed to States-General of Holland, Zealand (and the other Provinces of the North), Costerus explains how this New Testament was destined for the market in the Dutch Republic and especially for the Reformed part of its population. Costerus argued that the Reformers, who constantly appealed to the Bible, had unfortunately misinterpreted the Scriptures. For this reason, he had provided his edition with elaborate annotations providing a 'sound' interpretation of the scriptural texts, one that was in accordance with the Church fathers and the Tradition based upon their explanations. In more than one passage, the annotations take a fervent anti-Protestant tone, to convince the Reformed inhabitants of the erroneous character of their belief system and of the urgency of their return into the fold of the true Church.

It is striking that the edition does not contain any images, going against the established customs regarding Catholic biblical material, but this was a deliberate choice with regard to this specific edition in order to make it palatable to a Reformed readership. The Maurits Sabbe Library preserves, however, a copy of Costerus's edition, in which lots of images are carefully inserted or glued on the relevant pages of the New Testament. The work dates from the middle of the 17th century and contains images from engravers such as Cornelis Galle (1576–1650), Cornelis Schut (1597–1655), Martin van den Enden (1605–1673), Joannes Meyssens (1612–1670), and Caspar Huberti (1619–1684), among others. The aim was, of course, to adapt this New Testament for Catholic devotional practices, providing a meditative apparatus in both text and image that would nourish the soul of the user(s). At the prefatory letter to the 'Catholic' or 'Canonical' Epistles, we see coloured images of Saint Francis Borgia, as well as two images of Jesuit 'boy saint', to the right Stanislaus Kostka who, after have having invoked Saint Barbara, was brought Holy Communion by angels during a bout of illness, and to the left most probably Aloysius Gonzaga.

Franciscus Costerus
Het Nieu Testament onses Heeren Iesu Christi met korte uytlegghinghen
Antwerp: Joachim Trognæsius, 1614
[20], 1003, [48], [2 blank] p. · in 2°

Literature:
Els Agten, 'Costerus en Van den Leemputte: twee katholieke bijbelvertalingen uit de eerste helft van de zeventiende eeuw', in *De Bijbel in de Lage Landen: Elf eeuwen van vertalen*, ed. Paul Gillaerts, et al. (Heerenveen: Jongbloed, 2015), 395–405; Wim François, 'The Early Modern Bible between Material Book and Immaterial Word', in *The Agency of Things in Medieval and Early Modern Art: Materials, Power and Manipulation*, ed. Grażyna Jurkowlaniec, Ika Matyjaszkiewicz, and Zuzanna Sarnecka (New York and London: Routledge, 2018), 129–143, at 139–140.

Concilien, als [a] Laodicenum, [b] Carthaginense 3. ende d'oude Vaders, [c] *Origenes*, [d] *Athanasius*, [e] *Amphilochius*, [f] *Gregorius Nazianzenus*, [g] *Innocentius*, [h] *Augustinus*, [i] *Hieronymus*, [k] *Ruffinus*, &c. *die van't ghetal der Godlicker boecken schrijuen, noemen altijdt dese seuen Catholijcke oft Canonijcke brieuen, met hunne autheurs, Iacobo, Petro, Ioanne, Iuda; soo dat het maer eenen ketterschen vondt en is, daer aen te twijfelen: vvant altijdt heeft het aller ketteren ghebruyck ghevveest, de Schrifturen te vervverpen, oft te vervalschen, die merckelick hunne ketterijen omvverpen.*

[a] Can. 59.
[b] Can. 47.
[c] Hom. 7. in Iosue.
[d] In Synopsi.
[e] In Iambo ad Seleuc.
[f] In carm. de libris noui Test.
[g] Epist. 3. ad Exup.
[h] Libro 2. de doctr. Christ. c. 8.
[i] Epist. ad Paulin.
[k] In exp. Symb.

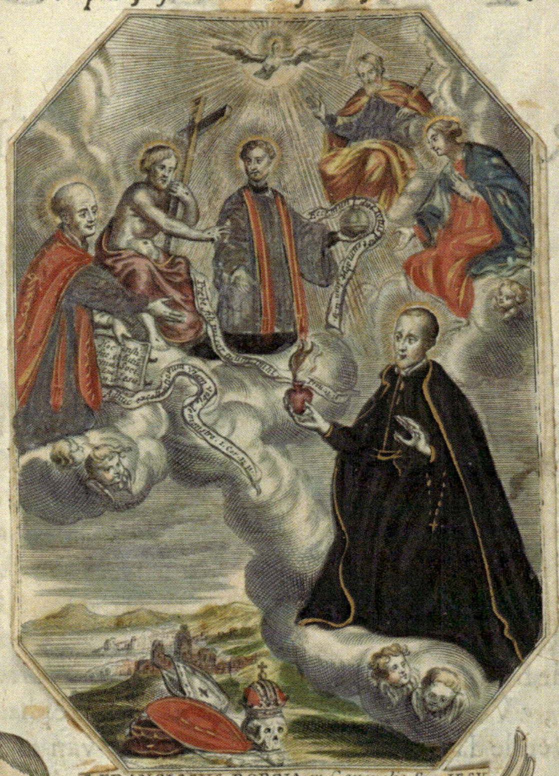

S. FRANCISCVS BORGIA III Generalis Soc. IESV.

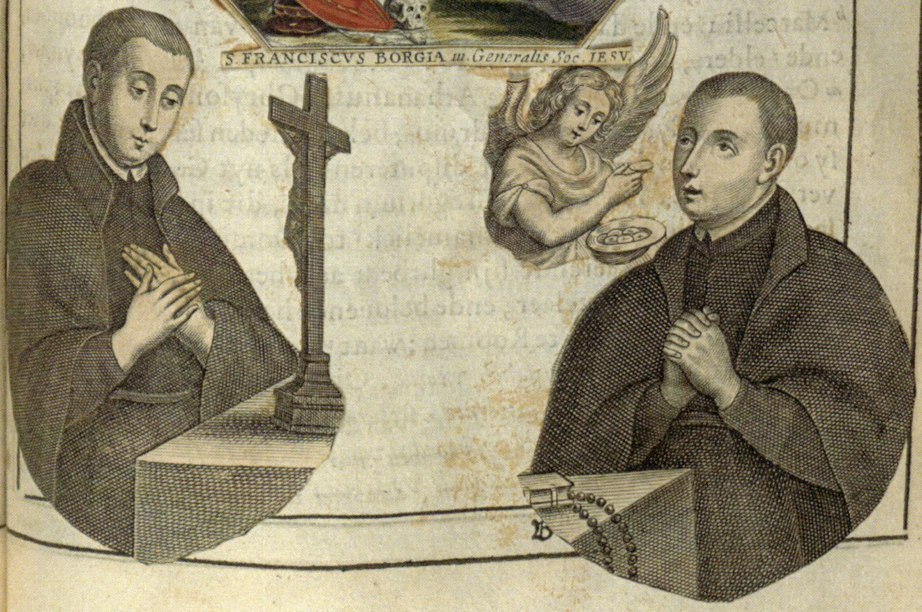

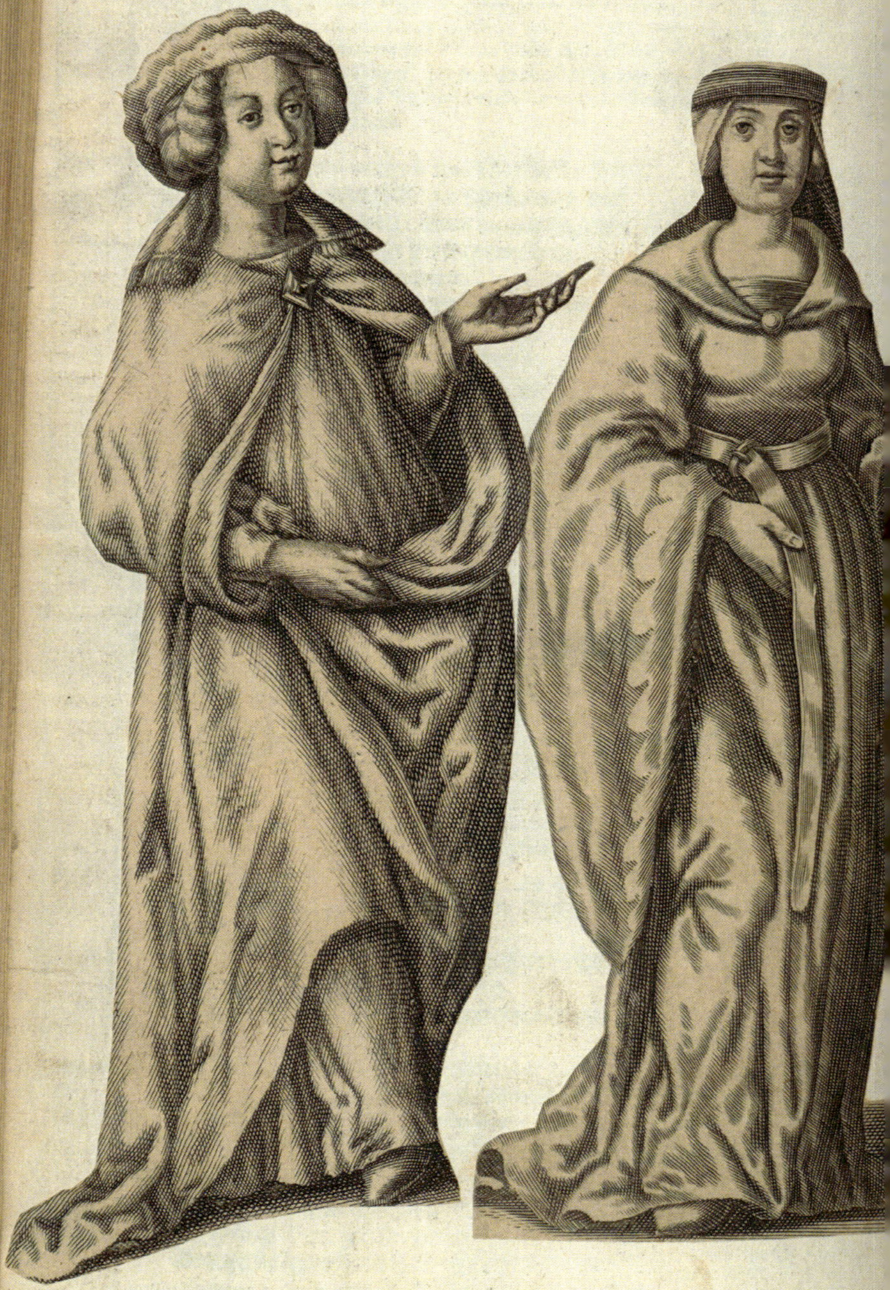

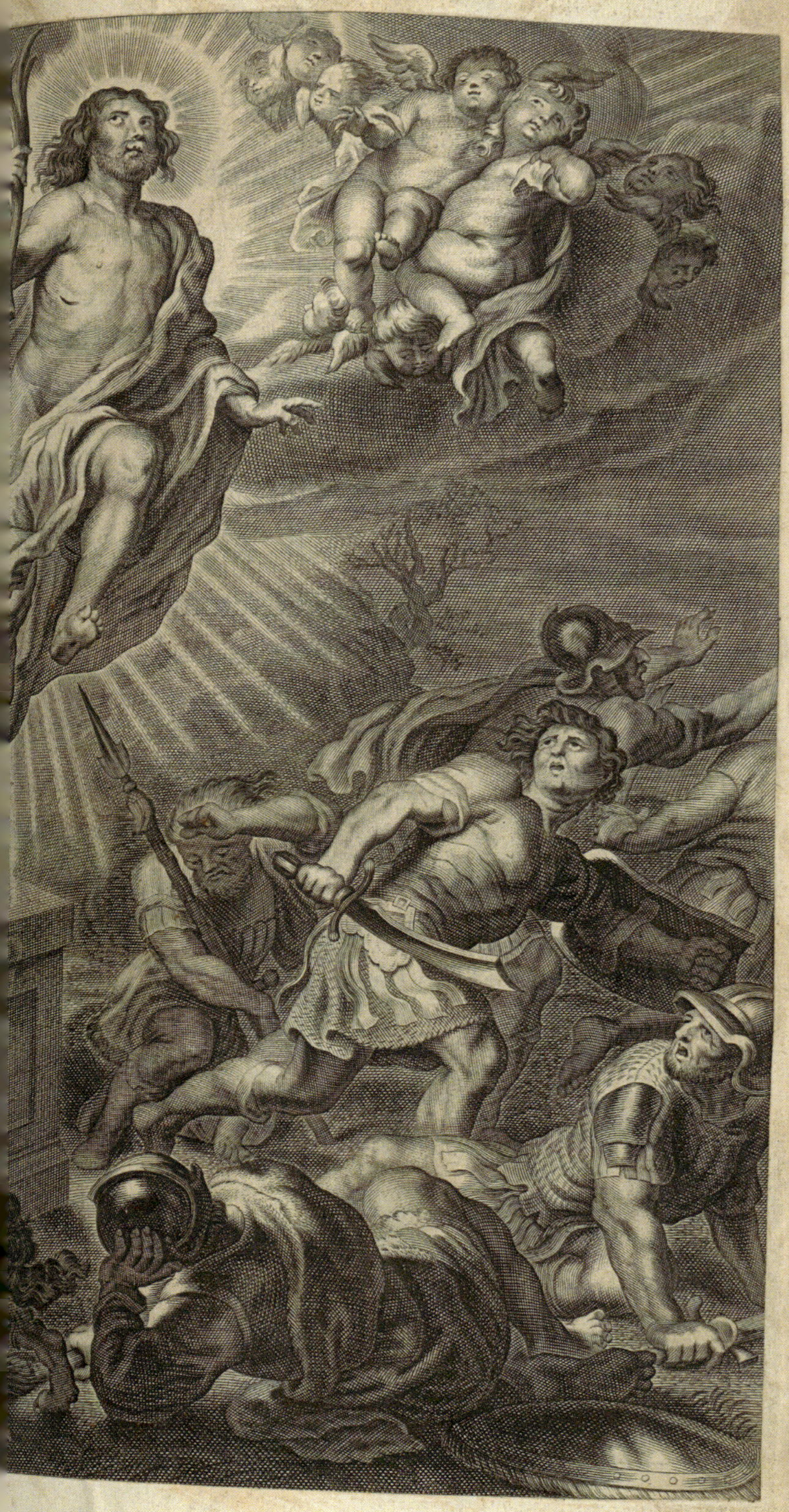

Lecture notes of Jansenius' Pentateuch commentary ~ 1631–1632

Cornelius Jansenius
Commentaria et primò præfatio in Pentateuchum
[Leuven], 1631–1632
[361] f. · 338 × 205 mm
PM0073/Q

Cornelius Jansenius (1585–1638) was without doubt the most important and best-known Louvain theologian during the Ancien Régime. His monumental and impressive work *Augustinus* attempted to offer an answer to the vexed question of the relationship between grace and free will. The work was based on a thorough reading of Augustine's anti-Pelagian works and often made use of other Latin and Greek Church fathers' works, as well as of the decisions of the councils.

Lesser known are Jansenius' activities as an exegete. Since 1630, Jansenius, very familiar with Greek and Hebrew, had been appointed as Royal Professor of Sacred Scripture. In 1630, he had already started commenting on the Pentateuch. The lecture notes – more than 750 pages of text – are the result of the lectures Jansenius offered starting in the summer of 1631. These lecture notes were put up for sale in London in 2011 and purchased by the Maurits Sabbe Library.

The lectures on Genesis were finished on 28 August 1631. No date is mentioned for the lectures on Exodus, but the Leviticus, Numeri, and Deuteronomy commentaries were finished on 11 October 1631, 11 February 1632 and 15 May 1632, respectively. In his commentaries, Jansenius avoided too far going mystical and allegorical interpretations of Scripture, warning his audience of the exaggerated allegories of Origen, and favouring a more literal interpretation of Scripture.

Jansenius' lectures were a success. Students loved his knowledge of the classical languages and his clarity, brevity, and impressive familiarity with the Church fathers. These notes make it clear how important Augustine was to Jansenius' exegetical work. Furthermore, they reveal Jansenius' pastoral concerns: often he warned his readers of Calvin's ideas. In 1638, while already Bishop of Ypres, Jansenius was given the privilege to publish his commentaries on the Pentateuch and on the four Gospels. However, on 6 May 1638, he passed away due to pestilence.

Nevertheless, the commentary on the Pentateuch was published posthumously in 1641 and went through six reprints. It would be very interesting to compare the handwritten notes with the version printed in 1641. Such a comparison would be of great help in understanding evolutions in Jansenius' views with regards to the Pentateuch.

Literature:
Jean Orcibal, *Jansénius d'Ypres (1585–1638)* (Paris: Études augustiniennes, 1989), 181–185; Bernard Chédozeau, 'Aux sources de la publication de la Bible catholique en français: C. Jansénius, L. Froidmont, Saint-Cyran', in *L'image de Jansénius jusqu'à la fin du XVIIIe siècle*, ed. Edmond J. M. van Eijl (Leuven: Leuven University Press, 1987), 93–103.

Eximij Domini Cornelij Janssenij
Commentaria et primò

PRÆFATIO IN PENTATEUCHUM

Pentateuchus quasi quinque voluminum liber vocatur: quam divisionem Philosophus libro de mundo (si tamen eius est) a Moyse factam esse indicat dum primum librum ab eo Genesin inscriptum tradit: sed in utroque videtur falli. Nam cum Hebræi omnibus reliquis Scripturæ libris a materia vel Authore nomen dederint, solos illos quinque a primis vocabulis nuncupant, quod potius continuationem narrationis quam separationem præ se fert. Unde cum Latini et Græci ab argumentis eos nomineut verisimile est septuaginta interpretes primum illam fecisse divisionem. Unde Christus Dominus eos non citat, nisi generaliter sub nomine Moysis, ut Lucæ 16. et 20. et Joannis 5. vel legis Moysis ut Lucæ ultimo, sicut etiamnum a Judæis vocatur. Ex quibus locis, et omnium tam Patrum quam Judæorum consensu, perspicuum est Pentateuchi authorem esse Moysen, adversus hæreticos Nazarræos, qui teste Epiphanio hæresi 8. Moysen quidem fatebantur, sed dicebant fictos esse illos libros, et nihil horum quæ narrabantur a Patribus factum esse: quos Manichæi scriptos a Moyse, sed Principe tenebrarum et dictatos esse delirabant, ut Aug. lib. de hæresibus. Non tamen a Moyse sic scripti sunt, quin aliquæ eius partes a nonnullis additæ dici possent, ut mors Moysi et nomen Dan Genes. 14. et quædam alia; quamvis et ista nonnulli et mortem ipsam suam Prophetice scripsisse Moysen sentiant, Philosophus in fine libri tertij de vita Moysis, et Josephus 4 Antiquitatum capite 8.

Moyses qualis fuerit.

Porro qualis et quantus fuerit Moyses, Philosophus tribus libris est persecutus, et uno Gregorius Nyssenus in quo totius vitæ gesta mystice ad exprimendos viri perfecti mores transfert. Sed ex nemine certius, quam ex his ipsis libris colligi potest. Ex eis namque constat fuisse summum historicum, sive veritatem primam historiæ laudem spectes sive longissimi temporis seriem. Fuisse Poëtam insignem probant pulcherrima duo cantica Exodi 15. et Deut. 32. Rhetorem eloquentem oratio Judæ ad Josephum: sublimem Philosophum ea quæ de mundo divinitus inspiratus tradidit: Theologum eminentissimum, sublimis illa divinorum attributorum commendatio;

Fuit Historicus

Poëta.

Rhetor.

Theologus.

tota

¢ Louvain safe again! Now students, return to your books! ~ 1635

Nicolaus Vernulæus
Oratio ad studiosam iuventutem cum calend. Augusti 1635 post solutam urbis Lovaniensis obsidionem studia resumerentur
Leuven: Jacob Zegers, 1635
23, [1 blank] p. · in 4°

In the last decade of the 16th century, the city and university of Louvain were dragged into a period of deep crisis. The war with the Northern Provinces was raging fiercely. After the siege by William of Orange in 1572 and the outburst of the plague in 1578, Louvain had been reduced to a rather desolate city in which troops were quartered among the citizenry. Only for a short period, the Archduke Albert of Austria and his wife Isabella could benefit from the Twelve Years' Truce (1609–1621). They consolidated Habsburg rule and ensured the triumph of the Counter Reformation in the Southern Low Countries. The university saw a short period of restoration too. Justus Lipsius' return from the Calvinist University of Leiden to Louvain paved the way for a successful Counter Reformation Age in which Erycius Puteanus (1574–1646), Nicolaus Vernulæus (1583–1649), Libertus Fromondus (1587–1638) and Valerius Andreas (1588–1655) united their intellectual efforts so as to reinstall some of the university's old luster. Yet, the political reality had changed again: the decease of Archduke Albert and a failed attempt at renewing the Truce in 1621 paved the way for new troubles.

The new governor of the Spanish Netherlands, the Cardinal-Infante Ferdinand had to face an alliance between France and the Dutch Republic. Raiding French and Dutch troops pillaged the city of Tienen in May 1635, and by the end of July their army had encamped outside Louvain. The city prepared for an imminent siege: the city walls were reinforced, a garrison of 4,000 soldiers was billeted. The city magistrate rallied companies of Walloon, Irish and German soldiers with an improvised militia of 2,000 citizens, students and clerics. After ten days, the siege was lifted. A deep sigh was heaved. Each year the liberation would be commemorated with a procession in honour of Our Lady – and this continued up until the French Revolution. Poets and rhetoricians put pen to paper in order to describe and eulogise these 'heroic' deeds and facts, both in prose and verse.

Puteanus, who had succeeded Lipsius in the chair of History, had described the siege from day to day. Moreover, he had compared the 'Ten days of Louvain' to the 'Ten years before Troye'. Following Puteanus' steps, Vernulæus, already appointed as *rhetor publicus* of the university, had composed a triumphal oration: the *Triumphus Lovaniensium*. A few weeks later, he summoned Louvain students to an *Oratio ad studiosam iuventutem*, instructing them to return to their books after the turbulent weeks of war and resistance under the command of François-Jean de Robles, canon of Saint Peter's. Both orations were issued in the Louvain printing office of Dormalius and Zegers; their high circulation testifies to an eager readership.

Literature:
Andries Welkenhuysen, "Erycius Puteanus, heer van Keizersberg, over het beleg en ontzet van Leuven in 1635: Voorstelling, vertaling en aantekeningen," *Loven Boven* 15, no. 3 (1985): 10–30; 16, no. 1 (1986): 16–41; 16, no. 3 (1986): 18–41; 17, no. 1 (1987): 12–29;
Toon Van Houdt and Erik De Bom, 'The Artistry of Civil Life: Deliberative Rhetoric and Political Pedagogy in the Work of Nicolaus Vernulæus (1583–1649)', *Rhetorica* 35, no. 3 (2017): 259–284.

NICOLAI VERNVLÆI

ORATIO

AD STVDIOSAM IVVENTVTEM

Cum Calend. Augusti 1635 post solutam Vrbis Louaniensis obsidionem Studia resumerentur.

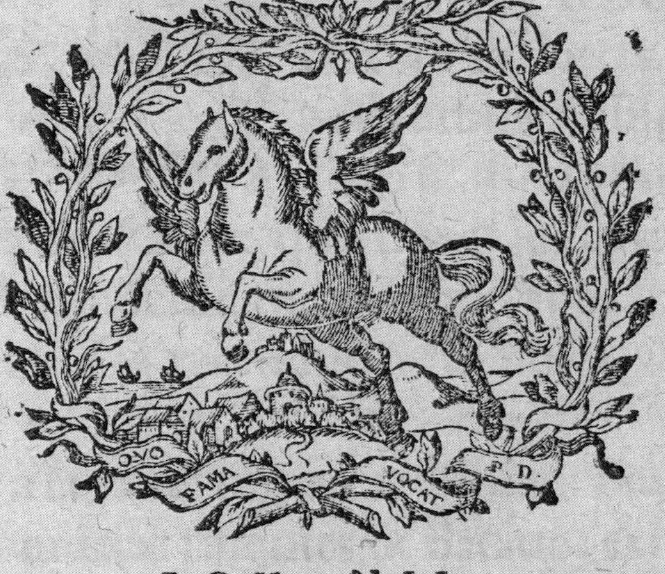

LOVANII,
Sumptibus IACOBI ZEGERS 1635.
Cum Priuilegio.

beenē/14. der tarse/te weten/twee hielbeenders/ twee astragalen/twee naviculare/ twee Cyboides, ende ses ongenoemde/10. in den voor-voet/ om in elcken voet 5. ende 28. inde teenen. Aengaende de Sesamoides, daer van zijnder soo veel inde voeten als inde handen. Dus is het ghetal van alle beenders des menschelicken lichaems 247. daer by ghevoecht wesende het been Hyoidis, ende de ses cleyne/ die inde hollicheyt der ooren besloten ligghen/ sonder nochtans daer onder te begrijpen de beenderkens Sesamoides, midtsdien dat de selve inde jonge menschen somtijts niet dan cartilagen en zijn/ ende daerom is haer ghetal altijt onseker. Voorts/ soo suldy observeren dat de drie cartilagen der laringe/ in de mans persoonen voor seker beenachtich zijn. Ende op dat ghy des te beter alle de beenderen des menschelicken lichaems ooghenschijnelick meucht sien/ soo hebben wy u hier dese figueren ghestelt.

Verclaringhe der letteren, vande eerste figuere der beenderen.

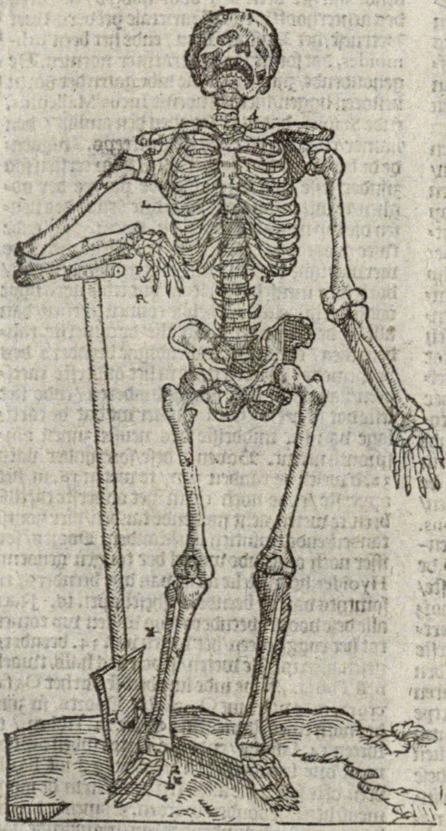

A. Het Coronaelbeen.
B. Twee parietale beenen/op elcke zijde een.
C. Twee petreuse beenders/een op elcke zijde.
D. Het Sygoma.
E. Het onderste caeckſbeen.
F. De rechte clavicule/ ende noch een ander op d'ander zijde.
G. De opperste Apophyse der Omoplate/ofte des schouderblats.
H. De voorste Apophyse der Omoplate/ die ghenoemt wort Coracoide, ofte den ravenberk.
I. Het Sternon, ofte het borstbeen dat de seven langhe ribben ontfangt.
K. De cartilage die ghenoemt wort Xiphoide.
L. De 24. ribben/op elcke zijde twaelfve/ waer onder datter seven langhe ribben zijn/ende vijf corte/de welcke alhier ghetepckent worden door 1. 2. 3. 4. 5. 6. etc.
M. Den arme/ ofte Brachium, ende Humerus, het welcke ghemeynelick het Adiutorium ghenoemt wort.
N. Het been des ellebogę/ ofte de groote Focile des arms.
O. Den Radius, diemen ghemeynelick de cleyne Focile des arms noemt.
P. De carpe/ofte het voorste der hant dat van acht beenderkens bestaet.
Q. De metacarpe der hant die van vier beenders ghescharpen is.
R. De beenders der vingheren/ in elcken vingher drie/ de welcke vijfthiene in als zijn.
S. Het been der heupe/datmen het Femur, ofte Crus noemt.
T. De knie-schijve.
V. De pijpe des beens.
X. De cleyne pijpe des beens/diemen de Fibula, ofte de cleyne Focile noemt.
Y. De Astragale.
Z. Het Naviculare been.
a. De vier beenderkens der Tarse.
b. De vijf beenderkens van het Pedion.
c. De veerthien beenders der teenen/in elcken teen drie/ende twee inden grooten teen.

Ver-

¢ A SURGEON'S GUIDE TO THE ANATOMY OF THE HUMAN BODY ∾ 1638

This is the Dutch translation of Ambroise Paré's *Les Œuvres* (Paris: Gabriel Buon, 4th ed., 1585), and the last one revised by the author himself. The translator was Carolus Battus, i.e. Carel Baten (Ghent c. 1540 – Amsterdam 1617), himself a physician and the first translator of French medical works into Dutch. This copy is a folio, comprising 940 pages, printed in two columns with marginal subtitles, to facilitate a quick consultation; it is printed in Gothic characters and lavishly illustrated; it is restored, and photocopies have been carefully inserted to replace the 16 pages missing from the original print.

Paré (1510–1590), since 1562 *premier chirurgien du Roy* in Paris had, as a barber-surgeon apprentice, no university education, but was a practician with a great reputation, especially as an army surgeon. Besides this experience in the field, he had also read medical literature broadly: the Medieval Arabic authors Razes and Mesua and the 12th-century alchemist Arnoldus Villanovanus, and his contemporaries Andreas Vesalius and Gabriele Falloppio (anatomy); Jean Fernel (physiology); Amatus Lusitanus, Jean Ruel and Pietro Andrea Mattioli (botany), and Paracelsus. His specialty comprised, apart from military surgery, also obstetrics and forensic pathology. He introduced, among others, the practice of tying blood vessels during amputations, the use of salve for curing wounds and, in obstetrics, a technique of child delivery with the feet of the baby coming first. He also invented a series of surgical instruments.

These *Opera Omnia* describe beasts; human anatomy; thorax; head; muscles and bones, tumours; bloody wounds; wounds caused by gun fire; gangrene, fistula; ligaments, fractures of legs; luxation, accidents and peculiar chirurgical interventions, gout, smallpox, measles and worms, rabies and other bites, the plague; prostheses; obstetrics; teratology; simples and compounds; alchemical distillations; embalming. This all-encompassing medical 'encyclopedia' is finished with an 'Apology' on his many travels.

Based as it was on reliable personal and competent observation, these *Opera Omnia* (first published in 1575) remained popular over the course of one century, and received various reprints and translations: in Latin (1582; 1610), German (1601), English (1634) and Dutch (1636; 1639; 1649; 1655). A Latin translation by F. Uffenbach (Frankfurt, 1610) arrived in the Jesuit library of Peking, and was partially translated into Chinese by Giacomo Rho (*Renshen tushuo*, c. 1638).

Ambroise Paré
De chirurgie, ende opera van alle de wercken van Mr. Ambrosius Paré …
Rotterdam: widow of Matthijs Bastiaensz, 1636
[16], 940, [12] p. · in 2°

Literature:
Janet Doe, *A Bibliography, 1545–1940, of the Works of Ambroise Paré, 1510–1590, Premier Chirurgien & Conseiller du Roi: Descriptive and Annotated Bibliography of the Original Books, Collected Works, Extracts and Translations, with an Introduction, Appendices and an Index* (Amsterdam: Van Heusden, 1976; repr. of the 1937 ed., with addenda of 1940 and 1970).

The Jesuits' *Imago primi sæculi*: a solemn pledge ∾ 1640

Imago primi sæculi Societatis Iesu a Provincia Flandro-Belgica eiusdem Societatis repræsentata
Antwerp: Balthasar Moretus, 1640
952, [22], [2 blank] p. · in [8°]
P271.5.018/F° Imag

From the very beginning, the *Imago primi sæculi,* the commemorative volume which the Jesuit order published in Antwerp in 1640 to celebrate its centenary, has provoked both positive and negative reactions. This is partly due to the nature and function of the work itself: it is a voluminous and visually opulent book in which long passages in prose alternate with learned emblematic poetry. At first glance, the work seems to offer an overview of the many achievements the order has accomplished in the Netherlands and elsewhere. However, the historical image which the prose texts offer easily gives way to collective self-praise.

Yet it would be wrong to consider the book in terms of conceitedness. For the memory of the glorious past proudly described entails an assignment: present and future generations of Jesuits are called to follow the example of their illustrious predecessors, starting with Ignatius of Loyola. Only by doing so, will they manage to face up to the numerous challenges and fierce resistance with which they are confronted.

Showing who and what you are in order to show who and what you ought to be: this message is emphasised by the literary-emblematic form in which the *Imago* has been cast. Its authors, young and talented Neo-Latin poets from the Southern Low Countries such as Sidronius Hosschius and Jacobus Wallius, appear to have drawn heavily from existing *imprese,* a much-appreciated genre of heroic symbols in which image and device are neatly intertwined so as to express one's commitment to a particular way of life. In the *Imago,* emblem and *impresa* as such merge, thereby strongly supporting the underlying message of the work as a whole. The Jesuits swear by it as a firm oath: they solemnly pledge to follow their predecessors' lead, to imitate or even emulate their glorious words and deeds.

In 1640, the Jesuits organised festivities all over the world. This was also the case in Antwerp where huge panels or *affixiones* were hung on the columns in the side galleries of the Jesuit church. The paintings were based on the engravings made by Cornelis I Galle for the *Imago* and its later Dutch counterpart *d'Afbeeldinghe van d'eerste eeuwe,* composed by Adriaen Poirters. Quite recently, approximately ten of those panels have been rediscovered: 'silent' yet telling witnesses of the baroque culture of spectacle to which the Jesuit order contributed so much and with which the *Imago* is inextricably connected.

Literature:
John W. O'Malley, ed., *Art, Controversy, and the Jesuits: The* Imago primi sæculi *(1640)* (Philadelphia: Saint Joseph's University Press, 2015).

Regnorum & Prouinciarum per Societatem conuersio.

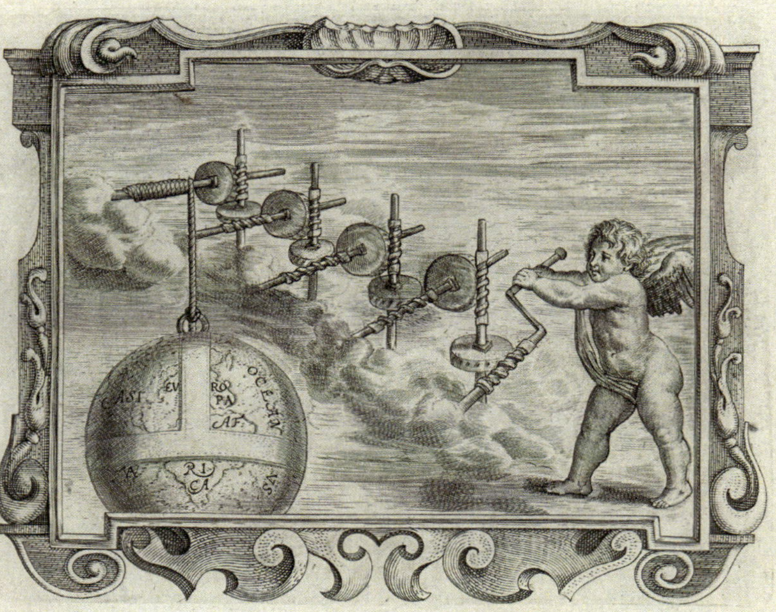

Fac pedem figat, & terram mouebit.

PArue puer, maiora tuis quid viribus audes?
Demens! non illâ est terra mouenda manu.
Risit; & , Hoc, inquit, fac pes consistat inani,
Mutabit medium pendula terra locum.
Illa quidem stat mole suâ, librataque magni
Arte Dei; nostris sed superanda rotis.
Nempe vbi vim totam rota versa coëgit in vnum,
Protinus appensum machina tollit onus.
Hoc quodcumque vides, Loiolæ sacra propago,
Quà vagus immensam Nereus ambit humum,
Quà Phœbi radios vltra iacet abdita tellus,
Virtutis spatium est metaque tota tuæ.
Hic fortem quacumque pedem defigis, in altum
Cuncta, graui quamuis mole premantur, agis.
Testis eris concussa tuis America Regnis,
Pænè tuo in Stygios pondere mersa lacus;
Sed validâ subducta manu pallentibus vmbris,
Cœpisti ignoti tecta subire poli.
Testis & Europe, medioque coërcita ponto
Africa; & hæc tenebris vtraque mota suis.
Vltima quin adeò nascentis limina Phœbi,
Vidimus hac etiam contremuisse manu.
Ima licet vastæ subsidant pondera terræ,
Euehet ad Superos ingeniosus amor.

¢ The good marriage according to Claude Maillard ~ 1647

Although the Catholic Church traditionally held married people in lesser esteem than virgins, marriage was nevertheless recognised as an honourable state of life in which one could be saved, on the express condition, however, that one had a true vocation to it and lived it virtuously. This theme was discussed at length by the French Jesuit Claude Maillard (1586–1655) in *Le bon mariage,* a hefty quarto of over 600 pages. The first edition was published in 1643 in Douai by Jean Serrurier; the second edition presented here was printed in Paris in 1647 by Jean de Launay. The book covers the following subjects: the excellence and purpose of marriage, its positive and negative aspects, and the obligations of spouses to one another, their children and their domestic staff. The final chapter deals with widowhood.

Any spouse aspiring to happiness in this life, and salvation in the next, had better take the covenant between Christ and the Church as a model. This mystical marriage is depicted on the title plate, engraved by J. Houlanger. God (at the top in the middle) is the 'author' of the match between Christ (pictured as Lamb of God) and the Church (personified by the Bride crowned with a tiara). The crowd gathered to the left and right of the pedestal (as a symbol of the eternal and unshakable foundation upon which the Church is built) shows the fruitfulness of this marriage. The patriarchs, prophets, martyrs, clergy, virgins, etc. are flanked by the two 'witnesses': Moses (Old Testament) and Paul (New Testament). The page facing the frontispiece offers a detailed explanation of its deeper meaning.

At the bottom we see the coat of arms of Sébastien II de Rosmadec († 1653), the nobleman to whom the printer dedicated the work. At that time the marquis was already a widower, and according to de Launay a shining example for fellow widowers: "vous estes comme la tourterelle qui ayant vescu avec sa compagnie en grande union & amour durant sa vie, ne cesse de gemir apres sa mort." It did not prevent the Marquis from remarrying later…

Claude Maillard
Le bon mariage; ou le moyen d'estre heureux et faire son salut en l'estat de mariage, avec un traité des vefves
Paris: Jean de Launay, 1647
[32], 631, [26] p. · in 4°

Literature:
Hans Storme, *Die trouwen wilt voorsichtelijck: Predikanten en moralisten over de voorbereiding op het huwelijk in de Vlaamse bisdommen (17e–18e eeuw)* (Leuven: Universitaire Pers, 1992); Agnès Walch, *La spiritualité conjugale dans le catholicisme français (XVIe–XXe siècle)* (Paris: Le Cerf, 2002).

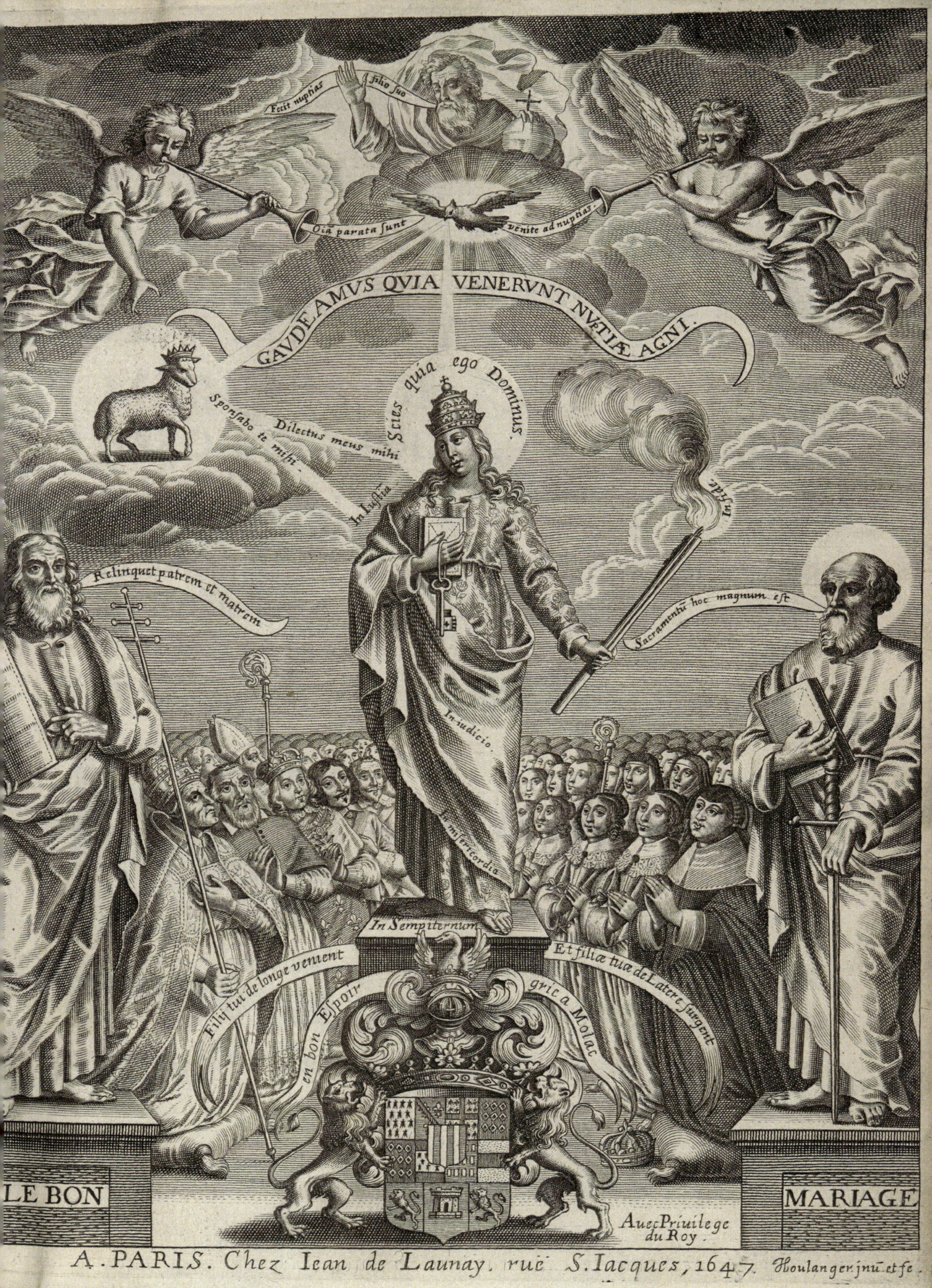
Fecit nuptias
filio suo
Oia parata sunt
venite ad nuptias
GAVDEAMVS QVIA VENERVNT NVPTIÆ AGNI.
Sponsabo te mihi
Dilectus meus mihi
Scies quia ego Dominus.
In Iustitia
In fide
Relinquet patrem et matrem
Sacramentu hoc magnum est
In iudicio.
In misericordia
In Sempiternum
Filij tui de longe venient
Et filiæ tuæ de Latere surgent
en bon Espoir
gric a Molac
LE BON
MARIAGE
Auec Priuilege du Roy.
A. PARIS. Chez Iean de Launay. rue S. Iacques, 1647.

¢ The Atlas of China by Martino Martini ∾ 1662

Martino Martini (1614–1661), the Trent-born Jesuit and former student of Athanasius Kircher, arrived in China in 1643. During the following years, he studied Chinese historical sources intensively and prepared an Atlas on China. He did this by visiting nine of the fifteen provinces, using (provincial) maps as his basis – specifically those of *Guang Yu tu* (1st ed. 1555) – as well as official statistic materials (censuses), and making original measurements of the latitude and longitude of a series of cities. All this converged into his *Novus Atlas Sinensis:* fifteen, plus two provincial maps, presenting the regional toponymy, hydrography and orography, mentioning c. 3,500 names all in (mostly original) Romanisation; the scale is expressed in German miles and Chinese *li.* Each map is accompanied by a long text, detailing the landscape, economic resources (mines of all kinds of ore!), population, human activities (handicraft, etc.), the local cuisine, natural and artificial *mirabilia,* the presence of Christian communities, the military defence works at the coast, all occasionally interspersed with comparisons to European situations, places, etc. The text is written in a polished Classic Latinity, with stylistic 'flowers' which are worth being selected for an anthology. There are traces of enhancement and updates introduced in the text after it had arrived with Martini in Europe in October 1653. New archival material shows that the original intention was to publish it – together with other materials (*De Bello Tartarico*; *Sinicæ Historiæ Prima Decas*) – with the Officina Plantiniana in Antwerp. After budgetary and logistical objections from the latter, the Governor Leopold in Brussels and Jean Bollandus, SJ, the hagiographer, arranged contact with Johan Blaeu in Amsterdam, who accepted the manuscript to be integrated in his major 'World Atlas' project. After arranging the maps and heavily adapting them to fit contemporary European standards, he published the Atlas in 1655, after some interventions of the Dutch Orientalist Jacob Golius (1596–1667), including the insertion of his *Additamentum de Cathayo* (on the identification of Medieval Cathay and China). The splendid frontispiece (two slightly different versions!) shows the opened gates in the Great Wall, with some pictures of Western measurements and observational instruments. In this form – as well as in German, Dutch, French and Spanish translations – it remained the most comprehensive source on China until the mid-18th century, shaping the European image of China, until it was replaced by the d'Anville atlases (Paris), which were based upon new observations and measurements.

Martino Martini
Novus Atlas Sinensis . . . In: Joannes Blaeu.
Asia, quæ est Geographiæ Blavianæ pars quarta, libri duo, volumen decimum
Amsterdam: Joannes Blaeu, 1662
[10], 171, [19] p. · 17 maps · in 2°
P PLANO 23–24

Literature:
Noël Golvers, 'Martino Martini S.J., *Novus atlas Sinensis* (1662)', in *Jesuit Books in the Low Countries, 1540–1773: A Selection from the Maurits Sabbe Library,* ed. Paul Begheyn et al. (Leuven: Peeters, 2009), 167–169; Luisa Maria Paternicò, Claudia von Collani, and Riccardo Scartezzini, eds., *Man of Dialogue: Proceedings of the International Conference "Martino Martini (1614–1661), Man of Dialogue" held in Toronto on October, 15–17, 2014 for the 400th Anniversary of Martini's Birth* (Trent: Università degli Studi di Trento), 2016.

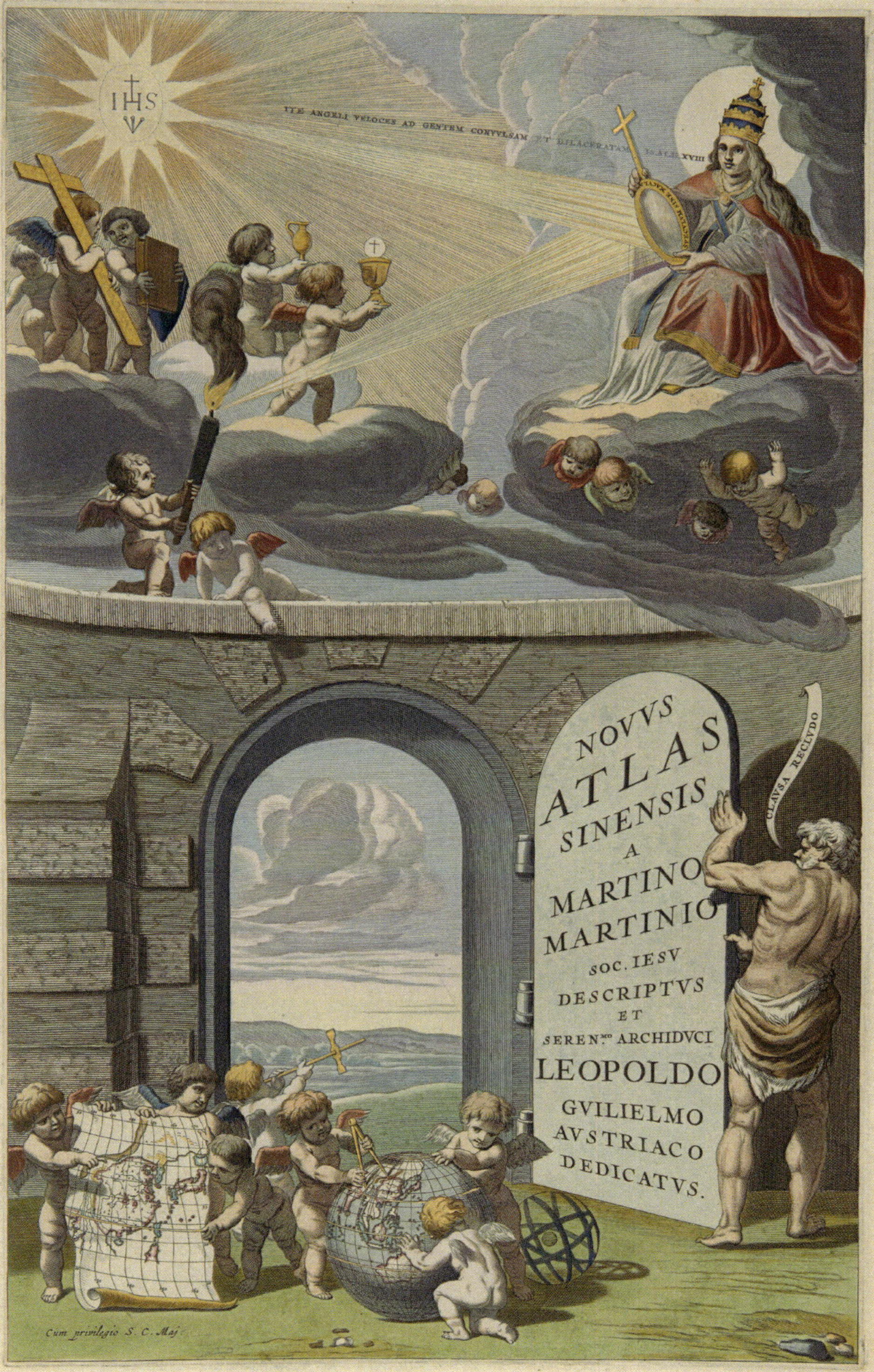
IHS
ITE ANGELI VELOCES AD GENTEM CONVVLSAM ET DILACERATAM ... XVIII
CLAVSA RECLVDO
NOVVS
ATLAS
SINENSIS
A
MARTINO
MARTINIO
SOC. IESV
DESCRIPTVS
ET
SEREN.mo ARCHIDVCI
LEOPOLDO
GVILIELMO
AVSTRIACO
DEDICATVS.
Cum privilegio S. C. Maj.

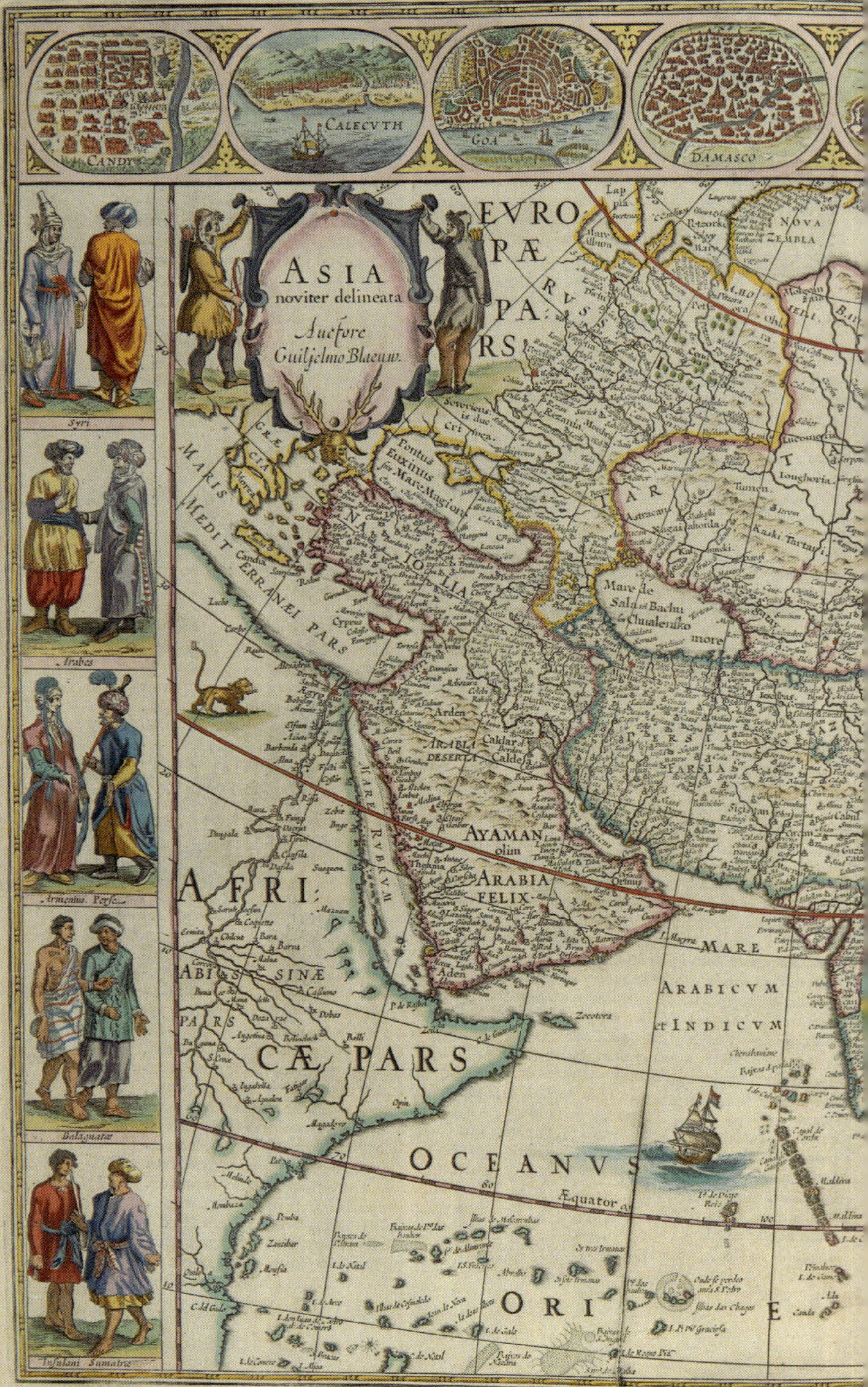

CANDY
CALECVTH
GOA
DAMASCO
ASIA
noviter delineata
Auctore
Guiljelmo Blaeuw.
Syri
Arabes
Armenius. Persa.
Balagatae
Insulani Sumatrae
EVROPÆ PARS
NOVA ZEMBLA
MARIS MEDITERRANÆI PARS
ARABIA DESERTA
AYAMAN olim
ARABIA FELIX
AFRI
ABISSINÆ
CÆ PARS
MARE ARABICVM ET INDICVM
OCEANVS
ORI
E
Æquator

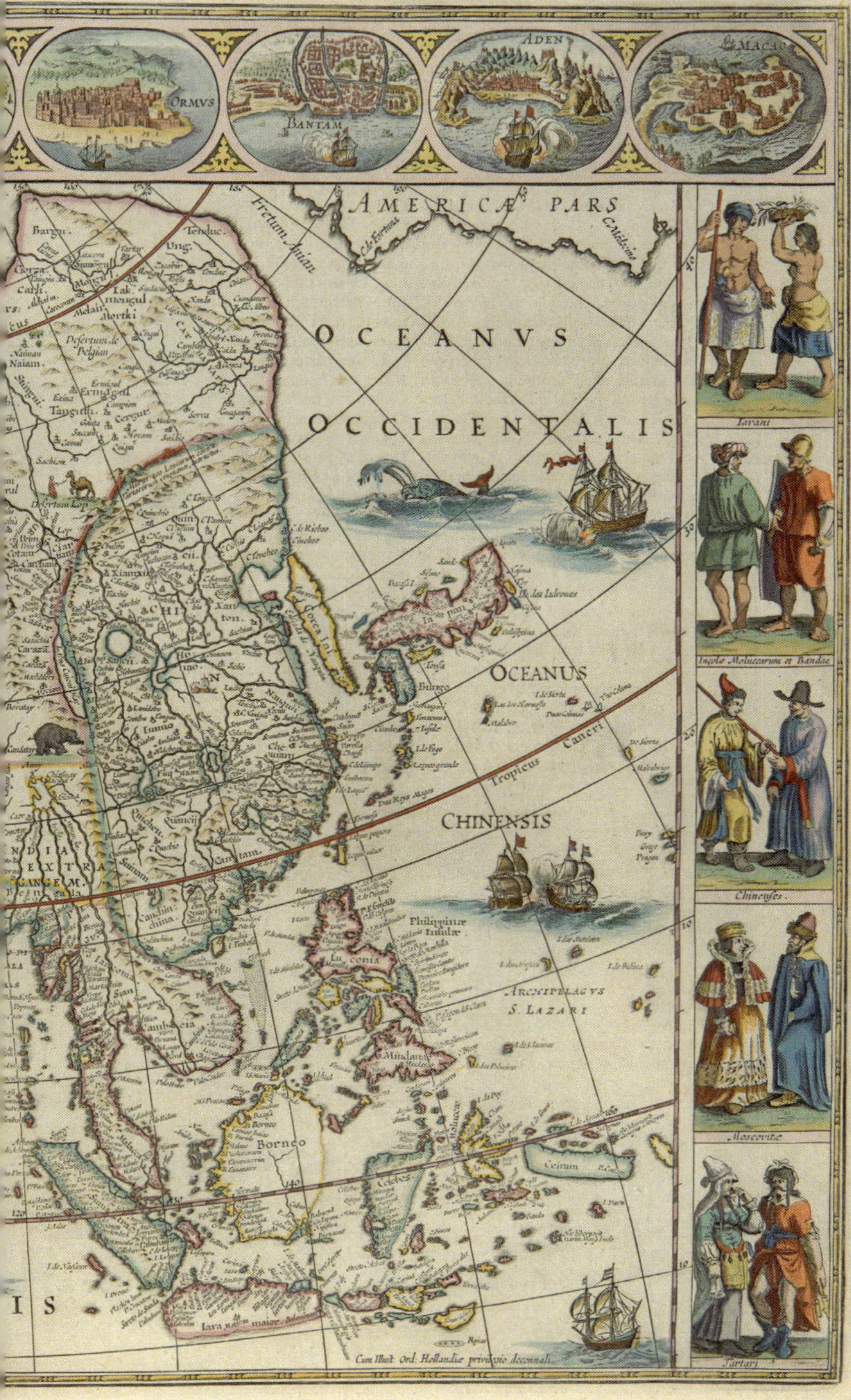

ORMVS
BANTAM
ADEN
MACAO
AMERICÆ PARS
Fretum Anian
OCEANVS
OCCIDENTALIS
OCEANUS
Tropicus Cancri
CHINENSIS
Philippinæ Insulæ
ARCHIPELAGVS S. LAZARI
Borneo
Iava major
Iavani
Incolæ Moluccarum et Bandæ
Chinenses
Moscovitæ
Tartari
Cum Illust. Ord. Hollandiæ privilegio decennali.

¢ College notes from a Louvain pedagogy ~ 1662–1664

Antonius Hermans
Logica. Physica. Metaphysica
Leuven, pedagogy of The Pig (*Het Varken*), 1662–1664
507 f. · 210 × 158 mm
PM0026/V

The young Antonius Hermans left his village of Schulen in September 1662. He moved into The Pig (*Het Varken*) pedagogy, one of the four pedagogies in Louvain that housed first and second-year students. There he was given room and board, and for two years he enjoyed an education in logic, physics and metaphysics, the usual curriculum of a student of the Artes Faculty.

Hermans neatly structured his notebook with titles and initials, embellished with illustrations of hunting scenes, heads, flowers and monsters. Noteworthy are the three engravings that he added to the section on physics, depicting the solar systems of Copernicus, Ptolemy and Tycho Brahe. These are the three oldest-known scientific engravings found in lecture notes in Louvain.

He was not only devoted to his studies but also to his pedagogy. He bought two frontispieces for his notebook, specially designed for The Pig. At the beginning of the logic course, The Pig is displayed adorned with a wreath and a banderol with the motto *Porcus alit doctos:* The pig breeds scholars. The patron saint of the pedagogy, Saint Anthony – with a pig as his attribute – is to the left, and Saint Anne with Madonna and Child are to the right. At the bottom there is a depiction of the University Hall; the pedagogy of The Pig was located nearby to this, in what is presently the Hogeschoolplein. On the blank middle section, Hermans recorded the name of his professor *primarius*, Egidius Martini. On the frontispiece of the course of physics, two putti hold a laurel wreath above a boar. On folio 193, Hermans drew a laurelled pig. As if this wasn't enough, on a separate sheet (f. 2) he sketched in among the letter 'P' (of *Præfatio*) his beloved animal again, depicted in a shrine, crowned and provided with the motto and emblems of the other pedagogies underneath. Between illustrations of a hunt for a wounded deer, floral tendrils, birds, and a woman's head, he signed his name.

Finally, the devotion to his pedagogy is made further apparent from a printed sheet that Hermans pasted at the back of his notebook. It concerns a donation of a six-volume work by Petrus Gassendi (his *Opera omnia*?) to the pedagogy library. Among the names of all the graduates from The Pig who put in their two pennies' worth, there is also – of course – Antonius Hermans.

The manuscript, originally created not far from its current repository, is a fine example of the lecture notes of a zealous student who was proud to be a Pig.

Literature:
Geert Vanpaemel, Katharina Smeyers, An Smets, and Diewer van der Meijden, eds., *Ex Cathedra: Leuvense collegedictaten van de 16de tot de 18de eeuw* (Leuven: Universiteitsbibliotheek KU Leuven, 2012), 172.

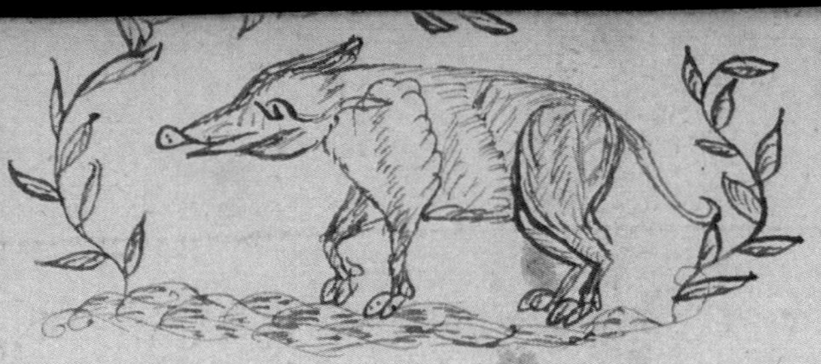

Præfatio

in

Physicam

Artis

¢ The *Mundus subterraneus* of Athanasius Kircher ∾ 1665

Athanasius Kircher
Mundus subterraneus
Amsterdam: Joannes Janssonius – Elizeus Weyerstraten, 1665
2 v. · in 2°

This publication on the geography of the earth was the first of several books that German Jesuit Athanasius Kircher (1602–1680) had printed in Amsterdam in order to avoid Roman censorship. In this spectacular publication, he combined ancient and medieval natural philosophy with observations of his own. He imagined the 'geocosm' as a living organism, and discovered a double system of canals and chambers containing water and fire which formed the foundation for the rest of the subterranean world. His theories were not only greatly indebted to predecessors such as Plato and Strabo in Antiquity and the 16th-century German humanist Georg Agricola, but also to contemporary Jesuits from South America.

The imprimatur was given in 1662 by Gian Paolo Oliva, Vicar-General of the Jesuits, and two others. The privilege of the States of Holland and West Frisia was signed in 1665.

Apart from the engravings (12 in vol. I, 9 in vol. II), each volume has a title-page and many geometrical figures, illustrations, charts and even a movable dial (vol. I, p. 156). The book opens with a portrait of Athanasius Kircher. The title-page of volume I shows the hand of God letting down the 'great chain of being' at the end of which is suspended the earth, hatched between the twin influences of sun and moon. Above it is a winged sphere pierced by a serpent and a hieroglyphic symbol of the Trinity with a quotation from Virgil. Twelve winds are blowing over the earth, acting as mediums for the influences of the twelve signs of the Zodiac. The two lowest figures represent the human attempt to survey and measure this planet.

The title-page in the second volume shows the multi-breasted statue of Artemis or Diana, which is identified by Kircher as both an image of Isis and of Mother Nature. In front of her sits a woman reading a book with obelisks, who is accompanied by Hermes. *Mundus subterraneus* was reprinted in Amsterdam in 1668, and a third and enlarged edition was issued in 1678. A Dutch translation was published in 1682.

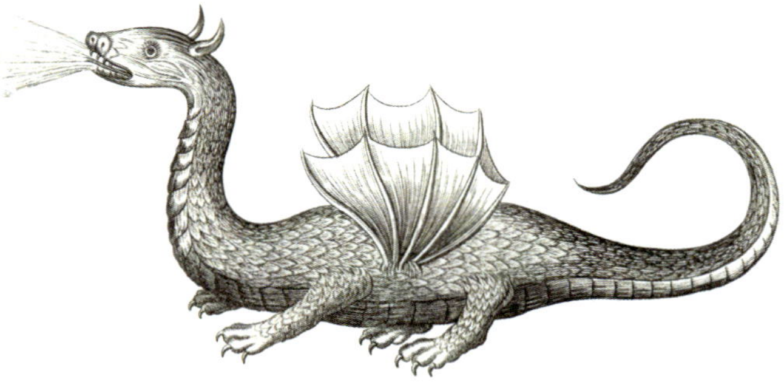

Literature:
Paul Begheyn, 'Athanasius Kircher S.J., *Mundus subterraneus* (1665)', in *Jesuit Books in the Low Countries 1540–1773: A Selection from the Maurits Sabbe Library*, ed. Paul Begheyn et al. (Leuven: Peeters, 2009), 173–176; Paul Begheyn, *Jesuit Books in the Dutch Republic and its Generality Lands 1567–1773: A Bibliography* (Leiden and Boston, MA: Brill, 2014), 147, 425–428.

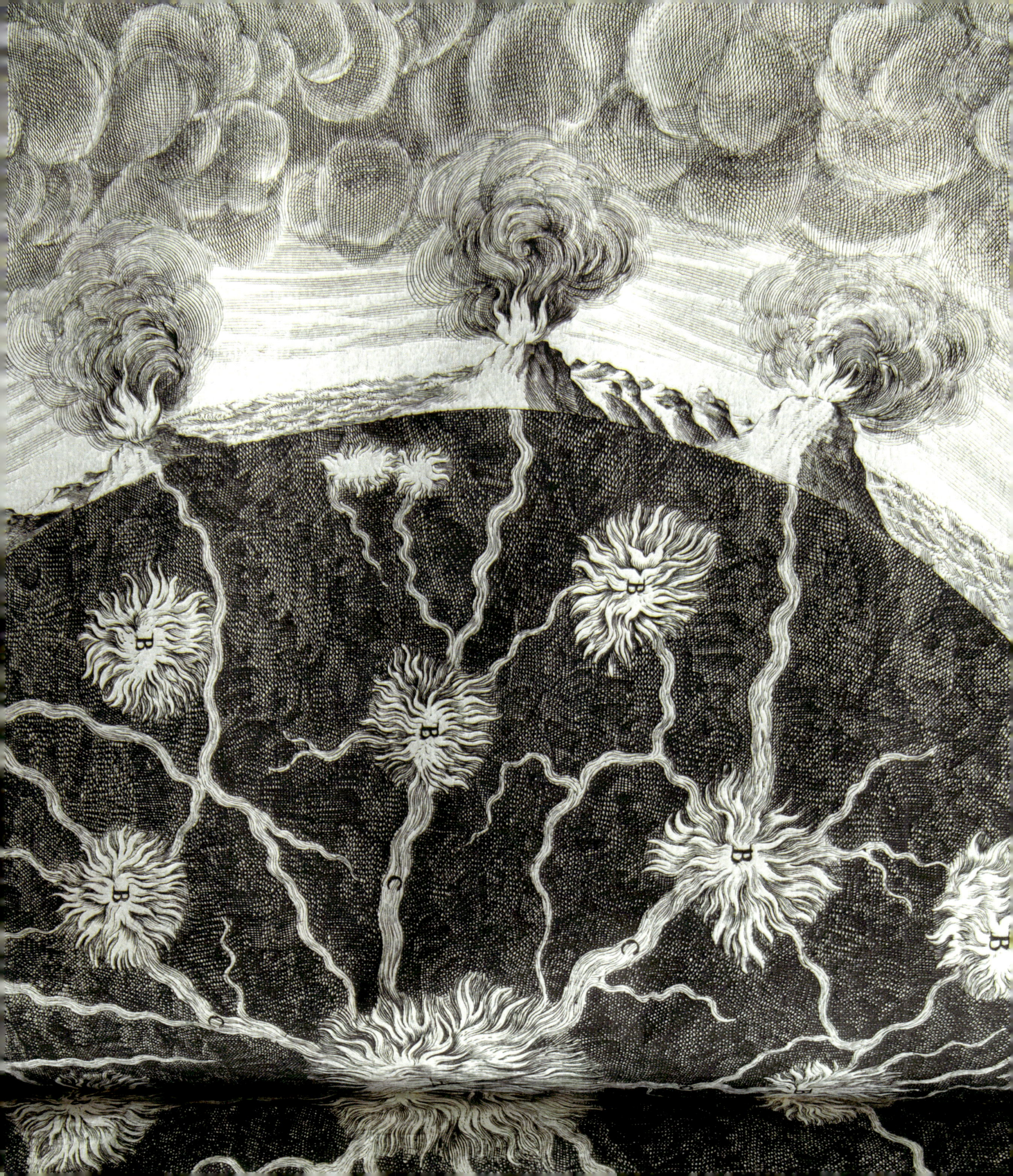
B
C

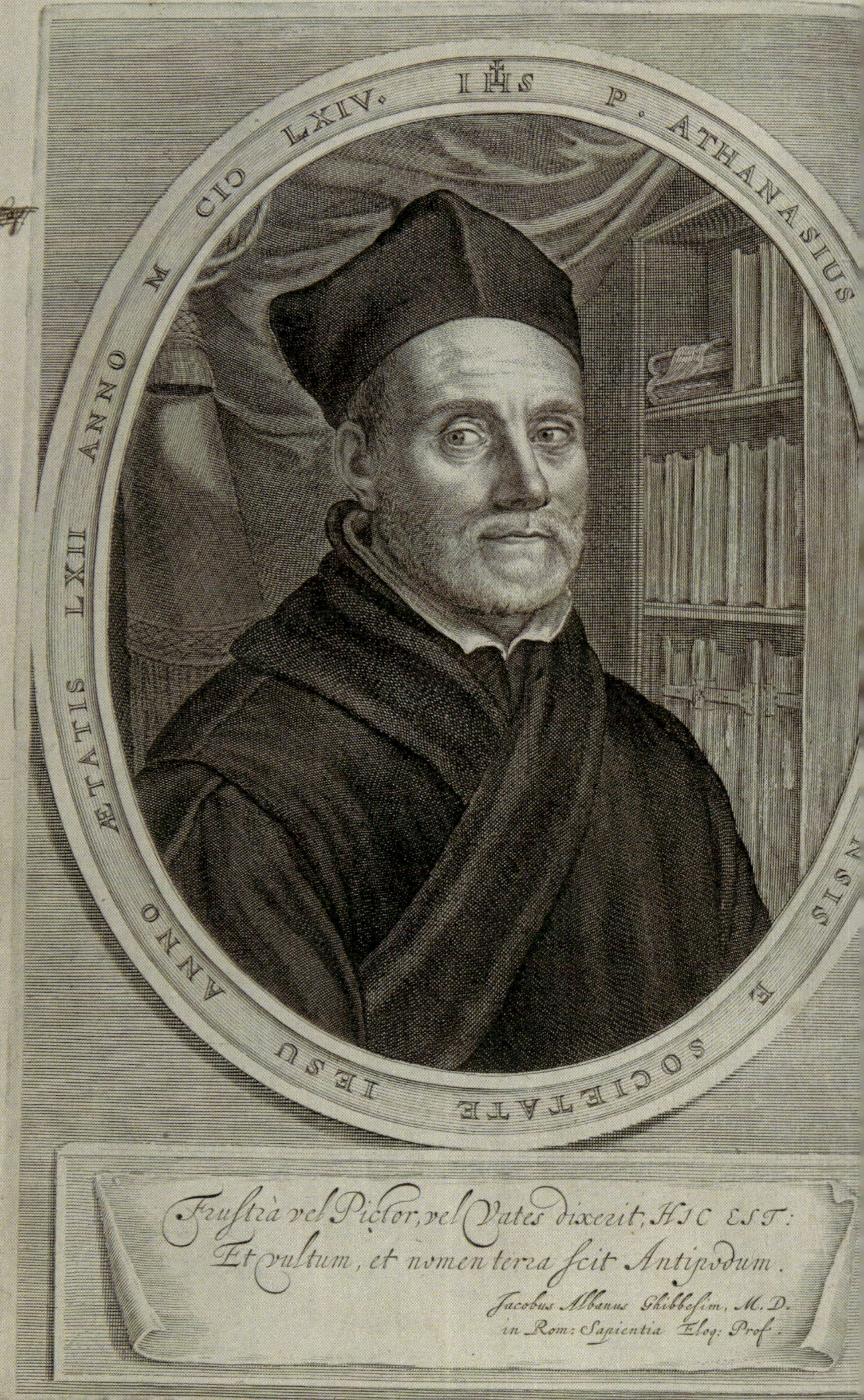
IHS
P. ATHANASIUS
NSIS E SOCIETATE IESU ANNO ÆTATIS LXII ANNO M CIↃ LXIV.
Frustrà vel Pictor, vel Vates dixerit, HIC EST:
Et vultum, et nomen terra scit Antipodum.
Jacobus Albanus Ghibbesius, M.D.
in Rom: Sapientia Æloq: Prof.

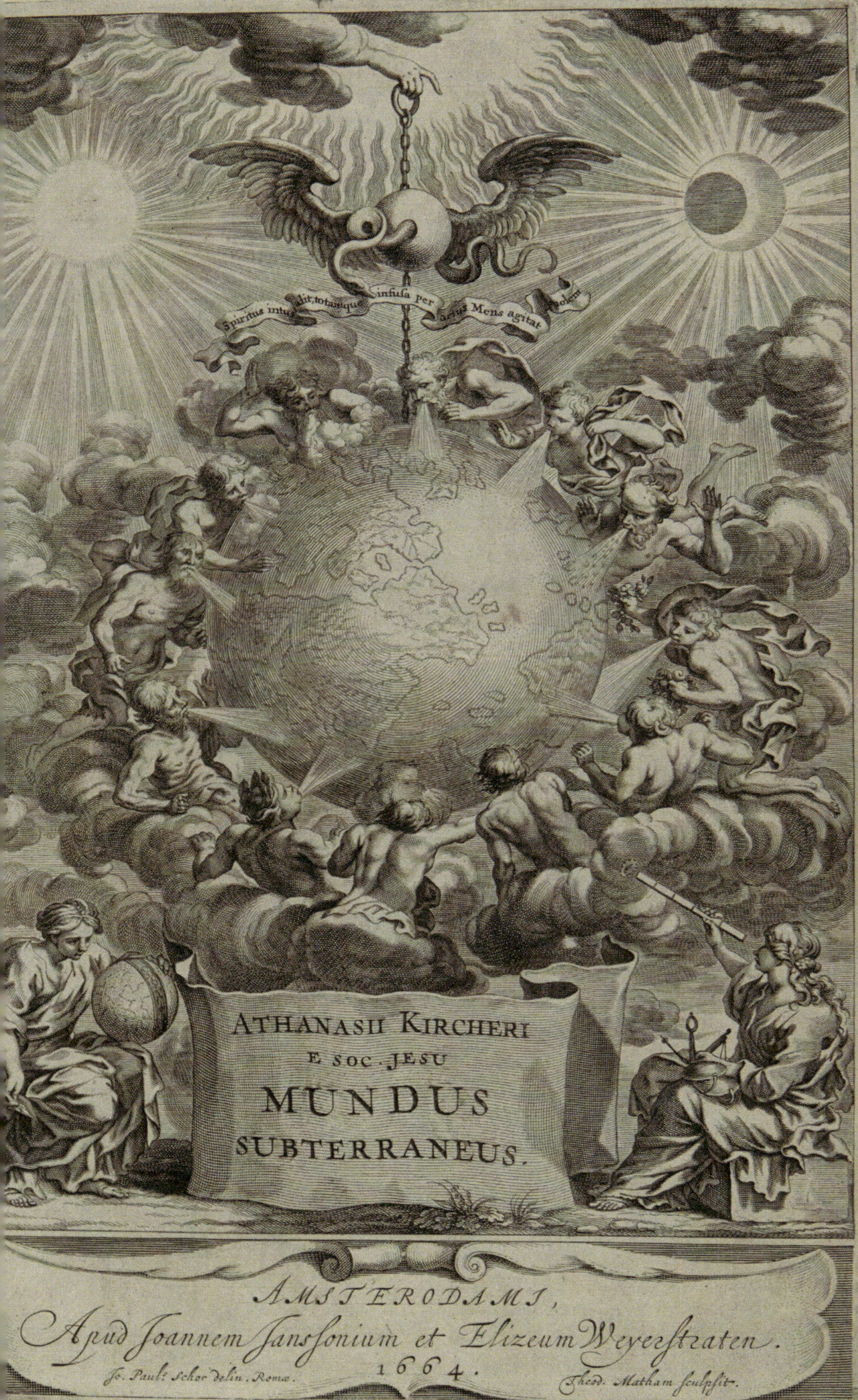
Spiritus intus alit, totamque infusa per artus Mens agitat molem
ATHANASII KIRCHERI
E SOC. JESU
MUNDUS
SUBTERRANEUS.
AMSTERODAMI,
Apud Joannem Jansſonium et Elizeum Weyerſtraten.
1664.
Jo. Paul. Schor delin. Romæ.
Theod. Matham ſculpſit.

Cornucopia of a new and unknown world ~ 1671

Arnoldus Montanus
De nieuwe en onbekende weereld: of Beschryving van America en 't Zuid-land, vervaetende d'oorsprong der Americaenen en Zuid-landers, gedenkwaerdige togten derwaerds ...
Amsterdam: Jacob Meurs, 1671
[8], 585, [27] p. · in 2°

The title of this heavy book by preacher Arnoldus Montanus, first published in 1671, could not be further from the truth: America was by no means unknown and certainly was not new at all. But the prudent Amsterdam publisher and Catholic Jacob Meurs knew how to put curiosity on the market. The addition in the title of a reference to the South Country (*Terra australis*) is significant. Although the travel report to this unspecified South (Australia, New Zealand and the Pacific) does not take up more than 10 of 600 pages, its inclusion demonstrated there was always more to know about the world. Montanus' *New and Unknown World* is above all an abundant description of people and goods from the American continent. Fact and fiction intermingle.

A skilled engraver, Jacob Meurs added marvellous engravings that give the book extra radiance. Just as exotic objects could be admired in a curiosity cabinet, the reader could discover America as a cornucopia continent via the stories in the book. The frontispiece shows that versatility. An Indian man wearing lots of plumes standing upright in a shell generously scatters gold and precious stones under the admiring glances of ornately dressed European administrators. A castle with cannons and high Spanish lances leave no doubt that the Spanish control the riches of the Americans. However, the abundance is more striking than the dreams of acquisition. Other Indians are busy with corn and tobacco under the watchful eyes of a llama, a beaver and a goat-like animal with an elaborate bushy tail. In America, opportunities were up for grabs and ecological diversity was a plus. The many illustrations of animals and nature in the engravings, and also the portraits, maps and images of cities, rituals and violent conflicts made the folio edition a desirable item, as was the continent.

The author of the book, Arnoldus Montanus (1625–1683), was a Reformed minister and taught at the Latin school in Schoonhoven. His compilation reads like a schoolbook. An English translation of *The New and Unknown World* by John Ogilby was published in 1671, and in 1673 a German translation appeared. That copies of the book are present in the collections of both the Mechelen Archdiocese and the Flemish Jesuits is no coincidence. The lure of America was indispensable for the promotion of a worldwide Catholic religion.

Literature:
Michiel van Groesen, *Amsterdam's Atlantic: Print Culture and the Making of Dutch Brazil* (Philadelphia, PA: University of Pennsylvania Press, 2017); Benjamin J. Schmidt, *Innocence Abroad: the Dutch Imagination and the New World, 1570–1670* (Cambridge: Cambridge University Press, 2001).

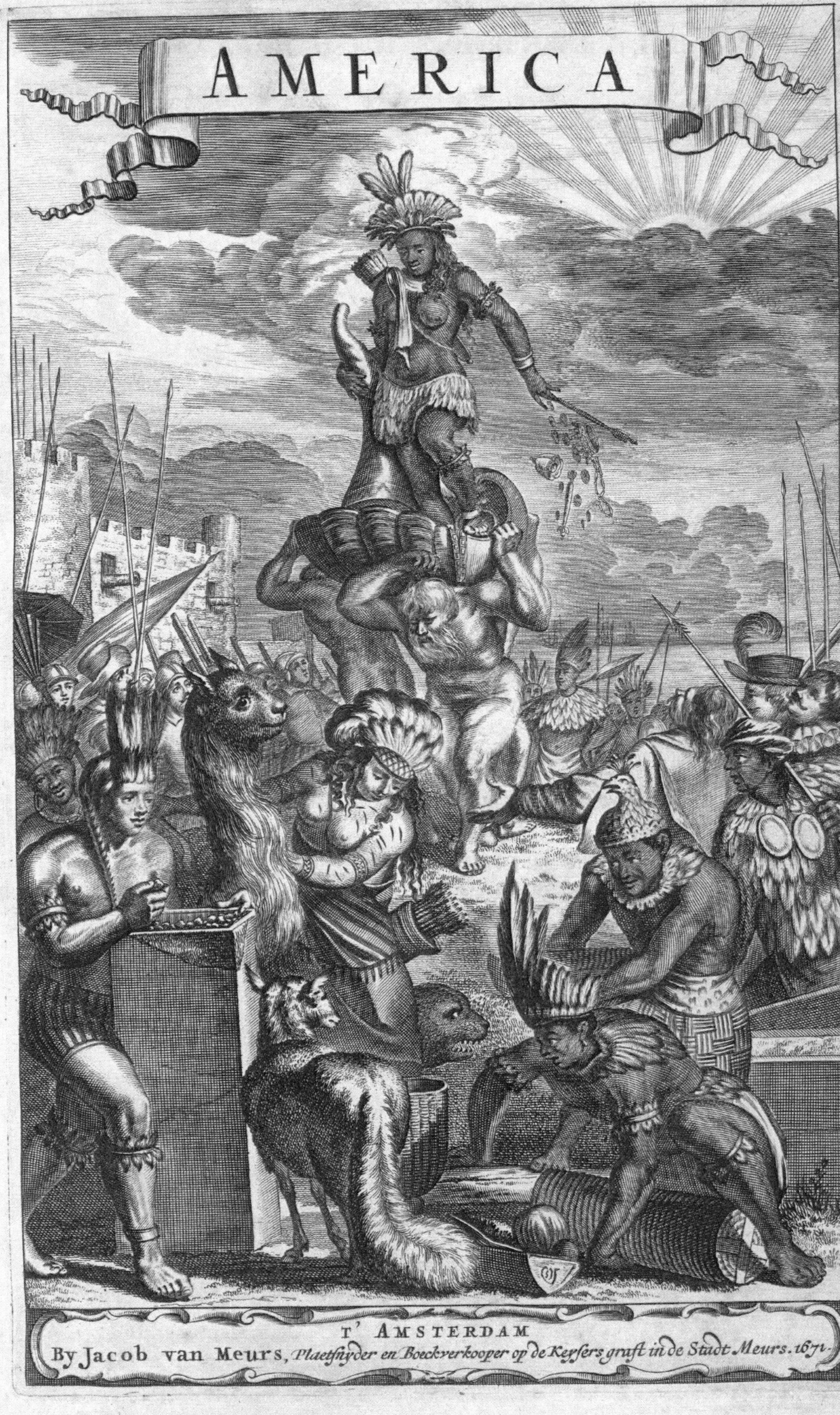
AMERICA
T' AMSTERDAM
By Jacob van Meurs, Plaetsnyder en Boeckverkooper op de Keysers graft in de Stadt Meurs. 1671.

₵ Calculation of the moon eclipses in imperial China ∾ 1671

Ferdinand Verbiest
Typus eclipsis lunæ
康熙十年二月十五日丁酉夜望月食圖
Beijing: s.n., 1671
scroll · 2400 × 283 mm
P MS SJ IG 112 K VERB 1671

The Jesuit Ferdinand Verbiest (1623–1688) travelled to China in 1657. Soon he was called to Beijing to work in the Astronomical Bureau, where he held leading positions from 1669 until his death. In the tenth chapter of his *Astronomia Europæa* (Dillingen, 1687; English translation by Noël Golvers), Verbiest describes how he, as the person responsible for the calendar, also had to calculate the eclipses: "There is still another burden, no less heavy and dangerous, I mean the calculation of all eclipses. Since this enormous empire is divided into seventeen provinces, and since an eclipse has to be calculated in relation to the latitude and longitude of the capital of each province, the calculations for one single solar eclipse, which differ for all seventeen provinces, swell into a fairly big volume." All eclipses had to be reported to the Emperor six months in advance, so that these calculations could still arrive in the most distant provinces in time and the eclipse could be observed there on the given day and hour. At the court in Beijing, the observation was accompanied by an elaborate ceremony attended by the highest mandarins, who knelt and bowed their heads to the ground in honour of the celestial lights at the time of the eclipse. "Immediately in all streets and especially in the temples of the idols, drums, cymbals and other similar instruments are beaten with great noise, so that the din echoes far and wide through the whole city. In doing this, they want to express their intention to help the sun and moon in their trouble, according to an old custom which the more educated people know to be groundless."

It is in this context that Ferdinand Verbiest had a figure or shadow drawing of an eclipse printed with a short summary for the benefit of the dignitaries. This scroll, in woodblock print, shows the phases of the lunar eclipse of 25 March 1671 in seventeen drawings, for each province (capital) one, with Korea (incomplete) last. The text is bilingual: in both Chinese and Manchu. The date is displayed according to the traditional Chinese calendar: the 15th day in the 2nd lunar month in the 10th year of the Kangxi emperor. A total of three such models of Verbiest's hand have been preserved. The Latin title page, a reflection of Verbiest's handwriting, indicates that these specimens also had a European target audience in mind.

Literature:
Noël Golvers, *The* Astronomia Europæa *of Ferdinand Verbiest, SJ (Dillingen, 1687): Text, Translation, Notes and Commentaries* (Nettetal: Steyler-Verlag, 1993).

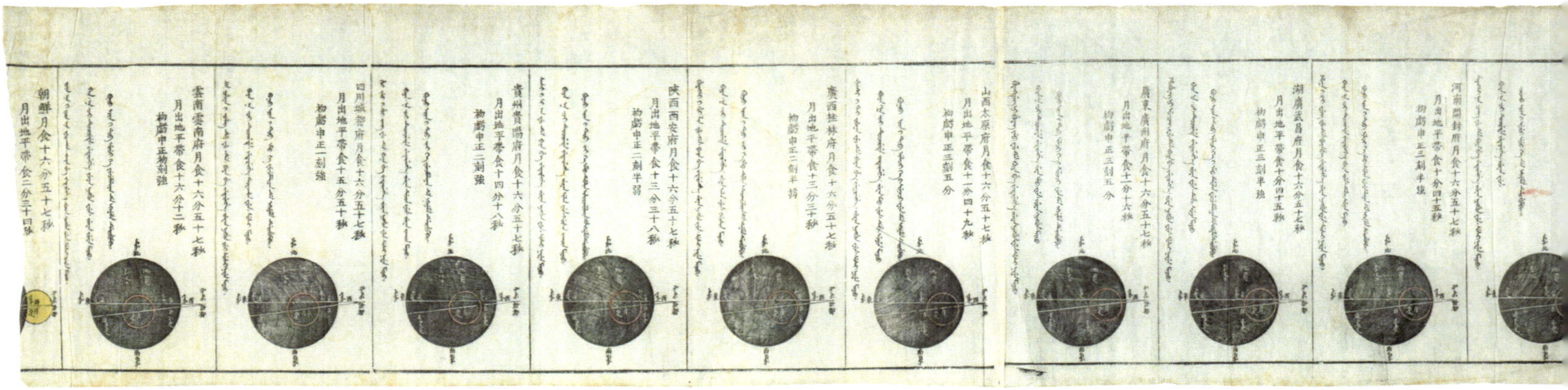

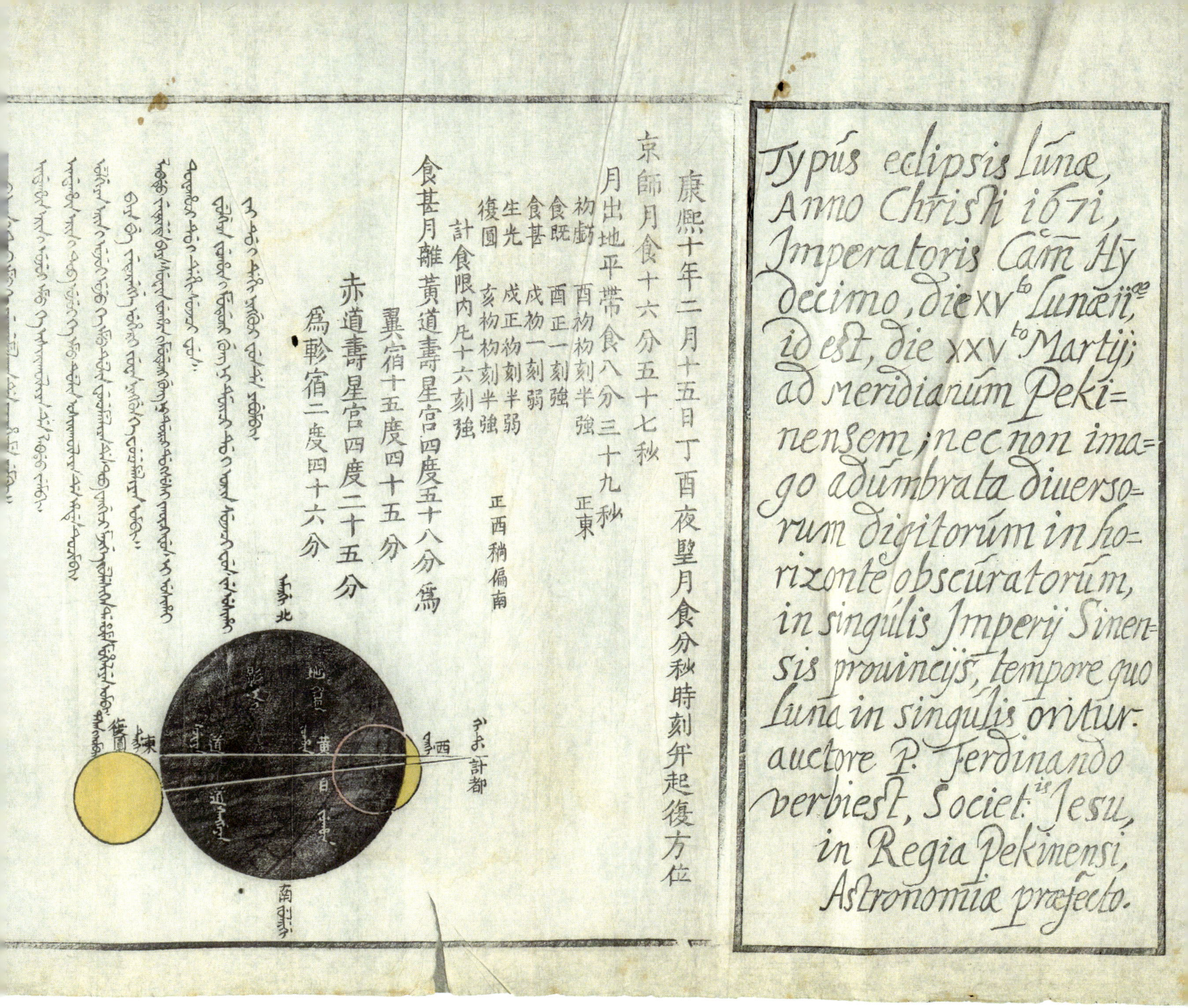

康熙十年二月十五日丁酉夜望月食分秒時刻并起復方位
京師月食十六分五十七秒
月出地平帶食八分三十九秒
正東
初虧 酉初初刻半強
食既 酉正一刻強
食甚 戌初一刻弱
生光 戌正初刻半弱
復圓 亥初初刻半強
計食限內凡十六刻強
正西稍偏南
食甚月離黃道壽星宮四度五十八分為
翼宿十五度四十五分
赤道壽星宮四度二十五分
為軫宿二度四十六分
北
復圓
東
西
南
Typús eclipsis lúnæ, Anno Christi 1671, Imperatoris Cam Hy decimo, die XV^to Lunæ II^æ, id est, die XXV^to Martij; ad meridianum Pekinensem; necnon imago adumbrata diuersorum digitorúm in horizonte obscúratorúm, in singúlis Imperij Sinensis prouinciis, tempore quo Luna in singulis oritur. auctore P. Ferdinando verbiest, Societ^is Jesu, in Regia Pekinensi, Astronomiæ præfecto.

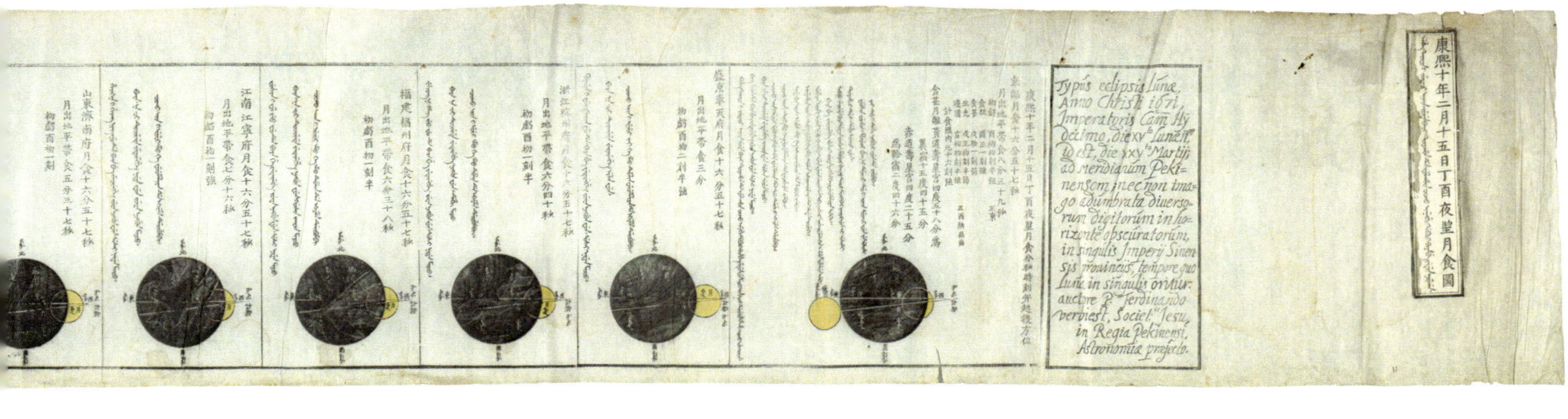

康熙十年二月十五日丁酉夜望月食圖

A curious botanical manuscript from the Philippines ∾ 1700

This 261-folio manuscript contains drawings of medicinal plants and herbs, commonly found and used in 17th-century Luzon (Philippines). This is believed to be the work of Moravian Jesuit brother-pharmacist Georg Joseph Kamel (Brno 1661 – Manila 1706), who collected and examined plants, and also drew them. See the leaf, flower and seedpod of the *banaba* tree, opposite, which is still used locally for treating diabetes. Kamel's name was immortalised when the Swedish botanist Carl von Linné (1707–1778) named the *Camellia* after him. Like other Jesuit scientists, Kamel sent drawings, descriptions and dry samples of his findings – all of which are preserved in the London Museum of Natural History and in the British Library – to his European correspondents, British botanist John Ray (1627–1705) and pharmacist-collector James Petiver (c. 1665–1718). Ray published Kamel's descriptions in the Appendix of his *Historia plantarum* (London, 1704), but without any drawings.

The exact link between the drawings kept in London and this Louvain manuscript is not clear, to say the least. Supplementary documentation allows us to observe that, following the donation of this manuscript to the Belgian Jesuits, there was an upsurge of research every fifty years, questioning its authenticity.

Can we shed more light on the problem? A brief handwritten note on the title page of the volume tells us that the manuscript was bought in 1858 by the Belgian botanist Count Alfred de Limminghe (1834–1861) at the Parisian auction of the estate of the de Jussieu family. He believed it to be an authentic work by Kamel. After his premature death in Rome in 1861, the manuscript ended up with the Jesuits, under whom he had studied in Namur. There, Fr. August Bellynck SJ (1814–1877), a botanist, knew about the manuscript, having already referred to it in his *Flore de Namur* (1855). Relevant events in the 150 years preceding the auction are still to be clarified.

The de Jussieu family, with its many botanists, possessed a huge library of 4,069 volumes as well as a network, extending all the way to England. Antoine-Laurent de Jussieu (1748–1836) probably had this volume bound. He even made personal annotations. Puzzling are the stylistically different botanical names, mainly in Tagalog, next to Latin and other tongues. Where is the hand of Kamel in all this? As of now, at least four drawings are considered authentic. Further, in 2015, a Czech scholar re-discovered two related volumes in the Parisian collection of Benjamin Delessert (1773–1847), previously unknown to 20th-century scholarship.

Georg Joseph Kamel
Herbarum aliarumque stirpium in Insulâ Luzone Philippinarum primariâ nascentium Icones ab autore delineatæ ineditæ, quarum syllabus in Joann. Raii historiæ plantarum tomo tertio
Philippines, [c. 1700]
[261] f. · 340 × 220 mm
PM0038/V (Leuven, Bibliotheek S.J., HS F° 112 K CAME 1700*)

Literature:

Sebestian Kroupa, '"Ex epistulis Philippinensibus": Georg Joseph Kamel SJ (1661–1706) and His Correspondence Network', *Centaurus* 57 (2015): 229–259; Raquel A. G. Reyes, 'Botany and Zoology in the Late Seventeenth-century Philippines: The Work of Georg Josef Camel SJ (1661–1706)', *Archives of Natural History* 36, no. 2 (2009): 262–276.

Ramus arb: Banaba.
c. Flore, et seminis
pericarpo.

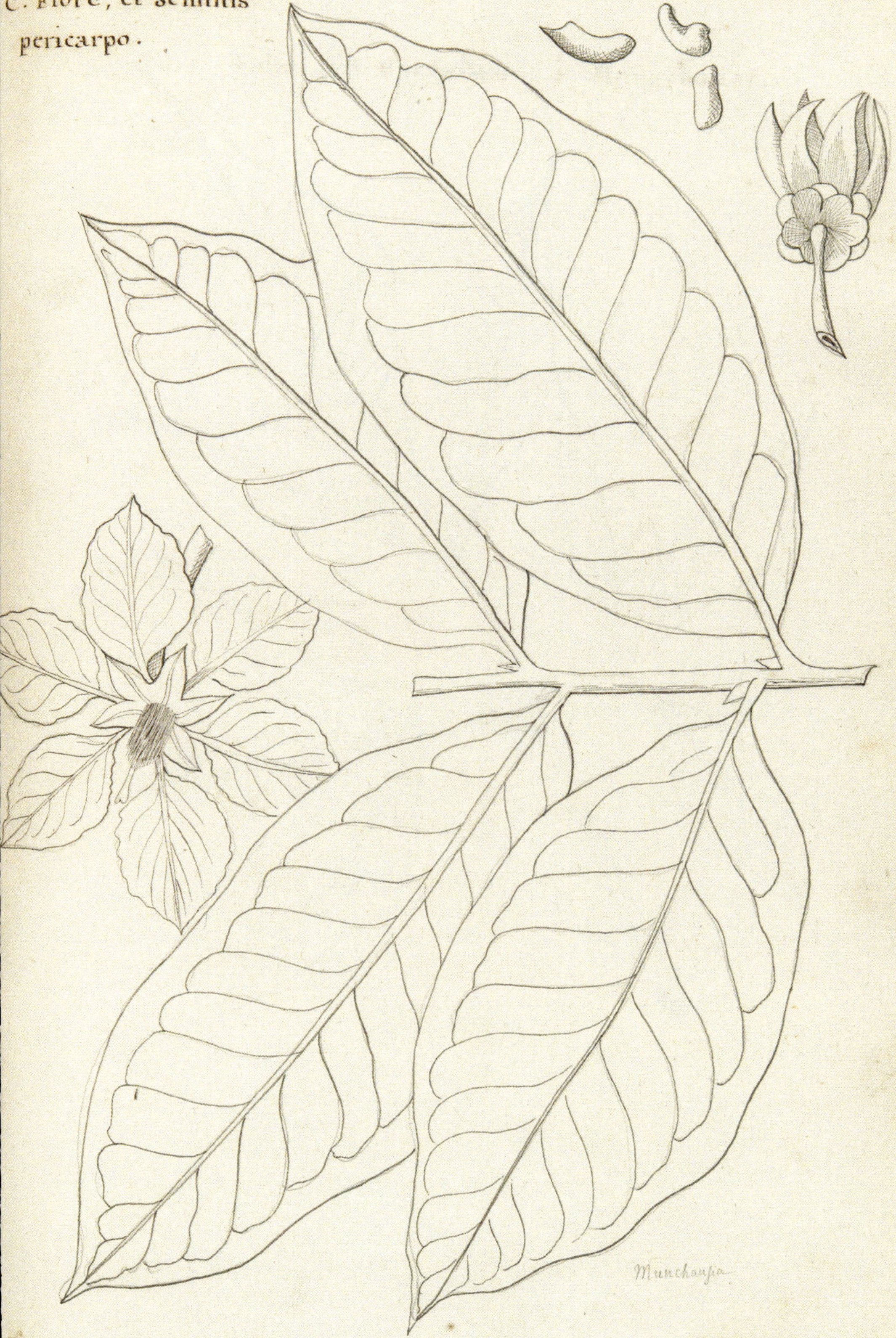

Camelli in Rai hist. 3. p. 80.

Rai. luz. 78. n. 1

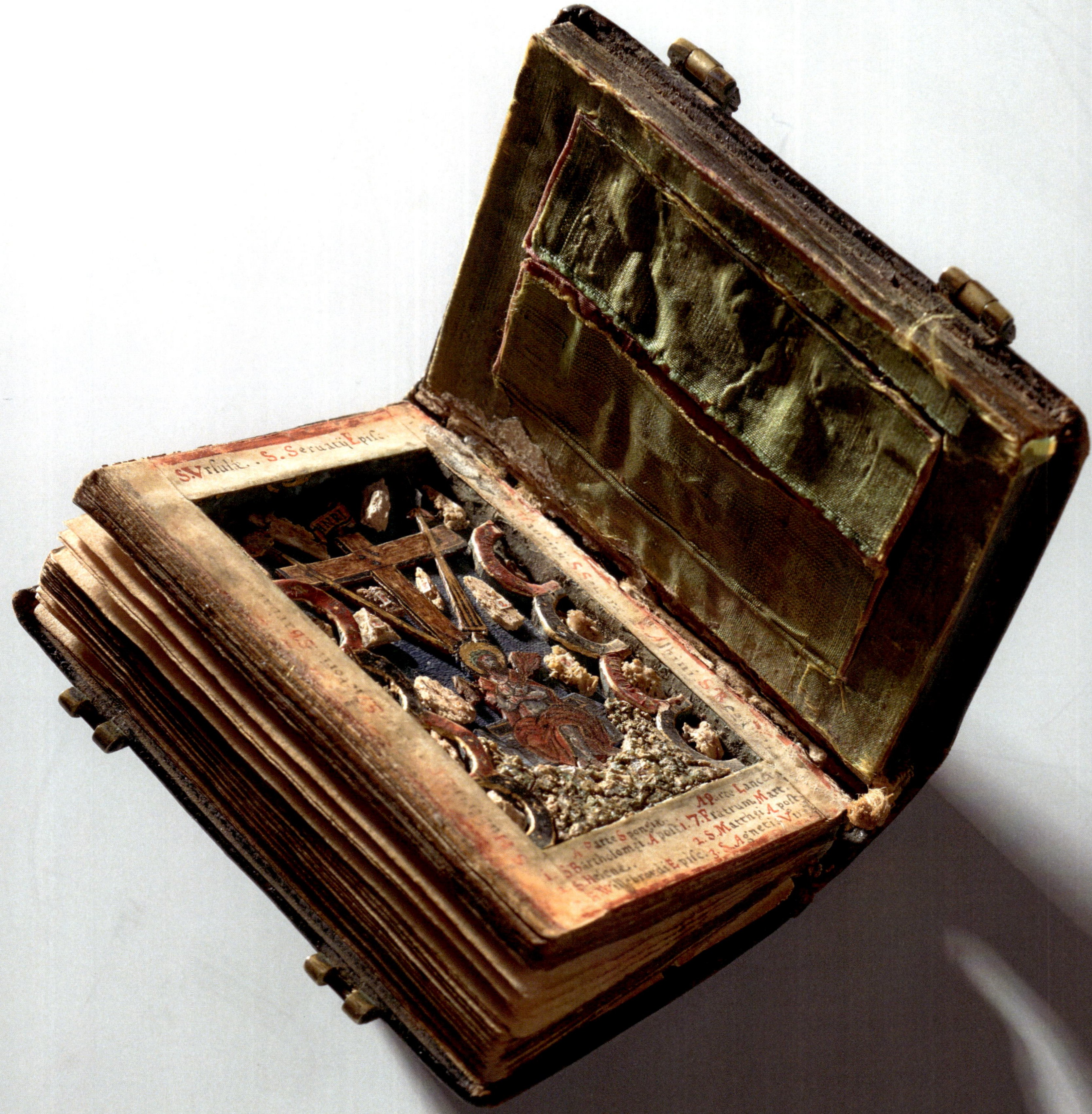
S.Vrsule. .S. Seruatij Episc.
INRI

A Capuchin booklet of spiritual guidance with relics ~ 1589

Den Reghel, ende Het Testament onses Heyligen Vaders Francisci
Antwerp: widow of Christopher Plantin, 1589
[192] p. · in 16°
PN0550

Around 1950, Hildebrand of Hooglede discovered this only known copy of the first Plantin edition of *Den Reghel, ende Het Testament onses Heyligen Vaders Francisci* (1589). This small (83 × 53 mm) book is one of the earliest publications of Capuchins in the Low Countries, together with a more extended Latin edition also printed by Plantin in 1589. A few years earlier, the Capuchins had founded a friary in Antwerp (1586), the first one in the Low Countries. Plantin printed five hundred copies of this Dutch edition, which further contains a selection of important texts relating to the Capuchin life, including Joannes of Fano's treatise on poverty. The Capuchins did not have to pay for this edition (cost: 68 fl. and 5 st.).

Unfortunately, this small book did not come down to us unscathed. Some initial pages are missing (A2–A4; p. 3–8), but the greatest loss is situated at the back: the book ends abruptly at page 63 (D8), while there should be 192 (!) pages in total (payment was made for typesetting and printing quires A to M8). Luckily, its complete content can be inferred from the 1624 Plantin edition, which also has collation A–M8, uses the approbation of the 1589 edition, and has the same text (apart from some spelling updates) on pages 9 to 63.

The two, originally three, intaglios (on pages 10, 50 and the missing page 88) were designed by Maarten de Vos and engraved by Julius Goltzius. Hundred copies were embellished with these intaglios; the remaining four hundred contained three woodcuts instead, designed by Peeter vander Borcht.

The most precious aspect of this little book explains why so many pages are missing at the back. By preserving the edges when cutting out the last 128 pages (E–M8; p. 65–[192]), a cavity in the book had been created, which was then turned into a beautiful miniature reliquary! On one side, eighteen relics are on display in a scenery of a bloodied Christ seated on an empty tomb before the Cross. Around the edge, the relics are identified: 'A Parte Spongiæ' we find, for instance, the relics of Saint Bartholomew, and of Saint Willibrord Bishop [of Liège]; 'A Parte Lanceæ' a relic of the Virgin Saint Agnes [of Rome].

The other side could perhaps best be described as a pigeonhole storage for the approximately sixty other relics, protected behind a slightly damaged transparent film, and concealed behind two shutters in bright green/red cloth.

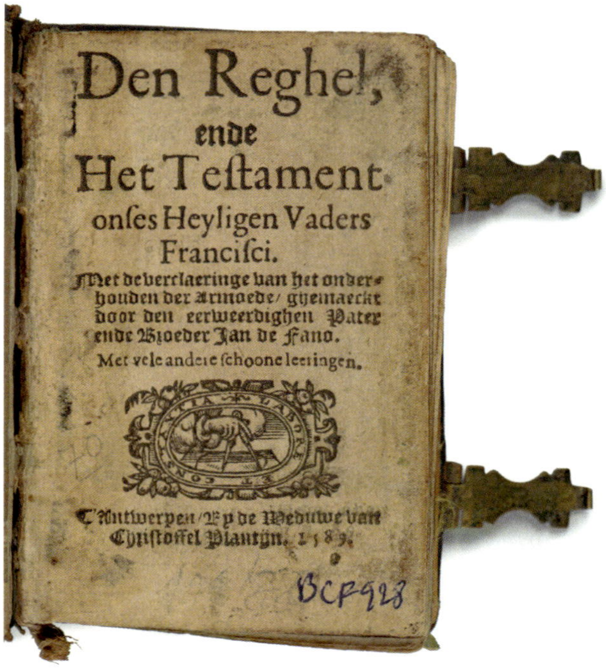

Literature:
Fidel Elizondo, 'Ediciones capuchinas de la regla franciscana publicadas en lengua inglesa y neerlandesa', *Estudios Franciscanos* 81 (1980): 223–261; Karen L. Bowen and Dirk Imhof, 'Book Illustrations by Maarten de Vos for Jan Moretus I', *Print Quarterly* 18 (2001): 259–289; Dirk Imhof, *Jan Moretus and the Continuation of the Plantin Press: A Bibliography of the Works Published and Printed by Jan Moretus I in Antwerp (1589–1610)* (Leiden: Brill, 2014), 601.

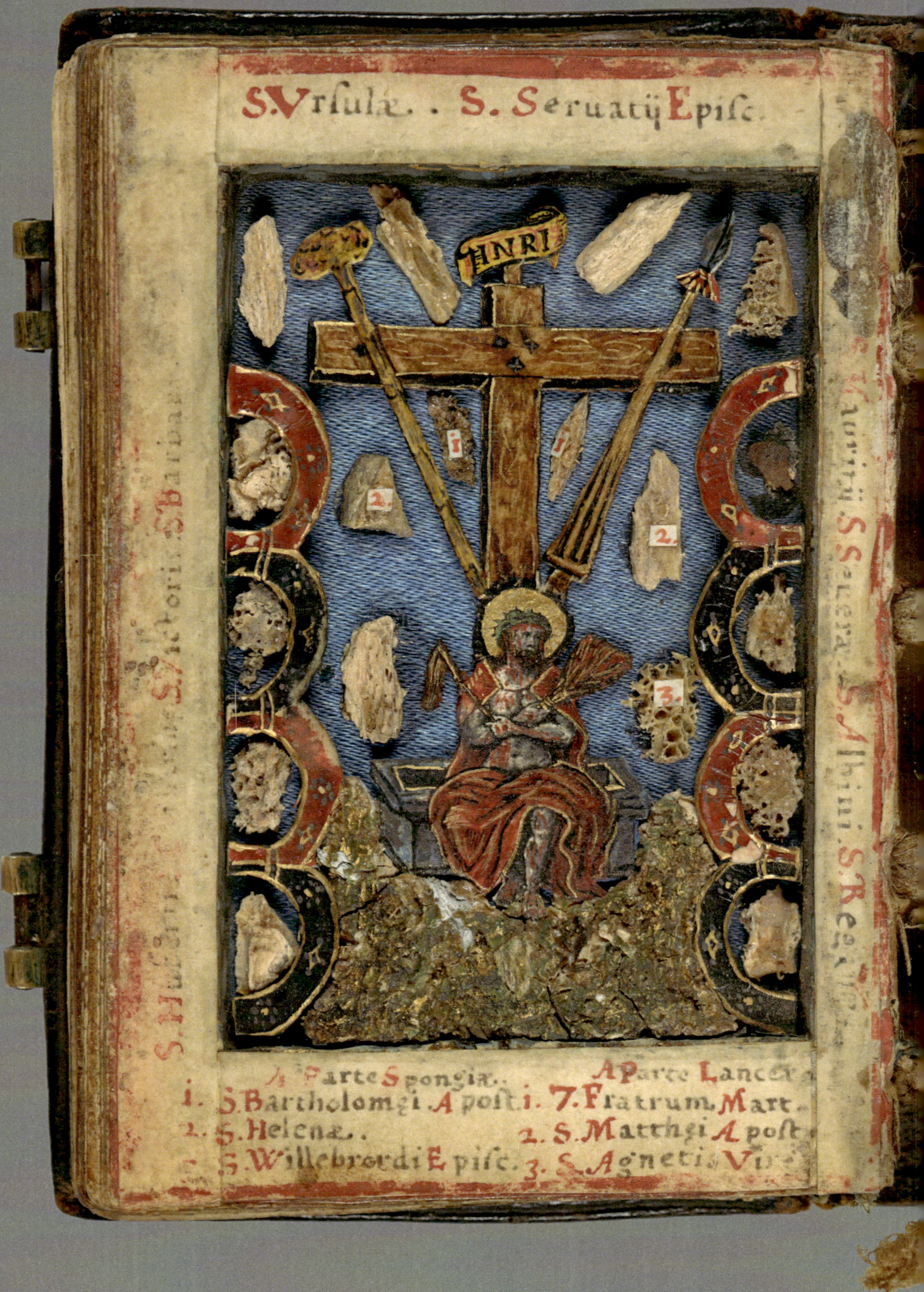
S.Vrsulæ . S. Seruatij Episc.
INRI
A Parte Spongiæ.
A Parte Lance
1. S.Bartholomæi Apost.
1. 7.Fratrum Mart.
2. S.Helenæ.
2. S.Matthæi Apost.
S.Willebrordi Episc.
3. S.Agnetis
S.Victoris. S.Barbaræ
S.Seuera. S.Albini. S.Reg

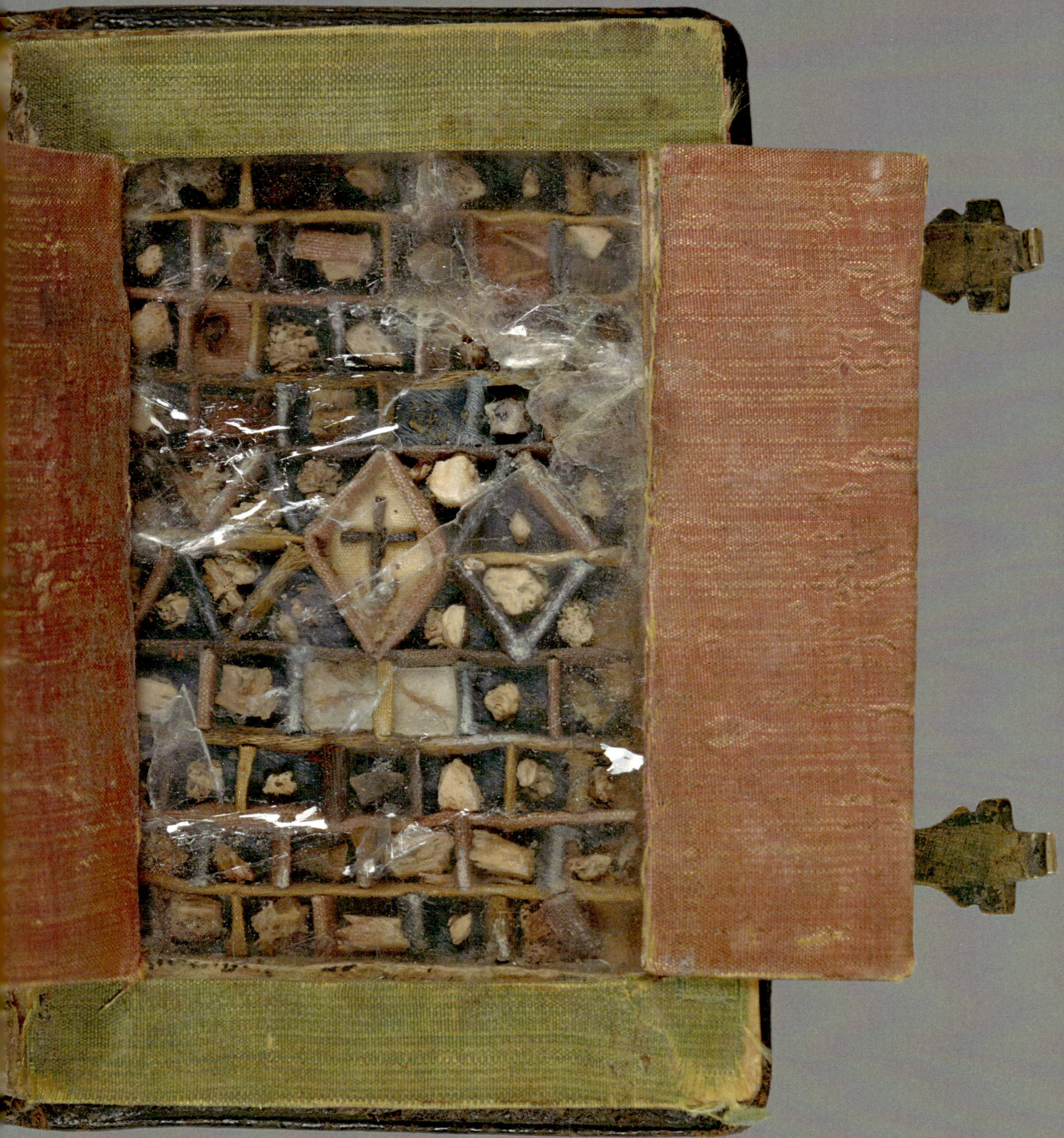

¢ The celebration of Cardinal Archbishop d'Alsace ∾ 1716–1719

The Jesuit order produced two booklets to celebrate the appointment of Thomas-Philippe d'Alsace (1679–1759) as Archbishop of Mechelen, and later on as cardinal. First, we have the typical congratulatory volume for episcopal ordinations, delicately adorned with engraved emblems, by the hand of pupils of the Mechelen Jesuit college. The second booklet consists of a Latin poem in a classical Jesuit style, by the Provincia Flandro-Belgica. Both volumes are bound together in a composite volume, which the Maurits Sabbe Library was able to acquire in 1995.

Like his forefathers, Thomas-Philippe de Hennin-Liétard de Boussu took up the name d'Alsace. As a young man he studied at the Latin college of the Brussels Jesuits and proved to be a gifted pupil. In 1716, he was consecrated Archbishop of Mechelen. During this time, he opposed Jansenism, by pronouncing his support for the Bull *Unigenitus*. Pope Clement XI responded kindly to this matter by creating the archbishop cardinal in 1719.

D'Alsace was a true bibliophile, constructing a large library in Mechelen, collecting books on exegesis, Patrology, Mariology, hagiography, Jansenism, humanism, as well as literary, historical and scientific works. Most books from the d'Alsace library were bound in the 18th century by Christiaan Jeghers in similar calfskin leather bindings, showing decorations of gold tooling with floral motifs on the spines and his coat of arms on the covers. The local clergy was allowed to consult the collection for studying purposes, thereby making the d'Alsace library the first semi-public library in the Low Countries.

In 1759 Thomas-Philippe d'Alsace died, leaving his library – at that time c. 11,500 volumes – *de facto* to the care of the cathedral chapter in Mechelen. In 1794, the French authorities ordered the transportation of the library. The most important books were packed into twenty-two cases and shipped to Paris. After a turbulent period in the first two decades of the 19th century, the remaining books of the depleted d'Alsace library could be found in Mechelen, either in the library of the Mechelen Seminary or in the Mechelen City Archives.

In 1970–1971, the largest part of the collection – some 3,000 titles – was moved, together with the original library of the Mechelen Major Seminary, to the Maurits Sabbe Library. In 2016, the Flemish Government included the Library Cardinal d'Alsace in its official List of Masterpieces, recognising the importance and uniqueness of this historical collection as a whole.

Illustrissimo ac reverendissimo Domino D. Thomæ Philippo de Alsatia, de Boussu ... Mechliniensium archi-episcopo primati Belgii, &c. recens inaugurato ... gratulatur et applaudit Gymnasium Societatis Jesu Mechliniæ [15] *Martii* M. D. CC. XVI
S.l.: s.n., 1716
31, [1] p. · in 4°
Eminentissimo ... Thomæ Philippo S. R. E. Presbyter Cardinali de Alsatia de Boussu ... cùm ... biretum scilicet purpureum à ... Clemente XI. *missum Mechliniæ reciperet, cardinalitiam dignitatem gratulatur Provincia Flandro-Belgica Societatis Jesu*
Mechelen: Laurens Vander Elst, [1719]
27, [1] p. · in 4°
P270.163.1/Q° GYMN Illu

Literature:
J. Laenen, 'L'ancienne bibliothèque des archevêques de Malines', *Bulletin du cercle archéologique, littéraire et artistique de Malines* 14 (1904): 133–156; L. Dequeker, 'De geschiedenis van de Bibliotheek Kardinaal d'Alsace', *Archief- en bibliotheekwezen in België* 39 (1968): 204–208; Goran Proot, '*Thomæ Philippo de Alsatia de Boussu gratulatur Societas Jesu* (1716, 1719)', in *Jesuit Books in the Low Countries, 1540–1773: A Selection from the Maurits Sabbe Library*, ed. Paul Begheyn et al. (Leuven: Peeters, 2009), 252–256.

EMINENTISSIMO
AC
REVERENDISSIMO
DOMINO
D. THOMÆ PHILIPPO
S. R. E.
PRESBYTERO CARDINALI
DE ALSATIA DE BOUSSU
ARCHI-EPISCOPO MECHLINIENSI
BELGII PRIMATI &c. &c.

Cùm præcipuum ex Cardinalitiæ Dignitatis insignibus, Biretum scilicet Purpureum à S. D. N. D. CLEMENTE XI. missum Mechliniæ reciperet,

CARDINALITIAM DIGNITATEM
GRATULATUR
PROVINCIA FLANDRO-BELGICA SOCIETATIS JESU.

MECHLINIÆ,
Typis LAURENTII VANDER ELST, Typographi sub Signo S. Francisci.

Booklets bound in gilded papers from Augsburg ∾ 18th century

In 1714 Thomas-Philippe d'Alsace was approved by the Emperor Charles VI as Archbishop of Mechelen. His appointment as archbishop took place on 16 December 1715. He was consecrated in January 1716. In March of the same year the congratulatory address to the archbishop from the Jesuit college in Brussels was published. This thin printed fascicle with sixteen leaves is wrapped in a splendid crimson paper embossed with gold coloured figures depicting running animals: dogs, deer, pigs, goats and hares in a web of floral branches.

A second wrapper in brocade paper in the d'Alsace collection is found on another congratulatory address: a fascicule printed in 1732 in Bruges by Paulus Roose. The light green brushed paper cover is lavishly decorated with gold coloured male and female dancing and playing figures, flying and standing birds, peacocks, ostriches, pigeons, chickens, grotesque heads and ornamental designs. These hunting and dancing themes were very popular and models of the animals were probably taken from engravings by Adriaen Collaert (c. 1560–1618). Through the Dutch paper market, the papers spread to bookbinders in the Low Countries and were used to cover dissertations and as end leaves.

The crimson brocade paper covering the 1716 fascicle lacks relief and belongs to the group of *bronsefernisspapir*, printed with woodblocks and a mixture of varnish and metallic colours (bronze-varnish) on colourful brushed paper. From the end of the 17th-century bronze varnished papers were made in the area of Augsburg and became popular in Europe: imitation gold leaf was pressed into sheets of paper by woodblocks, resulting in patterns or images in shiny metal foil.

The green brocade paper covering the 1732 gathering was produced in a slightly different way. The sheet of laid paper was first brushed with green paint and coated with an adhesive, then covered with gold coloured metal leaf and then placed on a soft support. The paper was embossed in a rolling press with a heated engraved plate which created a slight relief in the paper and transferred the metallic decorative pattern to the surface.

Neither of these decorative papers in the Library Cardinal d'Alsace is listed in the inventory of Albert Haemmerle, the German scholar who in 1977 published the most extensive study on 18th-century Augsburg brocade and bronze varnished papers to date.

Illustrissimo ac reverendissimo Domino D. Thomæ Philippo de Alsatia, de Boussu ... Mechliniensium archi-episcopo primati Belgii, &c. recens inaugurato ... gratulatur et applaudit Gymnasium Societatis Jesu Mechliniæ [15] *Martii M. D. CC. XVI*
S.l.: s.n., 1716
31, [1 blank] p. · in 4°

Applausus congratulatorius eminentissimo ac reverendissimo domino dno. Thomæ Philippo [...] *de Alsatia, de Boussu, archiepiscopo Mechliniensi*
Bruges: Paulus Roose, 1732
7, [1 blank] p. · in 4°

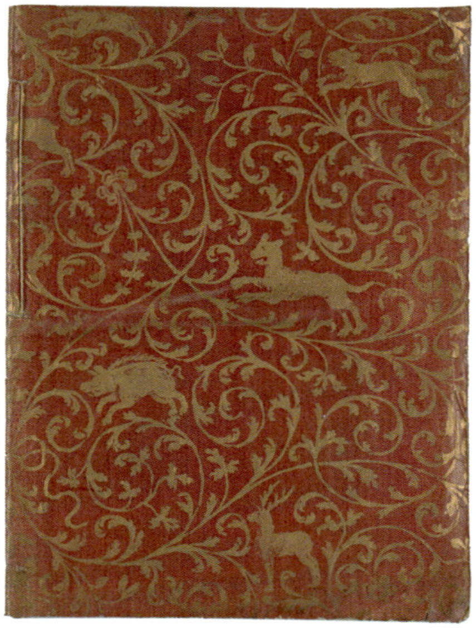

Literature:
Albert Haemmerle, *Buntpapier: Herkommen, Geschichte, Techniken, Beziehungen zur Kunst* (Munich: Callwey, 1977); Richard J. Wolfe, *Marbled Paper: Its History, Techniques, and Patterns, with Special Reference to the Relationship of Marbling to Bookbinding in Europe and the Western World* (Philadelphia, PA: University of Pennsylvania Press, 1990).

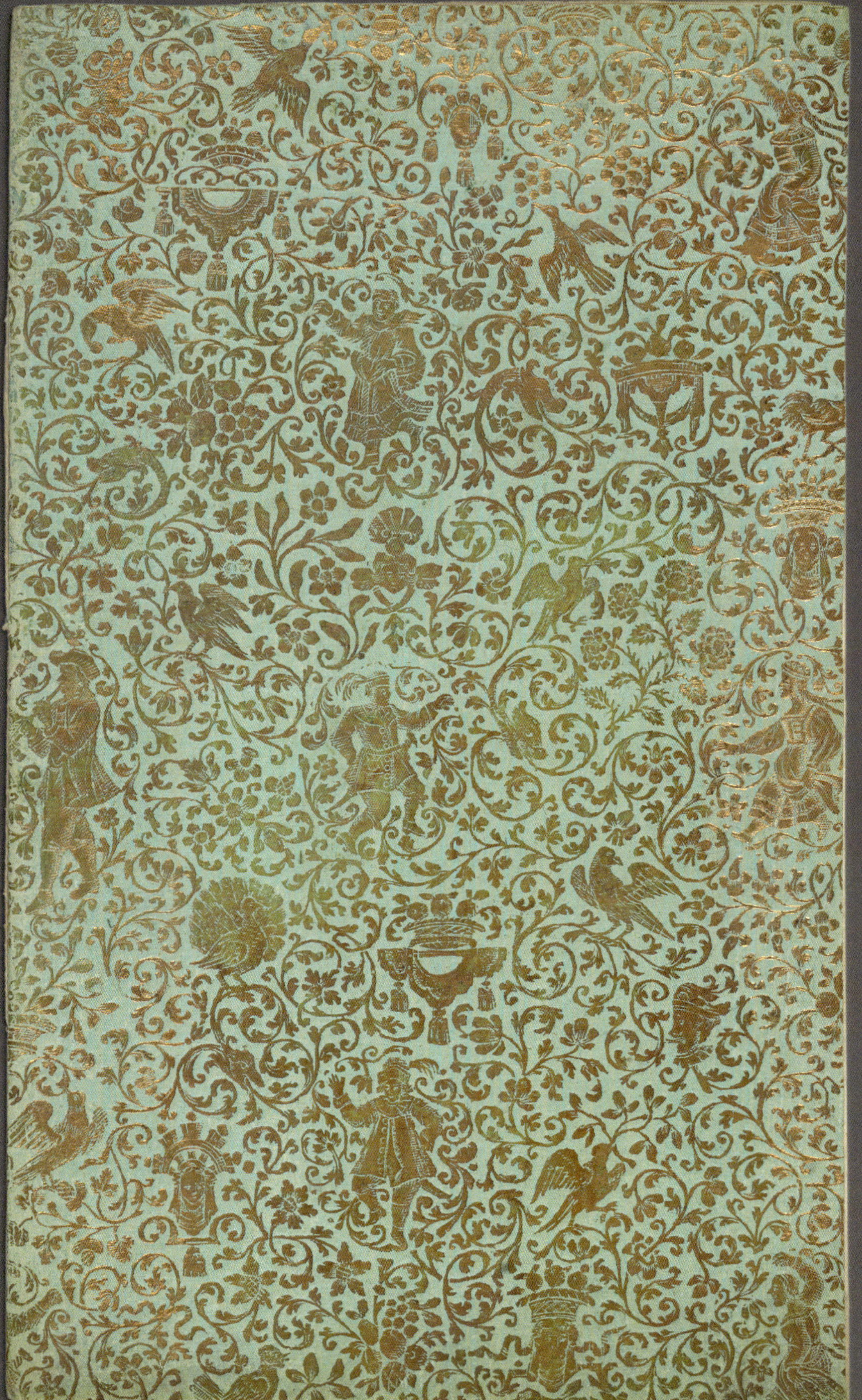

¢ Rubens reborn from his ashes ~ 1751

De plafonds, of gallerystukken uit de kerk der eerw. P. P. Jesuiten te Antwerpen. Geschilderd door P. P. Rubens; naer deszelfs echte schilderyen geteekent door Jacob de Wit, en in 't koper gebragt door Jan Punt
Amsterdam: Jan Punt, 1751
[3] f., [36] pl. · in plano oblong
P Plano 133 PLAF

This collection of engravings constitutes valuable visual evidence of the cycle of paintings created by Peter Paul Rubens around 1620–1621 for the ceilings of the upper and lower galleries of the Jesuits' Antwerp church (Saint Ignatius, now Saint Charles Borromeo). The cycle was destroyed by a fire that severely damaged the building on 18 July 1718 after it was struck by lightning. The Preface states that a series of drawings was made, under almost divine inspiration and before the destruction of the paintings, by the Amsterdam painter Jacob de Wit (1695–1754), presented as 'the Rubens of his age'. It also mentions that these drawings would have remained hidden forever if they had not been brought to light by the engraved versions of Jan Punt (1711–1779). Only long-lasting copper could guarantee the enduring existence of what had already been considered as masterpieces of the Antwerp master. The author of the Preface emphasises this motif of commemoration in images and in the immortality of the arts. The arts of painting, drawing and engraving compensate for the defects of our memory by presenting a clear and precise image of what once was.

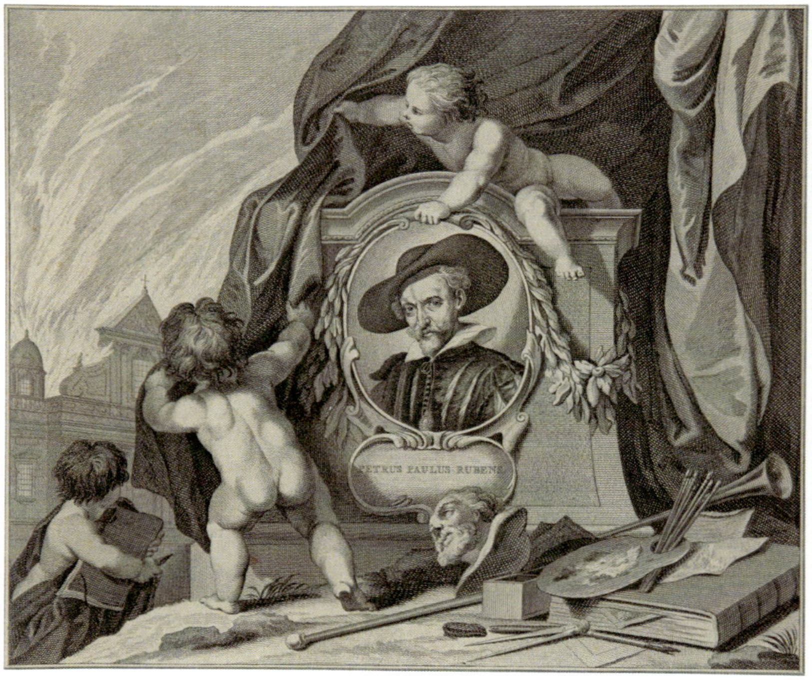

The frontispiece shows a medallion portrait of Rubens, accompanied by all the symbols of the arts and the trumpet of glory. It serves as a commemorative monument that putti seem to be trying to protect from the flames that are engulfing the Jesuit church in the background; it is highly likely that the sketchbook which the putto is bringing from the church symbolises the collection of drawings by Jacob de Wit. These drawings and engravings have thus saved these masterful works of art from fire and oblivion, allowing them to still be contemplated by connoisseurs and to arouse the admiration of art-lovers the world over. Indeed, the Preface concludes on the topic of the universality of the language of painting, with this collection being called on to spread the language of Rubens which is known, understood and welcomed everywhere. Concerning this language, we must bear in mind the transformations introduced by the hand of Jacob de Wit, a rococo painter who measured himself against Rubens. These transformations make the series a testimony to the 18th-century rather than to 17th-century style, with the artist re-appropriating the idiom of Rubens. Furthermore, we should note that the collection contributes to the conversion of the place of worship that is the Jesuit church into a temple of the arts containing jewels worthy not of religious adoration but of aesthetic admiration.

Literature:
John Rupert Martin, *The Ceiling Paintings for the Jesuit Church in Antwerp* (Brussels: Arcade, 1968); A. C. Knaap, 'Seeing in Sequence: Peter Paul Rubens' Ceiling Cycle at the Jesuit Church in Antwerp', *Netherlands Yearbook for History of Art* 55 (2004): 155–196; A. C. Knaap, 'Meditation, Ministry and Visual Rhetoric in Peter Paul Rubens's Program for the Jesuit Church in Antwerp', in *The Jesuits II: Cultures, Sciences, and the Arts, 1540–1773*, ed. John W. O'Malley, Gauvin Alexander Bailey, Steven J. Harris, and T. Frank Kennedy (Toronto: University of Toronto Press, 2005), 157–181.

P. P. Rubens pinxit in Templo Societ. Jesu Antverpiae

S. Michaël Archangelus triumphans de antiquo illo Serpente et angelis ejus Apoc. 12 V. 7. 8.

J. de Wit delineavit. J. Punt sculpsit. [illegible]

¢ Autographs of Melanchthon glued in a scrapbook ∾ c. 1804

Jan Frans Van de Velde
[. . .] *Continentur Philippi Melanchthonis imagines* [. . .] *sigilla* [. . .] *epistolæ autographæ* [. . .]
[1], 17, [3 blank] f. · 320 × 225 mm
HS F° 44 R MELA

Jan Frans Van de Velde (1743–1823) was a theologian and the last librarian of the University of Louvain before the university was closed by the French revolutionary regime in 1797. During his German exile from 1798 to 1804, Van de Velde became familiar with German Protestantism, even making plans to compile the correspondence of Philipp Melanchthon (1497–1560). Melanchthon was a classicist, theologian and close collaborator of Martin Luther in Wittenberg, who played a key role in the establishment of the Reformation.

Apart from many copies of letters, Van de Velde also came into possession of three autographs of Melanchthon which he included in a volume (using glue), together with some engravings showing a portrait of Melanchthon, one made by Lucas Cranach and another by Albrecht Dürer, among other materials. The Maurits Sabbe Library acquired this peculiar object through the Jesuit collection.

The first autograph concerns a letter written by Melanchthon from Leipzig on 15 October (obviously in 1555), to Valérand Poullain or Pollanus Francofurtensis, who was an alumnus of Louvain and pastor of a French-Flemish Protestant refugee congregation in Frankfurt. The letter was a gift to Van de Velde from Wilhelm Friedrich Hufnagel, a leading evangelical pastor and theologian in Frankfurt (29 August 1803). A second autograph that we find glued in the book is a letter written by Melanchthon on 5 February 1551 (most probably from Wittenberg), to Justus Menius, pastor in Gotha. The third is a letter from Melanchthon to Tileman Heshusen or Heshusius, general superintendent of the Palatinate in Heidelberg, written on 9 January 1558 (most likely also from Wittenberg). Letters 2 and 3 were gifts to Van de Velde from Heinrich Philipp Conrad Henke, *propræses* of the Council of the Duke of Wolfenbüttel (*consistorii ducalis Guelpherbytani Propræses*), 'abbot' of the seminary for pastors established in the former monastery of Michaelstein, and professor of theology in Helmstädt (27 August 1804).

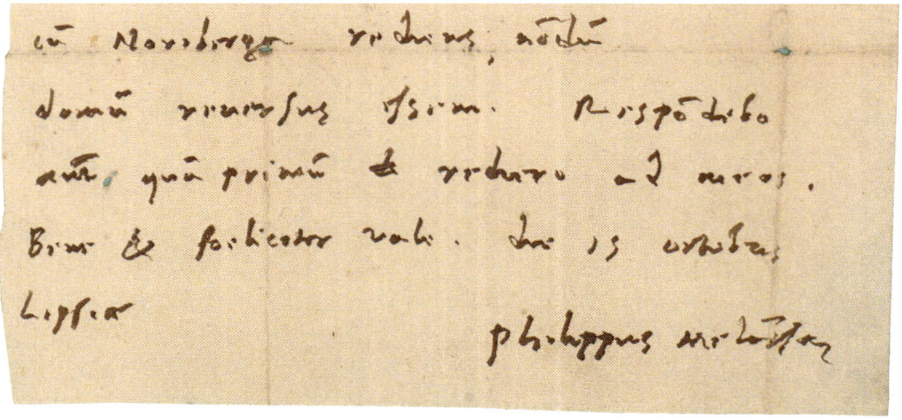

Literature:
Jan Roegiers, 'Jan Frans Van de Velde (1743–1823)', in Marcus de Schepper, Ann Kelders, and Jan Pauwels, *Les Seigneurs du livre: Les grands collectionneurs du XIXe siècle à la Bibliothèque royale de Belgique* (Brussels: Bibliothèque royale de Belgique, 2008), 46–56; *Catalogue des livres, rares et précieux, au nombre de 14435 lots, de la bibliothèque de feu monsieur Jean-François Vande Velde* (Breda: Van Gulick et Hermans, 1830–1833); *Melanchthons Briefwechsel: Kritische und kommentierte Gesamtausgabe*, ed. Heinz Scheible and Christine Mundhenk (Stuttgart-Bad Cannstatt: Verlag Frommann-Holzboog, 1977ff.).

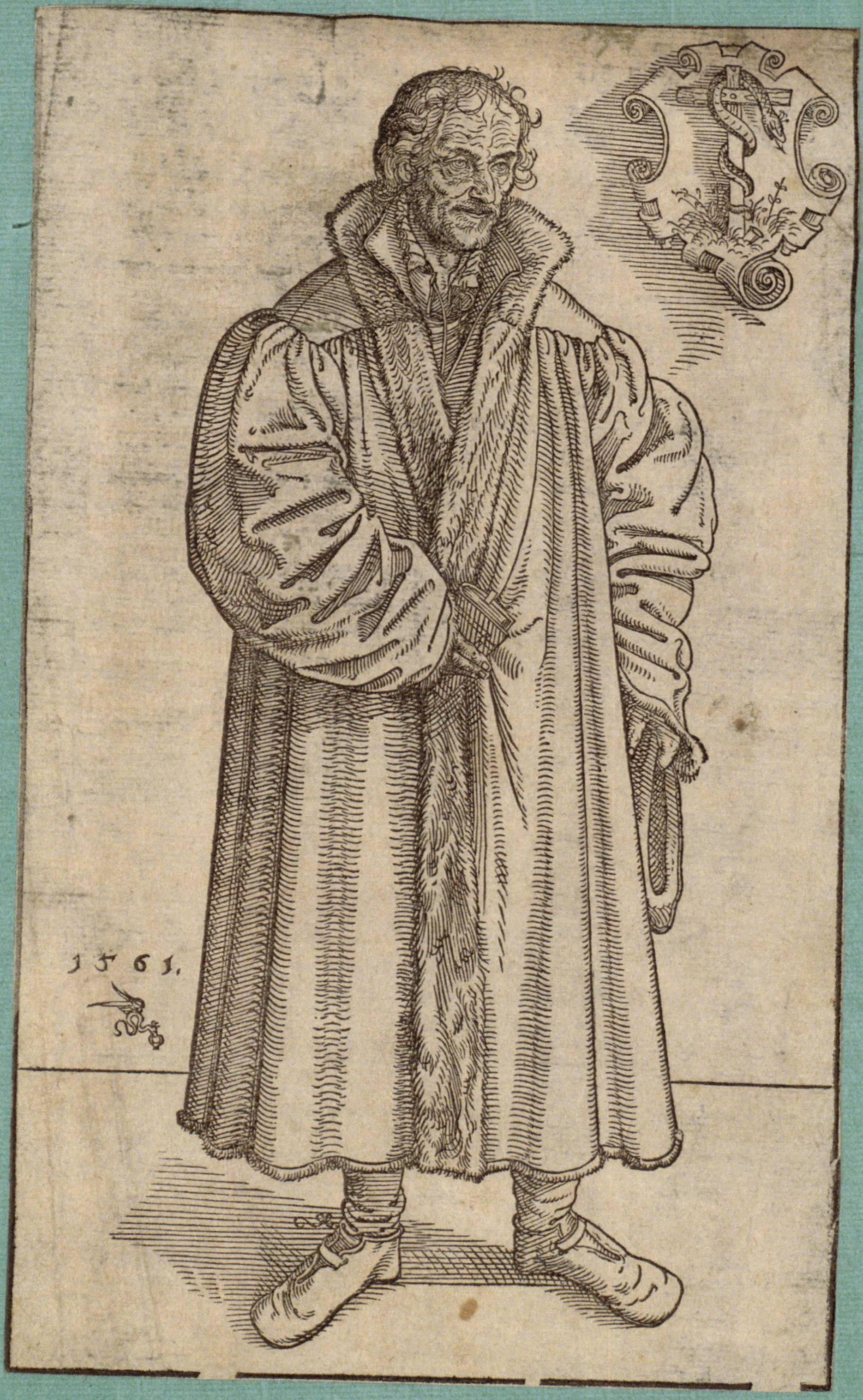
1561.

COLLEC
D'ANCIE
EVANG
TOM IV
TOM III
THEOLOGIE
CHRETIENNE
TOM I

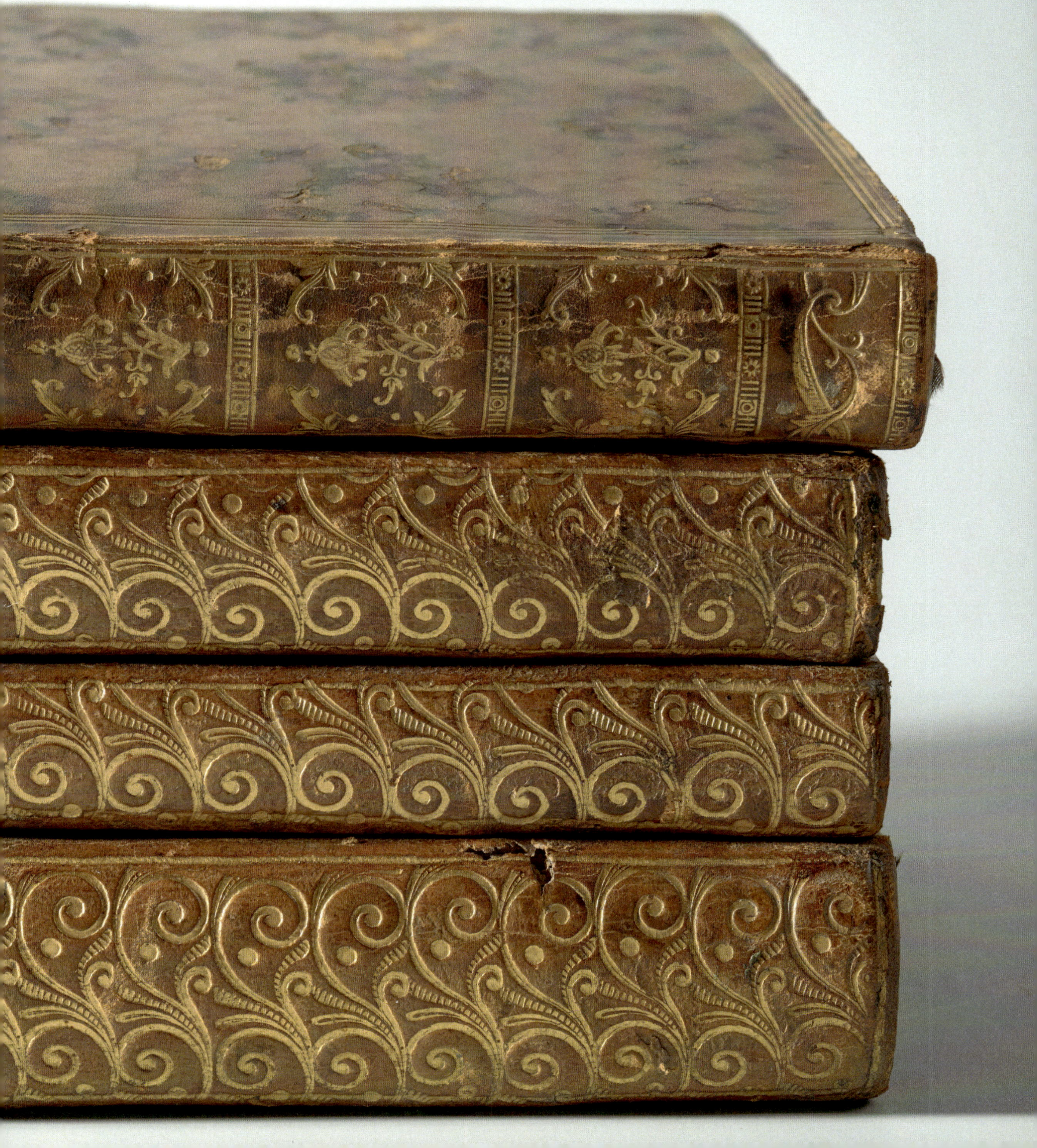

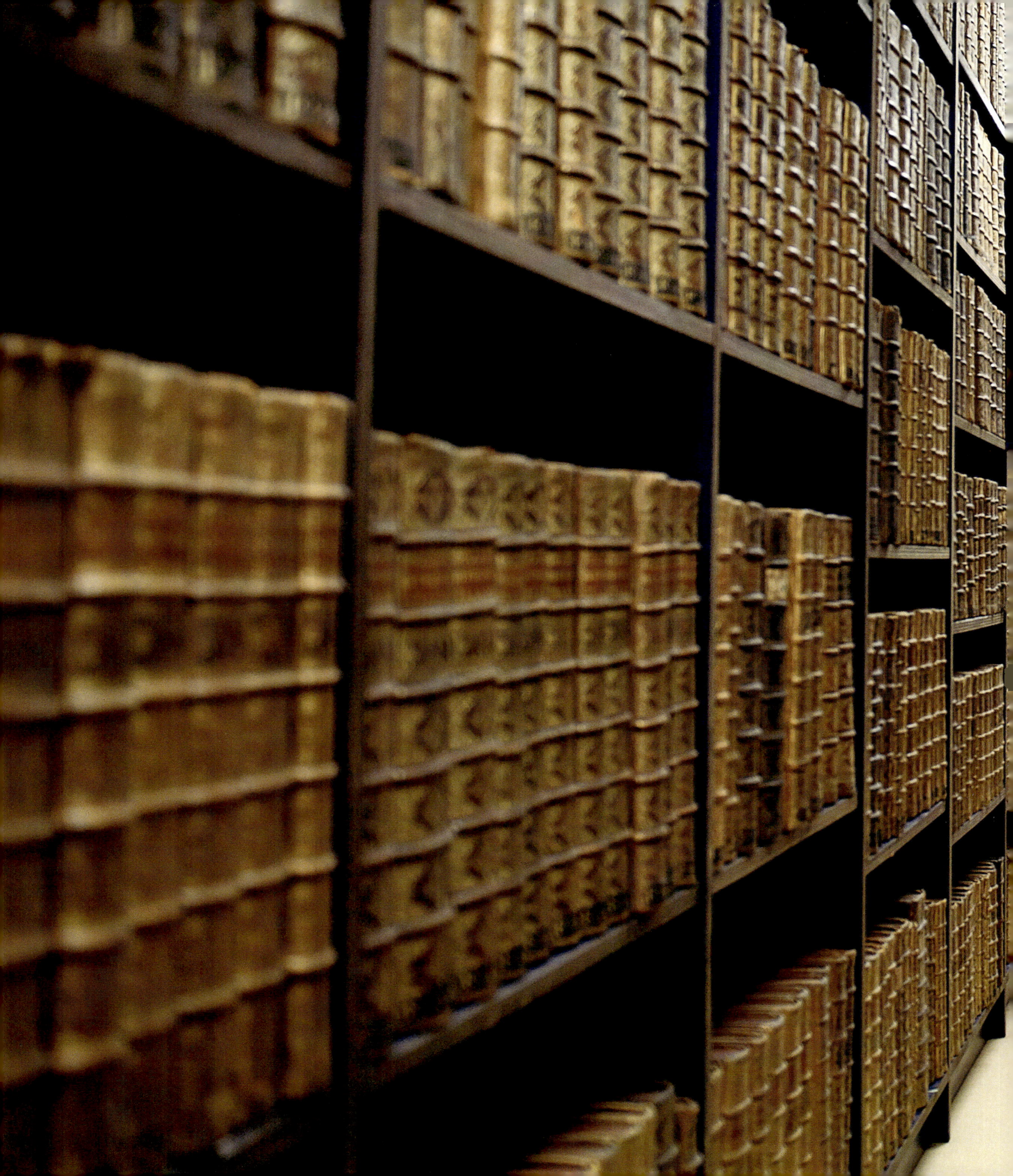

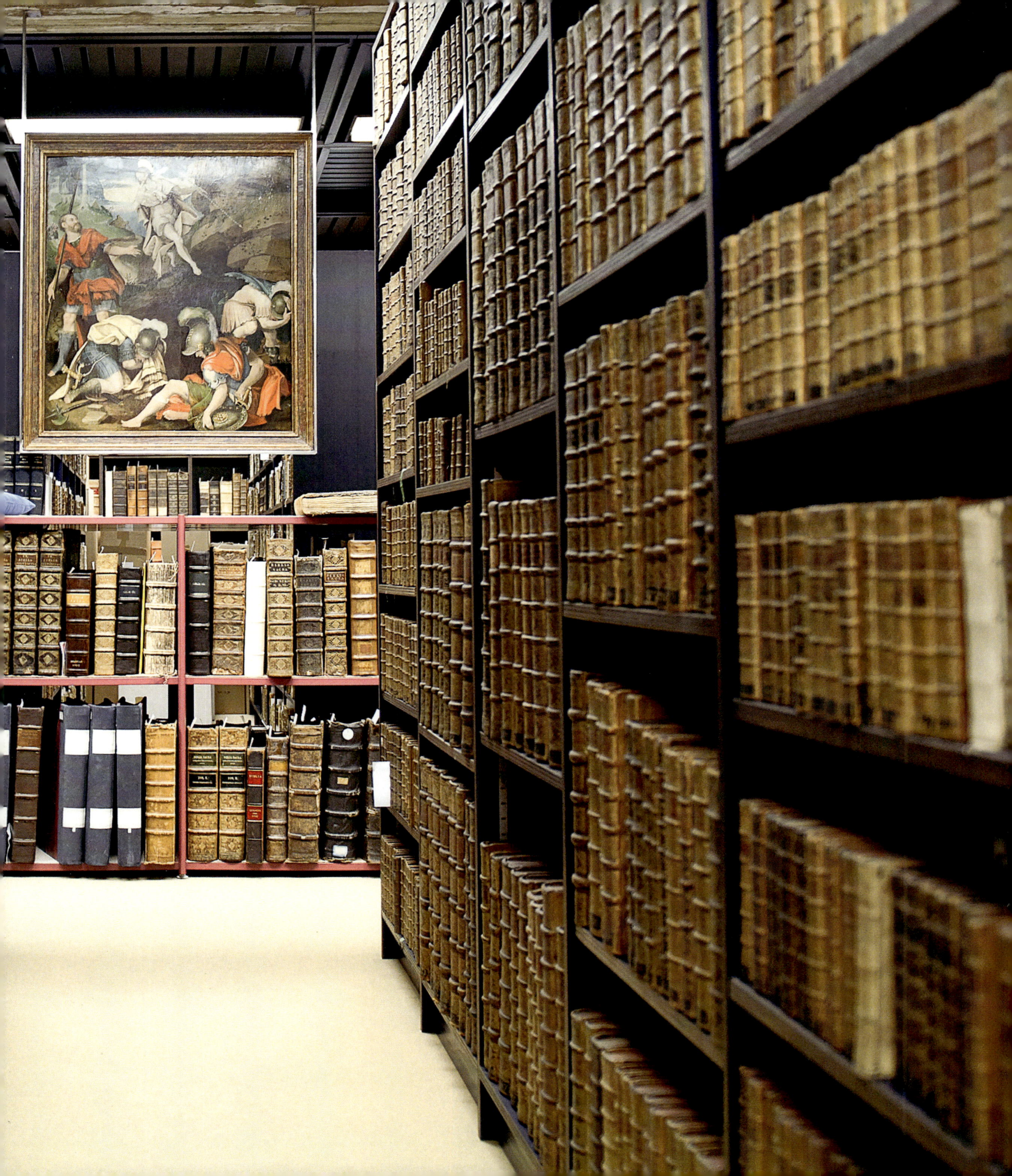

EDITORS Wim François, Lieve Watteeuw, Leo Kenis

GRAPHIC DESIGN Frederik Hulstaert

TEAM Hans Storme, Yannick Van Loon (copy-editing)
Eliza Halling, Catherine Reynolds (proofreading)
Ward De Pril, Veronique Verspeurt (library management)

PHOTO CREDITS Imaging Lab · KU Leuven Libraries
Frederik Hulstaert

PUBLISHER Peeters, Leuven

MAURITS SABBE LIBRARY, Research and Heritage Library of the Faculty of Theology and Religious Studies, KU Leuven,
Charles Deberiotstraat 26, BE-3000 Leuven (Belgium)
https://bib.kuleuven.be/english/msb
2019

This publication was made possible with the support of the King Baudouin Foundation, Baillet Latour Fund

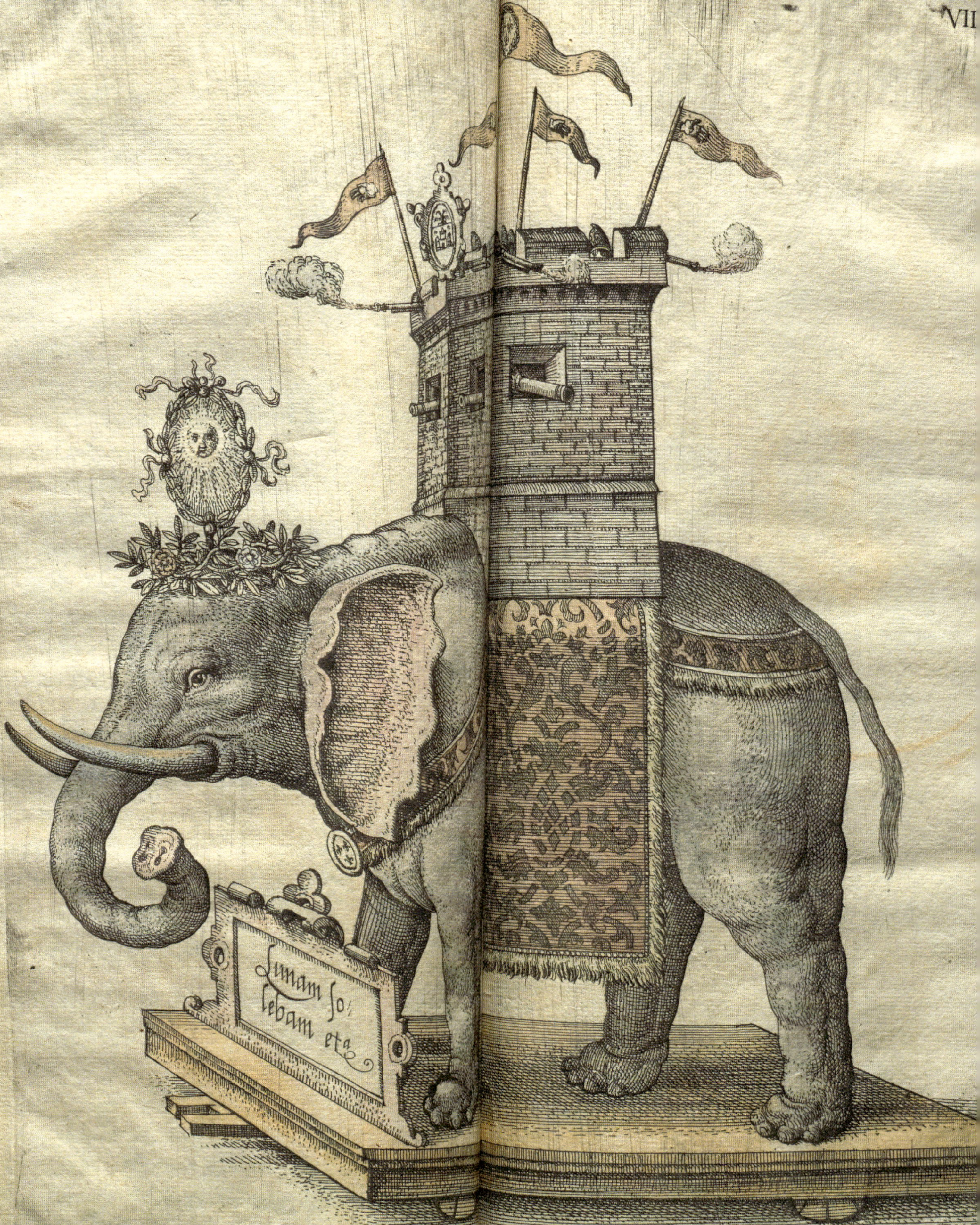
Lunam So/
lebam etc.